Resilient Global Supply Chains and Geopolitical Risk

Global supply chains, long seen as engines of efficiency and economic integration, have been increasingly disrupted by recent crises, including the COVID-19 pandemic, armed conflicts, and shifts in trade and industrial policy. These developments have raised costs, increased uncertainty, and reduced the predictability of cross-border production and exchange. Firms operating in Central and Eastern Europe (CEE) face particularly strong pressures as overlapping geopolitical forces reshape production networks, market access, and strategic choices.

This book examines how firms build and sustain supply chain resilience (SCRES) under persistent geopolitical uncertainty. It maps how research on SCRES has evolved and provides detailed empirical evidence on how firms in the CEE region respond to geopolitical risk. Focusing on practical adjustment mechanisms such as supplier diversification, nearshoring, inventory buffering, and route reconfiguration, this book analyses how firms adapt supply chains in environments shaped by sanctions, trade disputes, and regulatory fragmentation.

Using qualitative case studies and causal modelling, the analysis shows that resilience does not result from isolated decisions or single best practices. Instead, it emerges from the interaction of multiple strategic choices made over time. By combining insights from dynamic capabilities, institutional economics, and systems thinking, this book conceptualises SCRES as an economic outcome shaped by firms' responses to changing costs, governance constraints, and information conditions under geopolitical pressure.

The book is intended for researchers and graduate students in supply chain management, economics, international business, and related fields, as well as for policymakers and practitioners concerned with geopolitical risk, industrial adjustment, and resilience in global production networks.

Aleksandra Kania, PhD, is an assistant professor in the Department of International Competitiveness at Poznań University of Economics and Business. She holds a doctoral degree in economics and has participated in a range of national and international research and teaching projects conducted in cooperation with academic partners from the European Union and the United States. Her research is situated at the intersection of international business and strategic analysis, with a particular focus on firm behaviour, SCRES, and organisational adjustment under conditions of economic and geopolitical uncertainty.

Routledge Focus on Economics and Finance

The fields of economics are constantly expanding and evolving. This growth presents challenges for readers trying to keep up with the latest important insights. Routledge Focus on Economics and Finance presents short books on the latest big topics, linking in with the most cutting-edge economics research.

Individually, each title in the series provides coverage of a key academic topic, whilst collectively the series forms a comprehensive collection across the whole spectrum of economics.

Geopolitics, China, and the Global Supply Chain
Issues and Implications
Sarah Chan

Proactivity in Economics
Between Resourcefulness and Entrepreneurship
Jakub Bożydar Wiśniewski

The Geoeconomics of Global Value Chains
Navigating Geopolitical Complexity and Industrial Policy Shifts
Katarzyna Mroczek-Dąbrowska

Dollar Dominance
Fundamentals, Nature and Present Structure
Junji Tokunaga

Resilient Global Supply Chains and Geopolitical Risk
Evidence from Central and Eastern Europe
Aleksandra Kania

For more information about this series, please visit: www.routledge.com/Routledge-Focus-on-Economics-and-Finance/book-series/RFEF

Resilient Global Supply Chains and Geopolitical Risk

Evidence from Central and Eastern Europe

Aleksandra Kania

Routledge
Taylor & Francis Group
LONDON AND NEW YORK

First published 2026
by Routledge
4 Park Square, Milton Park, Abingdon, Oxon OX14 4RN

and by Routledge
605 Third Avenue, New York, NY 10158

Routledge is an imprint of the Taylor & Francis Group, an informa business

British Library Cataloguing-in-Publication Data
A catalogue record for this book is available from the British Library

ISBN: 978-1-041-22592-8 (hbk)
ISBN: 978-1-041-22593-5 (pbk)
ISBN: 978-1-003-73308-9 (ebk)

DOI: 10.4324/9781003733089

Typeset in Times New Roman
by KnowledgeWorks Global Ltd.

Contents

List of tables

List of figures

Acknowledgement

This manuscript benefited from language-editing support using an AI-based tool (ChatGPT 5.2). The use of AI was strictly limited to improving grammar, phrasing, and stylistic consistency. No ideas, interpretations, analyses, or substantive content were generated by the tool. The research design, empirical analysis, and conclusions are entirely the responsibility of the author.

About the author

Aleksandra Kania, PhD, is an assistant professor in the Department of International Competitiveness at Poznań University of Economics and Business. She holds a doctoral degree in economics and has participated in a range of national and international research and teaching projects conducted in cooperation with academic partners from the European Union and the United States. Her research is situated at the intersection of international business and strategic analysis, with a particular focus on firm behaviour, SCRES and organisational adjustment under conditions of economic and geopolitical uncertainty.

Her scholarly work has been published in internationally recognised academic journals and monographs and contributes to ongoing debates on resilience formation, uncertainty, and adaptive behaviour in the global economy. She was a Rotary Scholar at the University of Mannheim, Germany, and is a member of the Academy of International Business and the European International Business Academy. Prior to entering academia, she gained professional experience in multinational enterprises in the automotive and chemical sectors in Poland and Germany, which informs the empirical interpretation of firm-level adjustment processes examined in her research.

Glossary of abbreviations and key terms

Terminology governance note

This glossary is preceded by a terminology governance note to clarify how key concepts and abbreviations are used consistently throughout the volume. The monograph integrates bibliometric mapping, qualitative case analysis, and causal modelling, which necessarily involves the use of overlapping labels across different empirical and methodological contexts. To avoid semantic drift and post-hoc construct inflation, the following principles govern the use of terminology throughout the book.

SCRES is treated as a single analytically defined construct. The term supply chain resilience (SCRES) is used when referring to the focal capability under investigation, while the shorter term resilience appears only in generic discussion or synthesis sections and does not denote a distinct construct.

Capability domains are standardised across all chapters. The integrated analytical framework developed in Chapter 2 is organised around four capability domains—readiness, responsiveness, resurgence, and collaboration—which serve as the master categories for theory development, empirical analysis, and causal modelling. These domains represent a synthetic conceptual structure used consistently across the monograph rather than categories derived mechanically from any single empirical method.

Bibliometric clusters identified in the bibliometric-systematic literature review in Chapter 3—operational resilience, strategic reconfiguration, collaborative ecosystem, and digital readiness—are treated as empirically emergent thematic patterns rather than theory-level constructs. These clusters reflect dominant emphases within the literature and are interpreted through qualitative synthesis of the reviewed publications. For analytical integration, they are mapped interpretively onto the four capability domains as follows: operational resilience corresponds primarily to responsiveness; strategic reconfiguration to resurgence; collaborative ecosystem to collaboration; and digital readiness to readiness. This mapping provides a coherent bridge between inductively identified research streams and the deductive capability architecture used for cross-chapter integration and does not imply conceptual equivalence between bibliometric labels and capability constructs.

Digital phenomena are governed under the umbrella term digital readiness. References to digitalisation, analytics, artificial intelligence, machine learning, blockchain, platforms, or information systems are interpreted as empirical manifestations of digital readiness rather than as independent capabilities.

Clear distinctions are maintained between risk, exposure, vulnerability, and resilience. Geopolitical risk refers to the probability and intensity of politically driven disruption; exposure denotes structural positioning within risky environments; vulnerability captures potential loss given exposure; and resilience denotes adaptive capability under changing institutional, regulatory, and cost constraints.

Methodological terminology reflects a non-linear mixed-method design. The bibliometric-systematic literature review, case studies, and Decision-Making Trial and Evaluation Laboratory analysis are treated as complementary evidence streams rather than sequential validation stages. The integrated framework is a synthetic outcome of triangulated interpretation across methods, not the product of any single analytical technique.

Theoretical perspectives such as dynamic capabilities, transaction cost economics, global value chain analysis, and systems thinking are employed as explanatory devices rather than prescriptive management frameworks. Their role is to clarify adjustment mechanisms under persistent geopolitical and institutional constraints.

The glossary entries that follow define key abbreviations and terms in line with these governance principles.

Artificial Intelligence (AI)

Computational systems capable of performing tasks that normally require human intelligence, such as pattern recognition, prediction, and decision support, increasingly applied to supply chain monitoring and risk analysis.

Bibliometric systematic literature review (B-SLR)

B-SLR combines systematic literature identification and screening with bibliometric techniques such as co-citation analysis, bibliographic coupling, and keyword co-occurrence mapping to identify empirically emergent thematic structures within the literature. These structures are subsequently interpreted through qualitative synthesis and used to inform theory development rather than treated as theory-level constructs.

Computer-Assisted Web Interviewing (CAWI)

A survey data collection method in which respondents complete questionnaires online through a web-based interface without interviewer involvement.

Central and Eastern Europe (CEE)

A group of European economies characterised by deep integration into EU value chains and heightened exposure to geopolitical and institutional change.

Context–Mechanism–Outcome (CMO) configuration

A realist analytical framework explaining how outcomes arise from mechanisms activated within specific contextual conditions.

Decision-Making Trial and Evaluation Laboratory (DEMATEL)

A causal modelling technique used to identify interdependencies, feedback loops, and influence hierarchies among system elements.

Dynamic capabilities (DCV)

Firm-level abilities to sense environmental change, seize opportunities, and reconfigure resources in response to shifting constraints and uncertainty.

Exposure

The extent to which a firm or supply chain is positioned within regions, networks, or structures where risks may materialise.

Geopolitical risk

The probability and potential intensity of politically driven disruptions arising from state actions, conflict, or policy intervention.

Global supply chain

A cross-border network of firms, production stages, logistics flows, and governance arrangements through which goods, services, information, and coordination are organised from input sourcing to final markets under heterogeneous institutional and regulatory conditions.

Global Value Chain (GVC)

An international production system in which value-adding activities are fragmented across countries and coordinated through cross-border governance arrangements.

Institutional environment

The formal and informal rules, regulations, policies, and norms shaping economic coordination and organisational behaviour.

Multinational Enterprise (MNE)

A firm that owns or controls production and value-adding activities across more than one country.

Polycrisis

A condition in which multiple, interdependent crises interact and amplify one another across economic, political, environmental, and social domains.

Readiness

The capability to anticipate and prepare for disruption through visibility, intelligence gathering, and digital infrastructure.

Responsiveness

The capability to stabilise operations during disruption through short-term tactical adjustments and coordination mechanisms.

Resurgence

Long-term strategic adaptation involving structural reconfiguration of supply chains, including location and footprint redesign.

Supply Chain Resilience (SCRES)

The capability of a supply chain to anticipate, absorb, respond to, recover from, and adapt to disruptions while preserving operational continuity.

Systems thinking

An analytical approach that examines interdependencies, feedback loops, and dynamic interactions within complex systems.

Transaction costs

The costs of coordinating economic exchange, including contracting, monitoring, enforcement, and adaptation under uncertainty.

Vulnerability

The degree to which a firm or supply chain suffers losses when exposed to disruption, given its structure and capacity to adjust.

1 Rethinking supply chain resilience under geopolitical constraints

Introduction

The question of whether to organise production through market transactions or internal coordination has long occupied a central place in the economic analysis of the firm. Williamson's (1975) formulation of the make-or-buy dilemma conceptualises this choice as a trade-off between transaction costs, coordination efficiency, and exposure to uncertainty. From this perspective, supply chains can be understood as hybrid governance arrangements that combine market-based exchange with elements of hierarchical control, relying on inter-firm contracting while retaining internal coordination where it reduces costs or mitigates risk. As noted by Handfield and Nichols (2002), a supply chain comprises interconnected entities that transform inputs into finished products and manage their distribution. Economically, supply chain configuration therefore reflects firms' efforts to allocate production and coordination activities efficiently while balancing transaction costs, uncertainty, and the need for adaptive capacity under changing market conditions.

Over recent decades, increasing specialisation and geographic concentration of production have intensified interdependencies across global supply networks. This deepening interdependence is closely associated with the expansion of global value chains (GVCs), in which production activities are fragmented across jurisdictions and coordinated through cross-border governance arrangements. GVCs thus provide the structural context within which supply chains are organised, linking firm-level coordination decisions to location-specific institutional, regulatory, and political conditions. Disruptions rarely affect isolated firms; shocks originating in a single node can propagate rapidly across interconnected production networks (Antràs & de Gortari, 2020; Gereffi *et al.*, 2005). At the same time, efficiency-oriented configurations such as lean production, just-in-time systems, and single sourcing have reduced inventories and slack, lowering costs under stable conditions while increasing the marginal cost of disruption. By limiting redundancy and substitutability, these arrangements constrain the rapid reallocation of inputs, suppliers, and production locations, thereby raising adjustment costs as uncertainty increases. Growing reliance on digital infrastructure has further altered the risk profile of

DOI: 10.4324/9781003733089-1

supply chains, as failures in information systems can interrupt coordination, delay transactions, and amplify the economic impact of other shocks.

As adjustment costs rise and coordination margins narrow, firms become increasingly exposed to multiple, interacting sources of disruption. Under conditions of intensified interdependence and constrained adjustment capacity, resilience has emerged as a focal concept in the analysis of GVCs (Gereffi, 2014; Gereffi *et al.*, 2022). A set of reinforcing megatrends—including digital readiness, demographic change, urbanisation, evolving consumer preferences, climate pressures, and rising geopolitical tension—has contributed to an environment characterised by concurrent and mutually amplifying disruptions. This condition is increasingly described as a *polycrisis*, in which multiple shocks interact in ways that are difficult to predict, disentangle, or address in isolation (Lawrence *et al.*, 2024).

The term *polycrisis* was first introduced by Morin and Kern (1999), who argued that the central challenge facing the global system lay not in a single dominant crisis, but in the complex interdependence of problems, antagonisms, and uncontrolled processes. Building on this insight, Swilling (2013, 2020) conceptualised *polycrisis* as the interaction of crises within the global political economy that mutually amplify their effects. More recently, the concept has been applied to describe the intertwined dynamics of war, climate change, and pandemics following Russia's invasion of Ukraine in 2022 (Tooze, 2022), and it was widely adopted in policy discourse during the World Economic Forum's annual meeting in Davos in 2023 (Serhan, 2023).

Geopolitical disruption in the contemporary supply chain environment

Within the *polycrisis* environment, geopolitical disruptions have become particularly significant. These disruptions extend beyond episodic armed conflict to include shifts in trade policy, sanctions, export controls, regulatory divergence, and organisational realignments. Such developments directly affect the institutional conditions under which firms organise cross-border production and exchange, making it increasingly important to understand how supply chain structures evolve in response to changing external constraints. Despite growing recognition of these dynamics, existing research offers limited explanation of how firms adjust supply chain structures and coordination mechanisms over time when geopolitical disruption becomes a persistent rather than episodic condition.

In the recent years, academic interest in geopolitical risk has expanded accordingly (Ali *et al.*, 2025; Bednarski *et al.*, 2024; Bouoiyour *et al.*, 2019; Iftikhar *et al.*, 2025; Kotcharin & Maneenop, 2020; Roscoe *et al.*, 2022). This growing attention coincides with a resurgence of nationalism and protectionism in many advanced economies (Charpin, 2022; Colantone & Stanig, 2019). The financial crises of 2008–2009 and 2011–2013 intensified social and political divisions, contributing to more interventionist policy regimes and a reassessment of openness in trade and investment. These shifts have had tangible consequences for global supply chains. The United Kingdom's withdrawal from the European Union introduced regulatory uncertainty and higher transaction costs for firms embedded in EU–UK value chains, prompting relocation and restructuring decisions aimed at preserving market access and compliance continuity (Moradlou *et al.*, 2021). In the United States, tariff escalation and industrial policy measures introduced during the Trump administration triggered a prolonged trade conflict with China, leading multinational enterprises to reconsider concentration risk and the resilience of China-centred sourcing strategies (Tao *et al.*, 2024; Zhang *et al.*, 2020).

Beyond trade conflicts in advanced economies, long-term geoeconomic initiatives have also reshaped the institutional landscape of global supply chains. China's Belt and Road Initiative, launched in 2013, has further reshaped the geopolitical and economic landscape by altering infrastructure connectivity, investment flows, and regional power relations. While the initiative seeks to enhance cross-border integration through large-scale infrastructure investment, it has also generated political frictions by expanding China's influence and reshaping regional trade and investment patterns (Bednarski *et al.*, 2024; Comerma, 2024; Kotcharin & Maneenop, 2020). Concerns related to debt sustainability, organisational dependency, and geopolitical leverage have intensified debates about the evolving structure of the global economic order and the risks associated with deep cross-border interdependence.

The COVID-19 pandemic added a further dimension to these dynamics by exposing the sensitivity of GVCs to state intervention and regulatory disruption (Aljuneidi *et al.*, 2024; Barbieri *et al.*, 2020; Mena *et al.*, 2022). In many sectors, it was government mandates rather than the epidemiological shock itself that halted production and restricted mobility, effectively raising barriers to exchange and interrupting contractual relationships (van Hoek, 2020). Vaccine nationalism and unequal access to critical medical supplies illustrated how public health crises can rapidly acquire geopolitical significance, influencing trade, investment, and supply allocation decisions (Duong *et al.*, 2024; Finkenstadt & Handfield, 2021). The pandemic also intensified strategic rivalry between major powers, particularly the United States and China, reinforcing existing political and economic tensions.

Shortly thereafter, the war in Ukraine triggered sharp energy price increases, shortages of key inputs, and disruptions to critical transport corridors across Europe. The conflict demonstrated how inter-state violence can rapidly reshape economic conditions by altering relative prices, constraining access to strategic resources, and increasing uncertainty in cross-border contracting. Firms operating in affected regions were compelled to redesign supply networks, renegotiate sourcing arrangements, and reassess geographic dependencies in order to contain exposure to escalating risk (Roscoe *et al.*, 2022).

Beyond the European theatre, disruptions in major global transport corridors, including the Red Sea and the Suez Canal route, further exposed supply chains to geopolitically induced logistics risk. Recurrent security incidents and rerouting decisions raised freight costs and extended lead times for firms reliant on Asian suppliers, reinforcing vulnerability to shocks originating far beyond firms' immediate regional environments (Mrowiec & Penczar, 2024; Politico, 2024).

Geopolitical risk, however, extends beyond armed conflict to include economic nationalism, regulatory discrimination, cyber threats, and shifting public sentiment (Mroczek-Dabrowska *et al.*, 2024). As Charpin (2022) observes, these forces can restrict foreign firms' access to markets, alter investment incentives, and destabilise cross-border production networks. Recent trends suggest that global business increasingly operates in an environment marked by heightened conflict and weakening multilateral cooperation, sometimes characterised as a geopolitical recession (Feingold & Torkington, 2024). Since 2014, the incidence of armed conflict has risen relative to earlier decades (World Economic Forum, 2024), and executives across Europe, Middle East, and Central Asia consistently identify geopolitical instability as a major threat to economic growth (McKinsey & Company, 2024). Survey evidence reinforces these perceptions: according to Maersk, a large majority of European shippers view geopolitical tensions and inter-state conflict as leading risks facing supply chains (Newman, 2024).

Alongside conflict and pandemics, additional sources of disruption—including terrorism, cyberattacks, sanctions, and the reconfiguration of trade blocs—continue to strain global production systems. Fragmentation and the securitisation of trade policy challenge long-standing assumptions about efficiency-driven globalisation, increasing uncertainty and the costs of coordination across jurisdictions. From an economic perspective, geopolitical developments matter insofar as they modify relative prices, access to markets, regulatory regimes, and the predictability of cross-border transactions, thereby reshaping the constraints under which firms make sourcing, production, and investment decisions. Firms exposed to such changes must therefore monitor political and regulatory developments and adjust their governance arrangements to preserve continuity and economic viability.[1]

Conceptual boundaries and core definitions

While existing studies often portray resilience as a desirable supply chain attribute (e.g. Ponomarov & Holcomb, 2009), they provide limited insight into how firms revise organisational arrangements and resource allocations over time as geopolitical conditions evolve. Comprehensive reviews point to persistent gaps in understanding the long-term and macro-level implications of geopolitical disruption for supply chain configuration and economic performance (e.g. Bednarski *et al.*, 2024). Empirical evidence on how firms concretely develop and deploy resilience mechanisms under conditions of sustained geopolitical volatility remains scarce. Accordingly, throughout this book resilience is treated not as a normative objective, but as the outcome of firm-level adjustment processes operating under changing institutional constraints and cost structures. The analysis remains grounded in the analytical logic of mainstream economics, understood not as a single school of thought but as a shared core of assumptions concerning incentives, constraints, coordination, and adjustment under uncertainty. Rather than relying on static optimisation or equilibrium benchmarks, the book adopts a dynamic perspective that emphasises transaction costs, institutional heterogeneity, and path-dependent firm behaviour. This perspective allows geopolitical disruption to be analysed as an economically meaningful source of changing constraints that shapes supply chain organisation over time.

For analytical clarity, it is important to distinguish between risk, exposure, vulnerability, and resilience, which are often conflated in the supply chain literature. Geopolitical risk refers to the probability and potential intensity of politically driven disruptions arising from state actions or conflict (Caldara & Iacoviello, 2018, p. 2). Exposure captures the extent to which a firm or supply chain is positioned within environments, regions, or networks where such risks may materialise, for example through geographic concentration, critical supplier dependence, or reliance on specific trade corridors (Antràs & de Gortari, 2020; Gereffi *et al.*, 2005). Vulnerability reflects the extent to which exposed firms incur disruption-related losses, given their cost structures, contractual arrangements, and capacity to substitute inputs or reallocate production (Pettit *et al.*, 2010; Sheffi & Rice, 2005). SCRES, in contrast, does not denote the absence of risk or exposure, but the ability of firms and supply chains to absorb shocks, limit losses, and adapt organisational arrangements under changing institutional and cost constraints (Dolgui *et al.*, 2018; Ponomarov & Holcomb, 2009). This distinction allows geopolitical disruption to be analysed not simply as an external hazard, but as an economically meaningful condition that interacts with firm-level structures and capabilities over time.

To establish a clear conceptual foundation for the remainder of the monograph, SCRES is defined as the capability of a supply chain to anticipate disruption, absorb and respond to shocks, and adapt its structures and coordination mechanisms over time in ways that preserve operational continuity and, where feasible, sustain economic performance. This definition synthesises recurring elements identified in foundational contributions by Ponomarov and Holcomb (2009), Pettit *et al.* (2010), Jüttner and Maklan (2011), and Dolgui *et al.* (2018, 2021). Within this study, SCRES is understood as an economically grounded condition that enables firms to sustain participation in international trade by limiting disruption-induced losses, stabilising revenue streams, and maintaining contractual reliability under conditions of persistent uncertainty.

Geopolitical disruptions are understood as events arising from tensions, conflicts, or strategic interventions among state actors—such as wars, sanctions, export controls, diplomatic deterioration, and policy realignments—that reshape the institutional and economic conditions governing global supply chains. These disruptions influence trade flows, access to suppliers and customers, the viability of logistics corridors, market stability, and the regulatory environment within which cross-border activities are conducted. Drawing on insights from macroeconomics and political economy (Caldara & Iacoviello, 2018, p. 2), geopolitical risk is conceptualised here as a source of exogenous shocks that modifies relative cost structures, constrains or redirects market access, and redefines the parameters under which firms make sourcing, production, and investment decisions.

These definitions establish the analytical boundaries for the monograph. Although the analysis draws on concepts from supply chain management and strategic management, all theoretical perspectives are employed here as analytical devices to explain economically grounded firm-level adjustment processes under changing geopolitical and institutional constraints, rather than as normative or prescriptive management frameworks.

The analytical foundation of this book is deliberately selective and anchored in new institutional economics, with transaction cost reasoning as its central analytical lens. Within this perspective, institutions are understood as the formal and informal constraints that structure economic interaction and condition organisational adjustment under uncertainty (North, 1990). The analysis focuses on coordination, governance, and firm adjustment under changing institutional and geopolitical constraints. Rather than pursuing equilibrium outcomes or optimisation under stable conditions, the study examines how firms organise and reconfigure cross-border activities as transaction costs, regulatory conditions, and uncertainty evolve. Dynamic capabilities are incorporated as a complementary firm-level mechanism explaining how organisations respond and adapt within these constraints, while other economic perspectives are considered only insofar as they inform these core processes.

Research objectives and guiding questions

Against this backdrop, the study aims to advance theoretical and empirical understanding of how geopolitical disruptions reshape the functioning of supply chains and influence the formation, durability, and limits of resilience over time. Rather than describing isolated reactions to geopolitical shocks, the research explains the mechanisms and conditions through which resilience develops, persists, or weakens when geopolitical pressure becomes sustained. The analysis focuses on multinational enterprises operating in Central and Eastern Europe, where firms face overlapping geopolitical, institutional, and cost-related constraints that make adjustment processes particularly visible within international production networks.

Grounded in a realist research perspective, the study moves beyond observable practices to analyse how firms interpret geopolitical disruption and adjust their behaviour within existing institutional settings. Resilience is examined through the lens of dynamic capabilities, understood as firms' abilities to identify changes in geopolitical and regulatory environments, choose feasible adjustment responses, and reorganise supply chain resources, governance structures, and coordination mechanisms. From this perspective, resilience is treated as an economic outcome of firm-level adjustment under uncertainty, changing relative costs, and institutional constraints, rather than as a prescriptive management objective.

The investigation is guided by three interconnected research questions, each aligned with a distinct methodological component of the study:

RQ1: *How has scholarly understanding of the relationship between geopolitical disruptions and SCRES evolved over time, and what thematic developments and knowledge gaps characterise this field?*

This question is addressed through a SLR that provides a structured overview of research on SCRES under geopolitical uncertainty. The review organises the literature into thematic clusters, traces their evolution over time, and identifies gaps that inform the empirical stages of the study.

RQ2: *How do firms operating in Central and Eastern Europe interpret geopolitical disruptions, what mitigation strategies do they implement in response, and what outcomes do these strategies produce in strengthening SCRES?*

This question is explored through in-depth case studies of MNEs in the CEE region. The analysis captures how firms *sense* geopolitical risks, *seize* strategic opportunities for mitigation, and *reconfigure* their supply chain structures and capabilities. These three analytical dimensions—risk interpretation, reconfiguration response, and resilience outcomes—form a context–mechanism–outcome (CMO) configuration consistent with realist explanation and aligned with dynamic capabilities reasoning.

RQ3: *What is the structure and relative strength of causal relationships among mitigation strategies that enhance SCRES in geopolitically disruptive environments?*

This question is examined using the Decision-Making Trial and Evaluation Laboratory (DEMATEL) method. The analysis uncovers the interdependencies among resilience-building strategies, identifies feedback loops, and isolates leverage points—those mechanisms exerting the strongest systemic influence on resilience. This aligns with dynamic capabilities logic by clarifying which strategic reconfigurations most effectively enhance adaptive capacity.

Table 1.1 Mapping research stages to systems thinking elements

Research stage	*RQs*	*Research objective*	*Systems thinking element*
Conceptual framing	RQ1	Map the intellectual foundations of SCRES under geopolitical disruption; identify key concepts, thematic developments, and research gaps.	System awareness/ boundary definition
Mechanism discovery	RQ2	Understand how CEE-based MNEs interpret geopolitical disruptions, implement mitigation strategies, and generate resilience outcomes.	System environment, system response mechanisms, system output
Causal structure modelling	RQ3	Determine the interdependencies, causal strength, and leverage points among mitigation strategies that enhance SCRES.	Feedback loops/ leverage points

Source: Own elaboration.

The three research questions define a coherent analytical structure across complementary methodological components (c.f. Table 1.1). The literature review clarifies the conceptual and theoretical boundaries of the field. The case studies reveal how resilience mechanisms operate in practice under real geopolitical pressures. The DEMATEL analysis models the causal structures linking these mechanisms, offering insight into how different strategies reinforce or constrain one another within complex supply chain systems.

The study adopts a systems-thinking perspective (Arnold & Wade, 2015), conceptualising supply chains as dynamic and interconnected systems whose components interact over time (Senge, 1990; Wieland *et al.*, 2023; Wilden *et al.*, 2024). Within this perspective, SCRES is understood as an emergent property arising from interacting firm-level adjustment processes, shaped by transaction costs, institutional constraints, and path-dependent capability development over time. Rather than analysing supply chain elements in isolation, systems thinking emphasises how shocks affecting one part of the network propagate through interdependencies and feedback loops. In this book, this perspective is employed as an analytical device for examining how such interdependencies influence firms' adjustment costs, reallocation possibilities, and adaptive capacity under conditions of uncertainty.

When applied to geopolitical disruptions, systems thinking allows supply chains to be analysed as complex adaptive systems (CAS) exposed to exogenous shocks that alter their operating conditions. Geopolitical events function as contextual disturbances that unsettle the system's equilibrium by modifying prices, access constraints, and institutional parameters. Firms respond by activating adjustment mechanisms—such as diversification, collaboration, and digital readiness—whose economic effects are non-linear due to threshold effects, complementarities, and constraint interactions within supply chain systems. SCRES emerges from this interaction as an adaptive property of the system, reflecting firms' ongoing processes of sensing, response, and reconfiguration.

Systems thinking also facilitates the identification of leverage points by mapping causal relationships among mitigation strategies. By revealing how different interventions reinforce or constrain one another, this approach helps explain which strategic adjustments exert the greatest systemic influence on resilience formation in politically volatile environments.

Analytical framework and theory–method alignment

To operationalise the analytical boundaries established above, this book adopts a selectively pluralistic and systems-thinking framework aligned with its three research questions. Consistent with the guidance of Halldórsson *et al.* (2007), the analysis draws selectively on theoretical perspectives, treating them as analytical resources deployed in response to specific empirical problems rather than as parallel explanatory foundations. This pluralistic orientation accommodates the complexity of geopolitically exposed supply chains by integrating firm-level and system-level insights, thereby enabling a deeper understanding of how SCRES emerges under changing institutional and political constraints.

Chapter 2 provides a structured conceptual synthesis of the literature on SCRES, drawing on scoping review principles to trace the evolution of key concepts and to develop an integrated, capability-based framework. Building on established review approaches, the chapter documents the shift from recovery-oriented perspectives toward an understanding of resilience as a system of interrelated capabilities, positions geopolitical disruption as a structural source of supply chain risk, and connects macro-level institutional conditions with firm-level mitigation mechanisms. Through this synthesis, the chapter clarifies the theoretical foundations of the study and establishes the analytical framework that guides the empirical analyses presented in subsequent chapters.

To address **RQ1**, Chapter 3 conducts a SLR guided by the methodological principles of scientific knowledge mapping and bibliometric analysis. This approach enables the identification of dominant thematic clusters, influential publication networks, and underexplored research linkages within the SCRES–geopolitics literature. Rather than privileging a single explanatory theory, **RQ1** draws on the methodological rigour of the SLR tradition (Tranfield *et al.*, 2003) and the epistemological foundations of bibliometric research to establish a structured overview of how resilience has been conceptualised under geopolitical uncertainty.

RQ2, examined in Chapter 4, is anchored analytically in a systems-thinking perspective, which conceptualises supply chains as interconnected and evolving systems in which firm-level actions interact with institutional structures and external disturbances. Within this perspective, geopolitical disruption is treated as a systemic shock that propagates through interdependencies, generates non-linear effects, and reshapes firms' exposure and vulnerability over time. A CAS lens complements this view by explaining how external shocks trigger emergent and unpredictable responses within supply chain networks (Choi *et al.*, 2001; Pathak *et al.*, 2007).

Risk management reasoning is employed to clarify how firms operating within such systems identify, interpret, and prioritise sources of uncertainty affecting expected returns, volatility, and cross-border coordination (Kaplan & Mikes, 2012). Rather than assuming *ex ante* calculability, this approach highlights the interpretive processes through which firms make sense of geopolitical risk under conditions of uncertainty and incomplete information. Within a systems-thinking framework, these risk interpretations influence which adjustment mechanisms are activated and how firms position themselves within the broader network.

To explain how interpreted risk is translated into concrete mitigation strategies and resilience outcomes, the analysis draws on the dynamic capabilities framework. Dynamic capabilities are used to explain how firms sense changes in geopolitical and regulatory environments, seize feasible adjustment options, and reconfigure supply chain resources, governance arrangements, and coordination mechanisms under geopolitical pressure (Teece *et al.*, 1997). This framework is applied as an explanatory mechanism for firm-level adjustment embedded within a broader supply chain system, rather than as an independent theory of competitive advantage.

From a systems-thinking standpoint, the reconfiguration responses examined under **RQ2** are understood as mechanisms activated within a dynamic and interconnected production network. Their effectiveness depends on interactions with external shocks and internal system conditions, reinforcing an understanding of SCRES as an emergent and adaptive property of complex socio-economic systems rather than as a set of isolated firm-level practices.

Finally, **RQ3**, examined in Chapter 5, incorporates systems-thinking concepts explicitly through the application of the DEMATEL method. DEMATEL enables the identification of causal relationships, interdependencies, feedback loops, and leverage points among resilience strategies—core elements of systems thinking (Arnold & Wade, 2015; Senge, 1990). This analysis clarifies which mitigation mechanisms exert the strongest systemic influence on resilience formation in geopolitically volatile environments.

Across the three research questions, theoretical perspectives are deployed in a sequenced yet non-linear manner, ensuring conceptual coherence while capturing the multi-level dynamics of resilience—from geopolitical drivers, through firm-level adjustment mechanisms, to emergent system-level patterns

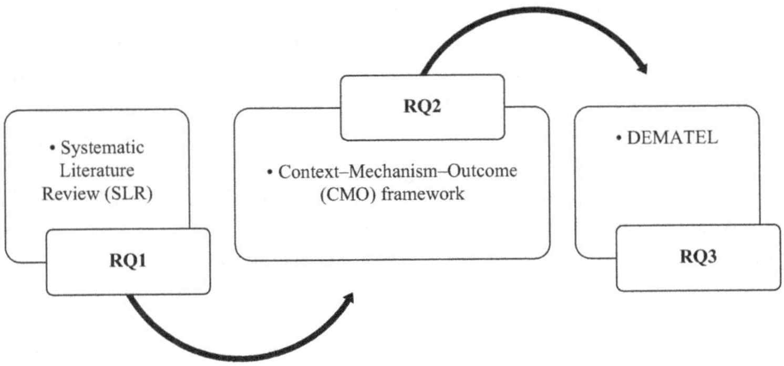

Figure 1.1 Research model.

(c.f. Figure 1.1). This theory–method alignment provides a coherent analytical foundation for understanding how multinational enterprises operating in Central and Eastern Europe navigate and adapt to geopolitical disruptions in their supply chains.

Research design and methodological approach

This study adopts an integrated mixed-method research design to examine how multinational enterprises operating in Central and Eastern Europe respond to geopolitical disruption and develop SCRES. The combination of qualitative and quantitative approaches—central to mixed-method research (Guetterman *et al.*, 2020)—is particularly suited to analysing complex, multilayered phenomena such as resilience formation under conditions of sustained geopolitical volatility. Method integration enables a more nuanced understanding of adjustment processes than would be attainable through any single methodological approach (Timans *et al.*, 2019).

The research design combines three complementary empirical components: a SLR, in-depth case studies, and causal modelling using the DEMATEL method. These components are treated as interrelated evidence streams rather than as sequential research stages. Their integration enables methodological triangulation across conceptual synthesis, context-embedded mechanism analysis, and systems-level causal modelling, thereby strengthening explanatory validity by linking theoretical patterns, observed firm behaviour, and inferred causal structures. The SLR establishes the conceptual contours of the SCRES–geopolitics field by identifying dominant themes and patterns in existing scholarship, providing an analytical reference point against which empirical findings are interpreted.

Firm-level adjustment processes are examined through qualitative case studies of selected multinational enterprises operating in the CEE region.

These cases are analysed using the CMO framework, which enables systematic examination of how firms interpret geopolitical risks, activate mitigation mechanisms, and generate resilience outcomes under specific institutional and organisational conditions. This realist-informed approach captures the interaction between strategic agency and structural constraints shaping supply chain reconfiguration.

To examine interdependencies among resilience-building strategies, the study applies the DEMATEL method. DEMATEL facilitates the identification of causal relationships, feedback loops, and leverage points within the resilience system, offering a systems-level perspective on how different adjustment mechanisms reinforce or constrain one another. When interpreted alongside the qualitative mechanisms identified in the case studies, DEMATEL enhances analytical generalisation without abstracting from contextual specificity.

The philosophical foundations of the study integrate critical realism and pragmatism. Critical realism provides the ontological anchor by conceptualising reality as stratified across observable events, experienced outcomes, and underlying causal mechanisms. This perspective is particularly appropriate for analysing how institutional, organisational, and geopolitical structures condition firm-level resilience processes. Pragmatism complements this foundation as the guiding methodological stance, legitimising the use of diverse methods based on their explanatory value and capacity to generate analytically meaningful insight into complex real-world problems.

Rather than treating these philosophical perspectives as competing paradigms, the study combines critical realism and pragmatism to support a research design that is both theoretically grounded and empirically flexible (Elder-Vass, 2022; Johnson & Duberley, 2000). This integrated stance enables the analysis to move beyond descriptive accounts, offering explanatory insight into how SCRES is developed, enacted, and sustained under persistent geopolitical uncertainty in the Central and Eastern European context.

Empirical focus and geographical scope

This volume examines firm-level adjustment mechanisms through which SCRES is developed in response to geopolitical disruption. The primary focus is on how organisations reconfigure sourcing, production, and coordination arrangements to preserve continuity and economic viability under conditions of heightened political and institutional uncertainty. Rather than offering a general account of supply chain vulnerability, the analysis concentrates on deliberate mitigation and adaptation practices activated by firms facing sustained external constraints.

The scope of the study is limited to international supply chains characterised by cross-border flows of goods, information, and resources. Within this context, the book investigates how firms assess geopolitical risk and implement strategies such as supplier diversification, nearshoring, multi-sourcing, inventory buffering, transport route reconfiguration, and systematic policy monitoring to reduce exposure and manage disruption-related losses. These strategies are examined not as isolated practices, but as components of broader adjustment processes shaped by cost structures, governance arrangements, and institutional environments.

A deliberate geographical emphasis is placed on Central and Eastern Europe, with particular attention to Poland—a region that occupies a distinctive position within European and GVCs (Kisperska-Moron & de Haan, 2011; Mroczek-Dabrowska & Kania; 2020; Gorynia *et al.*, 2024; Khan *et al.*, 2023). As a logistical bridge between Western Europe and Eastern markets, and a frontline EU member in the context of the armed conflict in Ukraine, Poland has experienced both heightened exposure to geopolitical disruption and continued deep integration into EU production networks.

Central and Eastern Europe is therefore treated not as a peripheral empirical setting, but as a high-exposure environment in which the mechanisms linking geopolitical disruption and firm-level adjustment become especially visible. Deep integration into EU value chains, combined with proximity to geopolitical fault lines, renders the region a natural laboratory for examining how resilience is formed, configured, and enacted under compounded and persistent shocks.

The volume's structure

When these words are written in December 2025, Europe—and particularly the CEE region—finds itself at a critical juncture. Emerging pressures such as trade wars, rising political instability, and the resurgence of protectionism underscore the growing significance of geopolitical disruptions in shaping global economic dynamics. Although the COVID-19 pandemic and the armed conflict in Ukraine have revealed profound vulnerabilities in global supply chains, there is still no clear evidence of a comprehensive shift from globalisation toward tightly bounded regional production systems. As noted by Butollo *et al.* (2024), the current landscape is characterised less by deglobalisation and more by intensified state-led interventions aimed at securing strategic geopolitical objectives. These interventions increasingly influence corporate decision-making, especially in sectors deemed critical to national or regional security.

Given the escalating complexity of global supply chains, the United States, the European Union, and China have begun reshaping their industrial policies to navigate challenges arising from globalisation, rapid technological change, and volatile demand patterns. Traditional risk management techniques are no longer adequate to address the interdependencies and cascading risks inherent in today's supply networks. In response, these major economic blocs are adopting more comprehensive and organisational approaches to strengthen the resilience of their supply systems in the face of geopolitical tensions, climate-related shocks, and cyber threats.

This volume responds to these debates by examining how firms adjust supply chain organisation and governance under sustained geopolitical disruption, with a particular focus on Central and Eastern Europe. It integrates conceptual framing, evidence synthesis, mechanism-oriented case analysis, and causal modelling to clarify how resilience capabilities interact and accumulate under changing institutional constraints.

The volume comprises six chapters, which together form a coherent narrative that progresses from theoretical foundations to practical, firm-level insights:

- Chapter 1, the introductory chapter, sets the context and outlines the purpose, scope, and structure of the volume.
- Chapter 2 traces the development of SCRES thinking and develops the book's capability architecture, conceptualising SCRES as a cumulative system of readiness, responsiveness, resurgence, and collaboration under geopolitical and institutional constraints.
- Chapter 3 presents a SLR examining the relationship between SCRES and geopolitical disruption. It maps the intellectual structure of the field, identifies dominant thematic clusters, and highlights unresolved gaps that motivate the empirical analyses.
- Chapter 4 shifts the focus to the case-study level, analysing how multinational enterprises operating in the Central and Eastern European region interpret geopolitical disruptions and activate resilience-enhancing mechanisms in practice.
- Chapter 5 examines the interdependencies among resilience-building strategies in geopolitically disruptive environments. Using the DEMATEL method, the chapter identifies causal structures, influence hierarchies, and feedback loops shaping resilience formation in CEE-based supply chains.
- Chapter 6 concludes the volume by synthesising the main findings into an integrated capability framework of SCRES. Drawing on insights from recent global crises—including the COVID-19 pandemic, U.S.–China trade tensions, the war in Ukraine, and rising cybersecurity threats—the chapter outlines analytically grounded implications for future resilience trajectories.

Collectively, the chapters provide an integrated explanation of firm-level adjustment and SCRES formation under geopolitical disruption.

Conclusion

This chapter has framed SCRES as an economic and organisational response to a geopolitical environment characterised by persistent uncertainty. Rather than treating disruption as an exceptional event, the discussion has shown how contemporary supply chains operate under ongoing pressures arising from geopolitical rivalry and state intervention. In such contexts, resilience is not a static attribute or an optimal design choice, but the outcome of continuous adjustment processes through which firms seek to preserve continuity, manage costs, and sustain participation in international production networks.

By linking resilience to transaction costs, coordination challenges, and institutional change, the chapter has established a conceptual foundation connecting firm-level decision-making with broader geopolitical dynamics. Recent crises—including the COVID-19 pandemic, the war in Ukraine, and escalating trade and technology conflicts—have not resulted in a simple reversal of globalisation, but have altered the conditions under which global integration is organised. Firms increasingly balance efficiency with adaptability, openness with control, and global reach with selective localisation as geopolitical forces reshape relative prices, access constraints, and regulatory environments.

The chapter has also clarified the analytical boundaries of the study by defining SCRES and geopolitical disruption in economic terms. SCRES is treated not as a normative objective, but as a capability enabling firms to limit disruption-induced losses, stabilise performance, and adapt organisational arrangements under changing external constraints. Building on this foundation, three research questions and a mixed-method research design have been articulated to examine how resilience mechanisms are conceptualised, enacted, and interconnected.

Chapter 2 builds directly on this framing by tracing the evolution of SCRES research and synthesising the theoretical perspectives that inform the capability-based framework employed throughout the book, providing the conceptual architecture for the empirical analyses that follow.

Note

1 This context motivates a closer examination of how geopolitical disruption translates into specific sources of supply chain risk and adaptation pressure, which is undertaken in Chapter 2.

References

Ali, I., Gligor, D., Balta, M., & Papadopoulos, T. (2025). Leadership style's role in fostering supply chain agility amid geopolitical shocks. *Industrial Marketing Management, 124*, 212–223. https://doi.org/10.1016/j.indmarman.2024.11.015

Aljuneidi, T., Punia, S., Jebali, A., & Nikolopoulos, K. (2024). Forecasting and planning for a critical infrastructure sector during a pandemic: Empirical evidence from a food supply chain. *European Journal of Operational Research, 317*, 17. https://doi.org/10.1016/j.ejor.2024.04.009

Antràs, P., & de Gortari, A. (2020). On the geography of global value chains. *Econometrica, 88*(4), 1553–1598. https://doi.org/10.3982/ECTA15362

Arnold, R. D., & Wade, J. P. (2015). A definition of systems thinking: A systems approach. *Procedia Computer Science, 44*, 669–678. https://doi.org/10.1016/j.procs.2015.03.050

Barbieri, P., Boffelli, A., Elia, S., Fratocchi, L., Kalchschmidt, M., & Samson, D. (2020). What can we learn about reshoring after COVID-19? *Operations Management Research, 13*, 131–136. https://doi.org/10.1007/s12063-020-00160-1

Bednarski, L., Roscoe, S., Blome, C., & Schleper, M. C. (2024). Geopolitical disruptions in global supply chains: A state-of-the-art literature review. *Production Planning & Control, 36*(4), 536–562. https://doi.org/10.1080/09537287.2023.2286283

Bouoiyour, J., Selmi, R., Hammoudeh, S., & Wohar, M. E. (2019). What are the categories of geopolitical risks that could drive oil prices higher? Acts or threats? *Energy Economics, 84*, 104523. https://doi.org/10.1016/j.eneco.2019.104523

Butollo, F., Staritz, C., Maile, F., & Wuttke, T. (2024). The end of globalized production? Supply-chain resilience, technological sovereignty, and enduring global interdependencies in the post-pandemic era. *Critical Sociology*. https://doi.org/10.1177/08969205241239872

Caldara, D., & Iacoviello, M. (2018). Measuring geopolitical risk. *Political Economy: Government Expenditures & Related Policies eJournal*. https://doi.org/10.17016/IFDP.2018.1222

Charpin, R. (2022). The resurgence of nationalism and its implications for supply chain risk management. *International Journal of Physical Distribution & Logistics Management, 52*(1), 4–28. https://doi.org/10.1108/IJPDLM-01-2021-0019

Choi, T. Y., Dooley, K. J., & Rungtusanatham, M. (2001). Supply networks and complex adaptive systems: Control versus emergence. *Journal of Operations Management, 19*(3), 351–366. https://doi.org/10.1016/S0272-6963(00)00068-1

Colantone, I., & Stanig, P. (2019). The surge of economic nationalism in Western Europe. *Journal of Economic Perspectives, 33*(4), 128–151. https://doi.org/10.1257/jep.33.4.128

Comerma, L. (2024). The normative influence of the belt and road initiative in Europe. *Journal of Current Chinese Affairs, 54*(2). https://doi.org/10.1177/18681026241277215

Dolgui, A., & Ivanov, D. (2021). Ripple effect and supply chain disruption management: New trends and research directions. *International Journal of Production Research, 59*(1), 102–109. https://doi.org/10.1080/00207543.2021.1840148

Dolgui, A., Ivanov, D., & Sokolov, B. (2018). Ripple effect in the supply chain: An analysis and recent literature. *International Journal of Production Research, 56*(1–2), 414–430. https://doi.org/10.1080/00207543.2017.1387680

Duong, L., Sanderson, H., Phillips, W., Roehrich, J., & Uwalaka, V. (2024). Achieving resilient supply chains: Managing temporary healthcare supply chains during a geopolitical disruption. *International Journal of Operations & Production Management, 29*. https://doi.org/10.1108/IJOPM-03-2024-0243

Elder-Vass, D. (2022). Pragmatism, critical realism and the study of value. *Journal of Critical Realism, 21*(3), 261–287. https://doi.org/10.1080/14767430.2022.2049088

Feingold, S., & Torkington, S. (2024). What is a geopolitical recession and how could we avoid one? *World Economic Forum*. https://www.weforum.org/stories/2024/05/what-is-a-geopolitical-recession-and-are-we-heading-into-one

Finkenstadt, D. J., & Handfield, R. B. (2021). Tuning value chains for better signals in the post-COVID era: Vaccine supply chain concerns. *International Journal of Operations & Production Management*, *41*(8), 1302–1317. https://doi.org/10.1108/IJOPM-01-2021-0039

Gereffi, G. (2014). Global value chains in a post-Washington consensus world. *Review of International Political Economy*, *21*(1), 9–37. https://doi.org/10.1080/09692290.2012.756414

Gereffi, G., Humphrey, J., & Sturgeon, T. (2005). The governance of global value chains. *Review of International Political Economy*, *12*(1), 78–104. https://doi.org/10.1080/09692290500049805

Gereffi, G., Pananond, P., & Pedersen, T. (2022). Resilience decoded: The role of firms, global value chains, and the state in COVID-19 medical supplies. *California Management Review*, *64*(2), 46–70. https://doi.org/10.1177/00081256211069420

Gorynia, M., Nowak, J., Trąpczyński, P., & Wolniak, R. (2024). What drives export resilience? The case of post-transition country firms in the context of the COVID-19 pandemic. *Entrepreneurial Business and Economics Review*, *12*(1), 119–133. https://doi.org/10.15678/EBER.2024.120107

Guetterman, T. C., Molina-Azorin, J. F., & Fetters, M. D. (2020). Virtual Special Issue on "Integration in Mixed Methods Research." *Journal of Mixed Methods Research*, *14*(4), 430–435. https://doi.org/10.1177/1558689820956401

Halldórsson, A., Kotzab, H., Mikkola, J. H., & Skjøtt-Larsen, T. (2007). Complementary theories to supply chain management. *Supply Chain Management: An International Journal*, *12*(4), 284–296. https://doi.org/10.1108/13598540710759808

Handfield, R. B., & Nichols, E. L. (2002). *Supply chain redesign: Transforming supply chains into integrated value systems*. Ft Press.

Iftikhar, A., Ali, I., Zhan, Y., Stevenson, M., & Tarba, S. Y. (2025). Firms' strategic responses to rising uncertainty amid ongoing geopolitical tensions: The synergistic mediating role of network capability and innovation ambidexterity. *Transportation Research Part E: Logistics and Transportation Review*, *199*. https://doi.org/10.1016/j.tre.2025.104146

Johnson, P., & Duberley, J. (2000). Pragmatism and critical realism - transcending Descartes' either/or? In *Understanding management research* (149–176). SAGE Publications Ltd. https://doi.org/10.4135/9780857020185.n7

Jüttner, U., & Maklan, S. (2011). Supply chain resilience in the global financial crisis: An empirical study. *Supply Chain Management*, *16*, 246–259. https://doi.org/10.1108/13598541111139062

Kaplan, R. S., & Mikes, A. (2012). Managing risks: A new framework. *Harvard Business Review*, *90*(6), 48–60.

Khan, K., Khurshid, A., & Cifuentes-Faura, J. (2023). Investigating the relationship between geopolitical risks and economic security: Empirical evidence from central and Eastern European countries. *Resources Policy*, *85*, 103872. https://doi.org/10.1016/j.resourpol.2023.103872

Kisperska-Moron, D., & de Haan, J. (2011). Improving supply chain performance to satisfy final customers: "Leagile" experiences of a polish distributor. *Leading Edge of Inventory Research*, *133*(1), 127–134. https://doi.org/10.1016/j.ijpe.2009.12.013

Kotcharin, S., & Maneenop, S. (2020). Geopolitical risk and shipping firms' capital structure decisions in Belt and Road Initiative countries. *International Journal of Logistics Research and Applications*, *23*(6), 544–560. https://doi.org/10.1080/13675567.2020.1766003

Lawrence, M., Homer-Dixon, T., Janzwood, S., Rockström, J., Renn, O., & Donges, J. F. (2024). Global polycrisis: The causal mechanisms of crisis entanglement. *Global Sustainability*, *7*, 6. https://doi.org/10.1017/sus.2024.1

McKinsey & Company. (2024, March). Economic conditions outlook 2024. McKinsey & Company. https://www.mckinsey.com/capabilities/strategy-and-corporate-finance/our-insights/economic-conditions-outlook-2024

Mena, C., Karatzas, A., & Hansen, C. (2022). International trade resilience and the COVID-19 pandemic. *Journal of Business Research*, *138*, 77–91. https://doi.org/10.1016/j.jbusres.2021.08.064

Moradlou, H., Reefke, H., Skipworth, H., & Roscoe, S. (2021). Geopolitical disruptions and the manufacturing location decision in multinational company supply chains: A Delphi study on Brexit. *International Journal of Operations & Production Management*, *41*, 102–130. https://doi.org/10.1108/IJOPM-07-2020-0465

Morin, E., & Kern, A. B. (1999). *Homeland earth: A manifesto for the new millennium*. Hampton Press.

Mroczek-Dąbrowska, K., Cherubin, D., & Kania, A. (2024). The art of deception: The trade-off between the information distortion and perception of FDI location attractiveness. *Entrepreneurial Business and Economics Review*, *12*(3), 205–219. https://doi.org/10.15678/EBER.2024.120311

Mroczek-Dąbrowska, K., & Kania, A. (2020). Poland's competitive position between 2005 and 2017 – A road to success. In *Poland in the single market: Politics, economics, the euro*. Routledge. https://doi.org/10.4324/9780429285301-4

Mrowiec, M., & Penczar, M. (2024). The most important threats to economic policy, financial system stability and PLN credibility – Results of the 12th edition of the forecast consensus of the European Financial Congress. *Bezpieczny Bank*, (4), *93*(4), 7–28. https://repozytorium.bg.ug.edu.pl/info/article/UOG40a20fcd978d4e48ac59d9a4b65ef363/

Newman, S. (2024). *Discover New Paths to supply chain resilience: How are European businesses responding to disruption?* Maersk. https://www.maersk.com/~/media_sc9/maersk/news/insights/files/european-business-resilience-report-2024.pdf&ved=2ahUKEwiKl7Ly5Y-SAxU0HBAIHVyRDngQFnoECBkQAQ&usg=AOvVaw2N45ow5Q6DER67OLojcIVf

North, D. C. (1990). *Institutions, institutional change and economic performance*. Cambridge University Press.

Pathak, S. D., Day, J. M., Nair, A., Sawaya, W. J., & Kristal, M. M. (2007). Complexity and adaptivity in supply networks: Building supply network theory using a complex adaptive systems perspective. *Decision Sciences*, *38*(4), 547–580. https://doi.org/10.1111/j.1540-5915.2007.00170.x

Pettit, T. J., Fiksel, J., & Croxton, K. L. (2010). Ensuring supply chain resilience: Development of a conceptual framework. *Journal of Business Logistics*, *31*(1), 1–21. https://doi.org/10.1002/j.2158-1592.2010.tb00125.x

Politico. (2024). *Houthi rebels and the EU make your coffee more expensive*. *Politico*. https://www.politico.eu/article/coffee-trade-espresso-europe-covid-global-supply/

Ponomarov, S. Y., & Holcomb, M. C. (2009). Understanding the concept of supply chain resilience. *The International Journal of Logistics Management, 20*(1), 124–143. https://doi.org/10.1108/09574090910954873

Roscoe, S., Aktas, E., Petersen, K. J., Skipworth, H. D., Handfield, R. B., & Habib, F. (2022). Redesigning global supply chains during compounding geopolitical disruptions: The role of supply chain logics. *International Journal of Operations & Production Management, 42*(9), 1407–1434. https://doi.org/10.1108/IJOPM-12-2021-0777

Senge, P. M. (1990). *The fifth discipline: The art and practice of the learning organization*. Doubleday/Currency.

Serhan, Y. (2023, January 17). *Why 'polycrisis' was the buzzword of day 1 in Davos. Time*. https://time.com/6247799/polycrisis-in-davos-wef-2023/

Sheffi, Y., & Rice, B. J. (2005). A supply chain view of the resilient enterprise. *MIT Sloan Management Review, 47*(1), 41–48. https://sloanreview.mit.edu/article/a-supply-chain-view-of-the-resilient-enterprise/

Swilling, M. (2013). Economic crisis, long waves and the sustainability transition: An African perspective. *Environmental Innovation and Societal Transitions, 6*, 96–115. https://doi.org/10.1016/j.eist.2012.11.001

Swilling, M. (2020). *The age of sustainability: Just transitions in a complex world*. Routledge, Taylor & Francis Group.

Tao, Y., Yang, W., Ye, Y., & Kong, D. (2024). The shock of U.S.-China trade war and the job market: Downstream shrinkage and upstream employment. *Journal of International Financial Markets Institutions & Money, 96*, 16. https://doi.org/10.1016/j.intfin.2024.102057

Teece, D. J., Pisano, G., & Shuen, A. (1997). Dynamic capabilities and strategic management. *Strategic Management Journal, 18*(7). https://www.jstor.org/stable/3088148

Timans, R., Wouters, P., & Heilbron, J. (2019). Mixed methods research: What it is and what it could be. *Theory and Society, 48*(2), 193–216. https://doi.org/10.1007/s11186-019-09345-5

Tooze, A. (2022, June 24). Defining polycrisis – From crisis pictures to the crisis matrix. https://adamtooze.substack.com/p/chartbook-130-defining-polycrisis

Tranfield, D., Denyer, D., & Smart, P. (2003). Towards a methodology for developing evidence-informed management knowledge by means of systematic review. *British Journal of Management, 14*(3), 207–222. https://doi.org/10.1111/1467-8551.00375

van Hoek, R. (2020). Research opportunities for a more resilient post-COVID-19 supply chain – closing the gap between research findings and industry practice. *International Journal of Operations & Production Management, 40*(4), 341–355. https://doi.org/10.1108/IJOPM-03-2020-0165

Wieland, A., Stevenson, M., Melnyk, S. A., Davoudi, S., & Schultz, L. (2023). Thinking differently about supply chain resilience: What we can learn from social-ecological systems thinking. *International Journal of Operations & Production Management, 43*(1), 1–21. https://doi.org/10.1108/IJOPM-10-2022-0645

Wilden, D., Hopkins, J., & Sadler, I. (2024). System thinking skills and their effect upon supply chain resilience: A practitioner perspective. *Systems Research and Behavioral Science, 42*(6). https://doi.org/10.1002/sres.3072

Williamson, O. E. (1975). Markets and hierarchies: Analysis and antitrust implications: A study in the economics of internal organization. *University of Illinois at*

Urbana - Champaign's Academy for Entrepreneurial Leadership Historical Research Reference in Entrepreneurship.

World Economic Forum (WEF). (2024). The global risks report 2025. World Economic Forum. https://reports.weforum.org/docs/WEF_Global_Risks_Report_2025.pdf

Zhang, F., Wu, X., Tang, C. S., Feng, T., & Dai, Y. (2020). Evolution of operations management research: From managing flows to building capabilities. *Production and Operations Management*, *29*(10), 2219–2229. https://doi.org/10.1111/poms.13231

2 Building resilient supply chains

Evolution and theoretical frameworks

Introduction

The concept of resilience originates from the Latin *resiliere*, meaning to rebound or recoil, and has been used across disciplines to describe the capacity of systems to absorb disturbance while maintaining core functions. In ecological economics, Holling's (1973) seminal contribution marked a decisive departure from equilibrium-based interpretations by conceptualising resilience as the ability of systems to persist, adapt, and reorganise under conditions of uncertainty. This shift introduced an explicitly economic concern with stability, path dependence, and adaptive capacity. Subsequent contributions in psychology (Luthar *et al.*, 2000), engineering (Hollnagel *et al.*, 2006), and disaster management (Manyena, 2006) further emphasised learning, flexibility, and recovery, establishing conceptual foundations later adopted in organisational and production-system research.

As resilience entered supply chain scholarship, it became closely associated with economic vulnerability, coordination failure, and the costs of adjustment under uncertainty. Early SCRES research framed resilience as the capacity to restore operations following disruption, reflecting concerns with continuity and recovery in inter-firm networks. Over time, this focus broadened to encompass anticipatory capabilities, resource reallocation, and structural adaptation in globally fragmented production systems. Pettit *et al.* (2010) conceptualise supply chain vulnerability as a function of turbulence, external pressures, resource constraints, sensitivity, connectivity, and partner dependence, explicitly linking exposure to disruption with capability investment. Their subsequent analysis (Pettit *et al.*, 2013) demonstrates how targeted capability development reduces vulnerability and stabilises performance, reinforcing an economic interpretation of resilience grounded in adjustment costs and coordination mechanisms.

Within management and economics, SCRES has thus evolved from a narrow emphasis on post-disruption recovery toward a broader concern with adaptive efficiency in interconnected production systems. As supply chains became more specialised, geographically dispersed, and institutionally

DOI: 10.4324/9781003733089-2

exposed, research increasingly examined buffering costs, coordination breakdowns, and economic implications of reconfiguration. Contemporary contributions conceptualise supply chains as interdependent systems in which disruptions propagate through contractual linkages, capacity constraints, price mechanisms, and institutional frictions across firms and regions.

This chapter traces the evolution of SCRES thinking through an explicitly economic lens and synthesises the principal theoretical frameworks that have shaped the field. Attention is directed toward how different strands of theory conceptualise adjustment, capability development, and stability under uncertainty. By organising these perspectives chronologically and analytically, the chapter establishes the foundations for understanding resilience as a cumulative and path-dependent process of economically grounded adaptation. This synthesis provides the conceptual basis for the capability framework developed later in the chapter and informs the bibliometric and empirical analyses presented in subsequent chapters.

From recovery to capability systems: the evolution of supply chain resilience

SCRES has undergone a marked conceptual evolution over the past two decades. While its core meaning—anticipating, absorbing, responding to, and recovering from disruptions—remains consistent with the definition adopted in this monograph, scholarly interpretations have expanded as supply chains have become increasingly exposed to systemic and persistent sources of disruption, including geopolitical disturbances.

Early conceptualisations of SCRES were predominantly recovery-oriented, defining resilience as the ability to restore operations following discrete shocks (Caniato & Rice, 2003; Christopher & Peck, 2004). As global production networks became more fragmented and interdependent, subsequent contributions broadened this perspective by incorporating anticipation, adaptability, and strategic preparation. This shift reflected growing recognition of structural vulnerability, coordination complexity, and dependence across supply chain tiers (Jüttner & Maklan, 2011; Pettit *et al.*, 2010; Ponomarov & Holcomb, 2009).

From the late 2010s onward, resilience has increasingly been conceptualised as a capability-based and systemic construct. Rather than focusing on episodic recovery, more recent works emphasise interdependence, path dependence, and cumulative adjustment under persistent uncertainty (Dolgui & Ivanov, 2021; Dolgui *et al.*, 2018). Contemporary contributions further advance this systemic interpretation by framing resilience as an emergent property of interconnected production networks shaped by reinforcing feedbacks and long-term reconfiguration processes (Scholten *et al.*, 2025; Zheng *et al.*, 2025). Table 2.1 summarises this evolution and illustrates the shift from reactive recovery toward integrated, capability-based, and system-oriented interpretations of SCRES.

Table 2.1 Selected definitions of SCRES

Researcher/s	*Theoretical lens*	*Definition*
Caniato and Rice (2003)	-	The ability to react to unexpected disruption and restore normal supply network operations.
Christopher and Peck (2004)	-	The ability of a system [supply chain] to revert to its original state or transition to a new, more favourable state after experiencing a disruption.
Sheffi and Rice (2005)	-	The ability of a supply chain to adapt to and recover from disruptions while maintaining the continuity of operations. Resilient supply chains can not only withstand unexpected disruptions but also absorb shocks and recover quickly, allowing them to return to normal or even improve their performance following disturbances.
Tang (2006)	-	The ability to manage fluctuations efficiently and recover quickly from disruptions. A resilient supply chain not only continues operations smoothly under normal circumstances but also adapts and sustains itself during crises. SCRES requires balancing cost efficiency with agility, flexibility, and strategic planning.
Ponomarov and Holcomb (2009)	Dynamic Capabilities Resource-Based View (RBV)	The ability to anticipate unexpected events, respond effectively to disruptions, and recover by ensuring the continuity of operations while maintaining the desired level of connectivity and control over its structure and functions.
Pettit *et al.* (2010, 2013)	Resource-Based View (RBV) Dynamic Capabilities Systems Theory	It's the desired balance between capabilities and vulnerabilities that creates a firm's true competitive advantage.
Blackhurst *et al.* (2011)	Systems Theory Resource Based View (RBV)	The ability of a supply chain to anticipate, react to, and bounce back from disruptions.
Jüttner & Maklan (2011)	-	The adaptive capability of the supply chain to prepare for unexpected events, respond to disruptions, and recover from them based on the four formative elements: flexibility, velocity, visibility and collaboration.
Ponis and Koronis (2012)	-	The ability to proactively plan and design the supply chain network for anticipating unexpected disruptive (negative) events, respond adaptively to disruptions while maintaining control over structure and function and transcending to a post-event robust state of operations, if possible, more favourable than the one prior to the event, thus gaining competitive advantage.

(*Continued*)

Table 2.1 (Continued)

Researcher/s	*Theoretical lens*	*Definition*
Wieland and Wallenburg (2013)	Relational View (RV)	The ability of a supply chain to cope with change through either reactive or proactive interaction with the environment. Relationships between supply chain members have positive influence on resilience.
Brandon-Jones *et al.* (2014)	Contingency Theory Resource-Based View (RBV)	The ability of a system to return to its original state, within an acceptable period of time, after being disturbed.
Melnyk *et al.* (2014)	-	The ability of a supply chain to both resist disruptions and recover operational capability after disruptions occur.
Zhao *et al.* (2019)	Complex Adaptive Systems (CAS)	The ability of a supply chain to adapt to disruptions by restructuring its configuration and operations through decentralised and context-specific decision-making by individual firms.
Dolgui *et al.* (2018), Dolgui and Ivanov (2021)	-	The ability of a supply chain to resist, absorb, and recover from disruptions while maintaining its essential functions. SCRES is seen as a combination of robustness (preventing or minimising the impact of disruptions), redundancy (modifying operations in response to changing conditions), and recoverability (restoring performance levels after a disruption).
Zheng *et al.* (2025)	Organizational Information Processing Theory (OIPT)	The evolving organizational capability that emerges through adaptive learning, strategic reconfiguration, and proactive value creation in response to geopolitical disruptions.
Scholten *et al.* (2025)	Panarchy Theory	The authors argue that resilience should not be viewed as a fixed outcome or static trait but rather as a dynamic capability that evolves through interaction with internal configurations and external conditions.

Source: Own elaboration based on Caniato and Rice (2003), Christopher and Peck (2004), Sheffi and Rice (2005), Tang (2006), Pettit *et al.* (2010), Blackhurst *et al.* (2011), Jüttner and Maklan (2011), Ponis and Koronis (2012), Wieland and Wallenburg (2013), Brandon-Jones *et al.* (2014), Melnyk *et al.* (2014), Dolgui *et al.* (2018), Zhao *et al.* (2019), Dolgui and Ivanov (2021), Scholten *et al.* (2025), and Zheng *et al.* (2025).

Collectively, these definitions reveal a coherent analytical trajectory. Early work prioritised continuity and post-disruption recovery; later studies incorporated anticipatory and adaptive capacities; and recent research conceptualises resilience as a dynamic property of interconnected systems. Despite differences in emphasis, the literature converges on a shared logic: resilience reflects the capacity of supply chains to withstand disruption, coordinate effective responses, and renew their structures over time. This logic underpins the capability-based framework developed later in the chapter, which organises resilience around interdependent adjustment functions operating across disruption phases.

Theoretical perspectives underpinning supply chain resilience

Analysis of the definitions summarised in Table 2.1 indicates that only a subset of SCRES studies explicitly adopts a theoretical framework. Among these, the Resource-Based View (RBV) is most frequently applied. RBV emphasises the role of firm-specific tangible and intangible resources in shaping capabilities that influence responses to internal and external shocks (Barney, 1991; Prahalad & Hamel, 1990). In the SCRES literature, this perspective has been used to examine human, organisational, and inter-organisational capital (Blackhurst *et al.*, 2011) as well as logistics capabilities (Ponomarov & Holcomb, 2009). To address the static limitations of RBV, scholars increasingly combine it with complementary perspectives, most prominently the dynamic capabilities view (Teece, 2014; Teece *et al.*, 1997), alongside contingency theory (Lawrence & Lorsch, 1967), systems theory (Katz & Kahn, 1978), the relational view (Dyer & Singh, 1998), complex adaptive systems theory (CAS) (Anderson, 1999; Holland, 1992), organisational information processing theory (OIPT) (Zheng *et al.*, 2025), and panarchy theory (Scholten *et al.*, 2025).

Definitions lacking explicit theoretical grounding tend to emphasise descriptive attributes such as flexibility, resistance, or recovery speed, without specifying the mechanisms through which these properties emerge or the conditions under which they are effective. By contrast, theoretically grounded approaches articulate causal mechanisms, boundary conditions, and levels of analysis, thereby enabling more consistent operationalisation. The uneven use of theory has contributed to fragmentation within the SCRES literature, underscoring the need for more integrated explanatory frameworks, particularly in contexts shaped by geopolitical disruption.

The dynamic capabilities view plays a central role in advancing such integration. Building on foundations in Schumpeterian innovation (Schumpeter, 1942), firm growth theory (Penrose, 1959), and evolutionary economics (Nelson & Winter, 1982), The Dynamic Capabilities View (DCV) conceptualises firms' capacity to sense environmental change, seize feasible adjustment options, and reconfigure resource bases over time (Teece, 2014; Teece *et al.*, 1997). This logic is particularly relevant for SCRES, where firms must repeatedly reallocate resources and redesign coordination structures under conditions of heightened uncertainty and shifting constraints.

Applied to supply chains, DCV highlights the importance of cross-organisational integration of resources and routines in enabling adaptive responses. Prior research identifies agility, velocity, and visibility as key antecedents of effective adjustment (Christopher & Peck, 2004; Jüttner & Maklan, 2011), while empirical evidence demonstrates that dynamic reconfiguration of processes and relationships underpins resilience outcomes (Brusset & Teller, 2017). Complementary perspectives further enrich this account: contingency theory emphasises alignment with contextual conditions; systems theory and CAS perspectives illuminate interdependence, non-linearity, and feedback effects (Blackhurst *et al.*, 2011; Bode *et al.*, 2011; Choi *et al.*, 2001; Katz & Kahn, 1978; Pettit *et al.*, 2013; Zhao *et al.*, 2019); the relational view highlights joint routines and shared assets supporting coordinated action (Dyer & Singh, 1998; Wieland & Wallenburg, 2013); and OIPT and panarchy theory address informational complexity, cyclical adaptation, and multi-level dynamics under turbulence (Scholten *et al.*, 2025; Vural *et al.*, 2024; Zheng *et al.*, 2025).

Combined, these perspectives are treated not as competing explanations but as complementary analytical lenses for examining economically grounded adjustment processes. RBV and DCV explain how resilience capabilities are built and reconfigured; contingency and systems-based approaches clarify how effectiveness depends on contextual and structural conditions; and relational and information-processing perspectives specify coordination and information mechanisms. Given that geopolitical disruptions simultaneously affect costs, constraints, relationships, and information flows, such theoretical integration is necessary to explain the formation and activation of SCRES under persistent uncertainty.

A capability-based framework of supply chain resilience

Building on the theoretical perspectives outlined above, this section develops a capability-based framework of SCRES grounded in four interrelated capabilities: readiness, responsiveness, resurgence, and collaboration. These capabilities are aligned with the temporal logic of disruption—pre-disruption, during disruption, and post-disruption—while collaboration operates as a transversal mechanism across all phases.

The dynamic capabilities view provides the overarching explanatory logic of the framework. Through processes of sensing, seizing, and reconfiguring, firms adapt supply chain structures, routines, and resource allocations in response to changing external constraints (Teece, 2014; Teece *et al.*, 1997). In this study, dynamic capabilities are not used to explain sustained competitive advantage or rent generation but to account for firm-level adjustment processes under uncertainty, capturing how organisations respond to altered cost structures, regulatory conditions, and access constraints induced by geopolitical disruption.

Within this analytical framing, resilience emerges as an outcome of economically motivated reconfiguration decisions rather than as a normative managerial objective. Capability activation reflects firms' efforts to preserve operational continuity, stabilise transactions, and sustain participation in international value chains when existing supply chain arrangements become infeasible. The framework thus links resilience directly to observable adjustment behaviour under shifting institutional and geopolitical conditions.

Empirical research consistently supports a capability-based interpretation of resilience. Prior studies identify capabilities that prevent, mitigate, and enable adaptation to disruption (Pettit *et al.*, 2010), emphasise visibility and velocity as antecedents of agility (Christopher & Peck, 2004; Jüttner & Maklan, 2011), and conceptualise resilience as a composite capability encompassing agility, collaboration, information sharing, risk awareness, and trust (Pettit *et al.*, 2013; Um & Han, 2021). Related work highlights flexibility, visibility, velocity, and collaboration as core resilience dimensions (Dolgui & Ivanov, 2021; Dolgui *et al.*, 2018), while innovation and adaptive processes are identified as key drivers of resilience formation (Katsaliaki *et al.*, 2022). These contributions, together with foundational insights from Schumpeter (1942), Penrose (1959), Nelson and Winter (1982), and Prahalad and Hamel (1990), inform the capability factors summarised in Table 2.2.

Table 2.2 positions readiness, responsiveness, resurgence, and collaboration as complementary capabilities underpinning SCRES. Readiness captures pre-disruption sensing, planning, and buffering activities, reflecting both the dynamic capabilities logic of anticipation and the contingency perspective

Table 2.2 Capability factors

Capability factors	*Definition*
Readiness	The ability to anticipate and interpret emerging risks through sensing and scanning, and to adjust inputs, outputs, or structural configurations in advance to strengthen supply chain design prior to disruption.
Responsiveness	The ability to quickly and effectively react to changes and disruptions while maintaining continuity through built-in redundancies. It involves a balance between agility, (understood as velocity, visibility and flexibility) and redundancy.
Resurgence	Unlike recovery, which focuses on reinstating prior performance levels, resurgence involves re-optimising supply chain structures under newly established political, regulatory, and cost constraints.
Collaboration	The ability to work effectively with other entities for mutual benefit.

Source: Own elaboration based on Christopher and Peck (2004), Ponomarov and Holcomb (2009), Pettit *et al.* (2010, 2013), Jüttner and Maklan (2011), Chowdhury and Quaddus (2016), Dolgui *et al.* (2018), Dolgui and Ivanov (2021), Katsaliaki *et al.* (2022), and Nikookar *et al.* (2024).

on strategic fit. It is strengthened through adjustments to inputs, outputs, and structural parameters in advance of disruption, as well as through buffers such as safety stock or excess capacity that stabilise supply chains under geopolitical uncertainty. These mechanisms involve trade-offs between resilience and efficiency (Contractor, 2025; Kampton *et al.*, 2023) and are supported by advanced planning systems, predictive analytics, digital twins, and related digital tools that enhance information-processing capacity, scenario evaluation, and early-warning capabilities in complex and uncertain environments (Zheng *et al.*, 2025).

Responsiveness encompasses during-disruption actions that enable firms to maintain operational continuity once shocks materialise. Logistics, operations, and supplier network responsiveness jointly shape the ability to absorb disruption and prevent cascading failures across interconnected activities (Gunasekaran *et al.*, 2008; Matysek *et al.*, 2024). Effective responsiveness depends on balancing agility—enabled by flexible processes, rapid information flows, and decentralised decision-making—and redundancy, which provides short-term safeguards but generates transaction costs (Williamson, 1989), cognitive constraints linked to bounded rationality (Simon, 1990), and relational tensions associated with bounded reliability (Kano & Verbeke, 2015). Responsiveness therefore reflects a coping and stabilisation capability that operates within existing supply chain structures, relying on coordination, contractual flexibility, and short-term rebalancing rather than durable structural change.

Under persistent geopolitical disruption, resurgence becomes as important as responsiveness, as repeated short-term adaptation without structural adjustment leads to escalating cumulative costs. Resurgence represents the post-disruption capability through which firms restore performance while deliberately reconfiguring supply chain structures under new political, regulatory, and cost conditions. Drawing on dynamic capabilities and panarchy perspectives, resurgence integrates recovery with transformation, consistent with Schumpeterian creative destruction (Schumpeter, 1942) and continuous reconfiguration logic (Teece, 2014). Structural responses such as reshoring, nearshoring, regional diversification, and supplier base reconfiguration are central to resurgence, as they alter long-term exposure profiles and coordination architectures. Technologies developed as part of readiness, including additive manufacturing, artificial intelligence, and circular production practices, support resurgence by lowering switching costs and expanding feasible reconfiguration options, without constituting resurgence mechanisms in their own right (Alvarenga *et al.*, 2023; Belhadi *et al.*, 2024a; Chowdhury & Quaddus, 2016; Nakandala *et al.*, 2023; Pessot *et al.*, 2023).

Collaboration functions as a transversal capability supporting all disruption phases. Rooted in the relational view, it enables access to complementary resources, information sharing, joint risk management, and coordinated adjustment across organisational boundaries (Christopher & Peck, 2004; Dyer & Singh, 1998; Jüttner & Maklan, 2011). Long-term relationships reduce transaction costs, mitigate information asymmetries, and enhance network stability under geopolitical strain (Knoben, 2008; McEvily & Zaheer, 1999; Ratajczak-Mrozek, 2017; Swiatowiec-Szczepanska & Kawa, 2018; Peters *et al.*, 2022; Daghar *et al.*, 2023; Zhou *et al.*, 2024). At the same time, systems and complex adaptive systems perspectives caution that interdependence can amplify systemic vulnerability, necessitating governance mechanisms that balance openness and control (Blackhurst *et al.*, 2011; Bode *et al.*, 2011; Contractor, 2025; Kim *et al.*, 2011).

Collectively, readiness, responsiveness, resurgence, and collaboration constitute a coherent capability system spanning the disruption lifecycle. By integrating anticipation, concurrent response, post-disruption renewal, and network-level coordination, the framework captures the cumulative and path-dependent nature of resilience formation. This capability-based perspective provides the conceptual foundation for analysing how resilience interacts with vulnerabilities and mitigation mechanisms under geopolitical disruption, as examined in the following section.

Geopolitical disruption as a structural source of supply chain risk

The resilience capabilities discussed in this chapter become particularly relevant when supply chains are exposed to geopolitical disruptions, which generate forms of uncertainty that extend beyond conventional operational risk. In this book, geopolitical disruptions, as already defined in Chapter 1, are understood as risks associated with wars, interstate tensions, and politically motivated disruptions involving state and non-state actors (Caldara & Iacoviello, 2018, p. 2). Such disruptions encompass political conflict, sanctions, strategic rivalry, and abrupt policy shifts that reshape the institutional and economic conditions governing global production systems. Their effects materialise through altered trade flows, restricted access to strategic inputs, constrained cross-border mobility, heightened cyber vulnerability, and rapidly changing regulatory requirements, cascading across interconnected supply networks and destabilising established sourcing, manufacturing, and distribution arrangements. Empirical evidence confirms that geopolitical tensions affect operational continuity, investment behaviour, and long-term supply chain design decisions (Aldrighetti *et al.*, 2021; Alikhani *et al.*, 2023; Althaf & Babbitt, 2021; BlackRock Corporate, 2025; Kotcharin & Maneenop, 2020; Moradlou *et al.*, 2021).

Geopolitical disruptions operate simultaneously at macroeconomic, institutional, and supply network levels, shaping exposure, vulnerability, and adaptive capacity. Recent events—including the United Kingdom's withdrawal from the European Union, U.S.–China trade tensions, the COVID-19 pandemic, and renewed regional conflicts—illustrate how geopolitical shocks disrupt production architectures, increase costs, extend lead times, complicate border procedures, and generate uncertainty regarding the location and governance of manufacturing assets (Bier *et al.*, 2020; Küffner *et al.*, 2022; Moosavi *et al.*, 2022; Mroczek-Dąbrowska *et al.*, 2023; Azadi *et al.*, 2024; Echefaj *et al.*, 2024; Ghanbarzadeh *et al.*, 2024; Schleifenheimer & Ivanov, 2024). From a contingency perspective, these dynamics reinforce the need for organisational adaptation through alignment between external conditions and internal structures (Lawrence & Lorsch, 1967; Roscoe *et al.*, 2020).

In direct connection with **RQ2**, firms operating across borders face a constellation of interrelated risks driven by geopolitical instability. Trade policy volatility manifests through export controls, sanctions, and tariff changes that raise costs and restrict market access (World Trade Organization [WTO], 2023; PricewaterhouseCoopers [PwC], 2022). Disruptions to material flows further undermine reliability as conflict, border closures, or political instability interrupt the movement of intermediate inputs (IMF, 2022; McKinsey & Company, 2020). Regulatory uncertainty compounds these challenges through frequent changes in customs rules and compliance requirements, increasing administrative burdens and slowing shipments (Deloitte, 2021; OECD, 2023).

Geopolitical tensions also affect transportation and logistics systems via port restrictions, airspace closures, sanctions on carriers, and unsafe transit corridors, reducing logistical efficiency and predictability (BCG, 2022; World Bank, 2023). Financial risks arise through exchange-rate volatility, capital controls, and constraints on cross-border payments, complicating procurement and financial planning (ECB, 2021; KPMG, 2022). At the same time, cyber risks have intensified as state-sponsored attacks and politically motivated disruptions threaten digital infrastructure and operational continuity (World Economic Forum, 2023; IBM Security, 2022).

Exposure is further amplified by supplier concentration in geopolitically sensitive regions, increasing dependence on vulnerable sourcing locations (McKinsey & Company, 2023). Labour-related risks also play a role, as civil unrest, political restrictions, and regulatory interventions disrupt workforce availability and production capacity (International Labour Organization [ILO], 2022; UNCTAD, 2023). Although these risks differ in form and transmission channels, they converge in highlighting how geopolitical uncertainty destabilises cross-border coordination and increases cumulative adjustment costs.

These dynamics underscore the structural nature of geopolitical disruption as a source of supply chain risk. Effective mitigation therefore requires coordinated configurations of readiness, responsiveness, resurgence, and collaboration. Readiness supports proactive monitoring and assessment; responsiveness enables rapid operational adjustment during disruption; resurgence facilitates longer-term technological, organisational, and structural upgrading; and collaboration strengthens information sharing and coordinated action across networks. These conceptual foundations provide the basis for examining macro-level resilience mechanisms in the following section.

Industrial policy and macro-level conditions shaping supply chain resilience

The risks outlined above increase the geopolitical exposure of multinational enterprises and elevate the strategic importance of state-driven interventions. As supply chains become more entangled in political, economic, and technological rivalries, resilience capabilities—readiness, responsiveness, resurgence, and collaboration—operate within increasingly constrained environments. Industrial policy has therefore re-emerged as a central mechanism for managing geopolitical risk, safeguarding critical sectors, and restructuring global supply chains. This section examines how the United States, China and the European Union, are reshaping industrial policy and how these shifts influence firm-level adaptive space.

A longer-term policy realignment began in the late twentieth century, when globalisation accelerated on the back of falling trade barriers and new manufacturing hubs. The trajectory reversed as protectionist sentiment grew from 2017 onward. Tariff escalations, renewed nationalist agendas, and political ruptures—including the U.S.–China trade war and Brexit—demonstrated how geopolitical tensions can rapidly alter the structure of production networks (Główka *et al.*, 2021; Jankowska *et al.*, 2021; Johnson & Haug, 2021; Shivakumar *et al.*, 2024). After the COVID-19 pandemic, concerns over technological sovereignty and supply chain fragility intensified state intervention.

In the United States, major legislative initiatives such as the Infrastructure Investment and Jobs Act (2021), the CHIPS and Science Act (2022), and the Inflation Reduction Act (2022) mobilised extensive public funding to rebuild domestic capacity in semiconductors and clean technologies. These measures introduced strong local content requirements aimed at increasing readiness by reducing strategic dependencies and strengthening domestic production ecosystems (Luo & Van Assche, 2023). In parallel, export controls directed at China sought to constrain technological diffusion and protect U.S. leadership in critical technologies (Schivakumar *et al.*, 2024). Tariff increases introduced in 2025 further intensified geopolitical frictions, raising costs for firms and consumers and limiting responsiveness by constraining rapid sourcing adjustments (Contractor, 2025), while China's retaliatory measures reinforced the cyclical nature of such policy escalation (Fajgelbaum & Khandelwal, 2022). Subsequent updates to export control rules and tariff enforcement in 2024–2025 tightened constraints on technology transfer and sourcing flexibility, consolidating policy volatility as a structural limitation on firms' short-term responsiveness.

Against this backdrop, China's policy direction has increasingly centred on technological self-sufficiency as a strategic response to external constraints. The Dual Circulation Strategy (2020) and the Fourteenth Five-Year Plan (2021–2025) prioritise domestic capabilities in semiconductors, artificial intelligence, and green technologies. Large-scale investments channelled through the Integrated Circuit Investment Fund (2023) aim to reduce external vulnerability and insulate critical sectors from geopolitical shocks (García-Herrero & Schindowski, 2024). These measures strengthen readiness and post-disruption resurgence by expanding domestic innovation and production ecosystems, while simultaneously constraining collaboration with foreign partners as regulatory controls and technology restrictions tighten. Implementation guidelines and enforcement measures adopted in 2024 signal a shift from strategic orientation toward operational consolidation of self-sufficiency objectives, further reinforcing resurgence and narrowing the scope for cross-border technological collaboration.

A different configuration of policy responses is evident in the European Union, where geopolitical concerns have translated into a coordinated strategy centred on strategic autonomy rather than full self-sufficiency. The revised EU Industrial Strategy (2020/2021), together with the European Chips Act (2022), the Critical Raw Materials Act (2023), the Green Deal Industrial Plan (2023), and the Net Zero Industry Act (2023), seeks to secure access to critical inputs, expand advanced manufacturing capacity, and reduce external dependencies at the regional level (Seidl & Schmitz, 2024). These initiatives enhance readiness through strengthened regional supply capacity and may support resurgence by incentivising technological upgrading and investment. At the same time, increasing compliance obligations, sustainability requirements, and regulatory fragmentation across member states can limit responsiveness for firms adapting supply chain operations within compressed timeframes. Institutional cybersecurity regimes such as the NIS2 Directive (European Union, 2022) further reinforce these constraints by expanding firms' responsibilities for data governance, incident reporting, and supply chain cyber risk management, thereby shaping digital readiness while increasing coordination and compliance burdens across networks. Economic security and de-risking implementation documents issued in 2024 indicate that strategic autonomy is increasingly operationalised through regulatory instruments, intensifying compliance demands and shaping firms' real-time adjustment capacity.

A cumulative picture emerges of a geopolitical environment marked by fragmentation, divergent regulation, and rising state involvement in strategic sectors (c.f. Table 2.3). Industrial policy has re-emerged as a structural force shaping the boundary conditions within which firm-level resilience capabilities operate. For Poland, positioned at the intersection of these transformations, the implications are particularly significant. As a Central and Eastern European manufacturing and logistics hub integrated into EU policy frameworks, the country benefits from regionalisation and nearshoring trends but remains vulnerable to regional security risks and dependencies on external technologies. The specific implications of these dynamics for Polish firms and supply chains are examined in greater detail in subsequent empirical chapters.

Industrial policy therefore functions simultaneously as an enabler and a constraint for firm-level resilience. Readiness, including digital readiness, is

Table 2.3 Relevant industrial policies in the United States, China, and European Union

Country/Region	*Strategic industrial policies since 2020 (Post-COVID-19)*
United States	• Infrastructure Investment and Jobs Act (2021) • Inflation Reduction Act (2022) • CHIPS and Science Act (2022) • Export controls on advanced chips and related manufacturing equipment to Chinese firms • Tariffs on Chinese exports (2025)
China	• Fourteenth Five-Year Plan including Dual Circulation Strategy (2020) • Launch of new Integrated Circuit Industry Investment Fund (2023)
European Union	• European Industrial Strategy (2020, 2021) • Further IPCEIs on batteries, hydrogen, cloud infrastructure, and microelectronics (2021–2023) • European Chips Act (2022) • European Economic Security Strategy (2023) • Green Deal Industrial Plan (2023) • Critical Raw Materials Act (2023) • Net Zero Industry Act (2023)

Source: Own elaboration based on Luo and Van Assche (2023), García-Herrero and Schindowski (2024), Schivakumar *et al.* (2024), Seidl and Schmitz (2024), and Contractor (2025).

strengthened through investment incentives, local content requirements, and the expansion of domestic or regional production capacity, which enhance firms' ability to anticipate, assess, and prepare for disruption. Responsiveness, by contrast, may be constrained when tariff regimes, export controls, or compliance obligations limit firms' capacity to adjust sourcing, logistics, or production rapidly during disruption. Resurgence is supported insofar as industrial policy incentivises digital capability development and green upgrading that facilitate longer-term structural reconfiguration, but it may be impeded when regulatory barriers restrict access to critical technologies or cross-border knowledge flows. Collaboration is enabled through public–private partnerships and regional alliances, while simultaneously challenged by geopolitical bloc formation and regulatory divergence. In this way, industrial policy both expands and circumscribes the adaptive space available to firms, shaping how readiness, responsiveness, resurgence, and collaboration can be mobilised in practice.

The transition toward the micro-level perspective now becomes essential. Examining how firms operationalise these capabilities—whether through supplier diversification, digital investment, inventory policies, network redesign, or coordinated partnerships—provides insight into the mechanisms through which resilience is built. The next subchapter therefore analyses post-pandemic micro-level strategies and the concrete pathways through which firms mitigate risks in an era of geopolitical uncertainty.

Firm-level mitigation mechanisms and resilience capability activation

Intensifying industrial competition, protectionist policies, and technological nationalism in the post-pandemic period have reshaped the risk environment faced by multinational enterprises. While traditional mitigation strategies remain relevant, they increasingly require adaptation to conditions characterised by frequent disruptions, digital interconnectedness, and deep interdependence across global networks. This section examines how firms translate systemic shocks into operational responses through the activation of readiness, responsiveness, resurgence, and collaboration. Digital technologies cut across all four capabilities, although their functional role varies by phase, supporting anticipation, rapid adjustment, structural learning, and coordination.

Pre-pandemic mitigation frameworks were largely developed for comparatively stable environments and episodic shocks. Tang's (2006) resilience strategies and Manuj and Mentzer's (2008) risk management framework emphasised postponement, strategic inventory, diversified sourcing, and hedging, alongside flexibility and inter-organisational learning. Pettit *et al.* (2010) framed resilience as a balance between vulnerabilities and capabilities, while Dolgui *et al.* (2018) distinguished proactive, reactive, and concurrent resilience logics. Evidence from Brexit illustrated how these principles were operationalised through supplier diversification, stockpiling, and asset reallocation (Jankowska *et al.*, 2021). However, the scale, persistence, and simultaneity of post-2020 disruptions exposed the limits of these approaches and prompted a shift toward more systemic and digitally enabled capability configurations.

Within this evolution, readiness captures the pre-disruption capacity to anticipate, interpret, and prepare for emerging risks through foresight, planning, and structural positioning. Geographic diversification reduces exposure to region-specific shocks (Jiang *et al.*, 2022), while total cost of acquisition analyses and local cluster formation support risk-adjusted location choices under heterogeneous institutional conditions (Huq *et al.*, 2021). Digital supply chain twins strengthen digital readiness by enabling *ex ante* simulation of system behaviour under alternative scenarios (Ivanov *et al.*, 2019), while artificial intelligence and advanced analytics enhance early-warning and forecasting capabilities (Ahmed *et al.*, 2023; Belhadi *et al.*, 2024; Hendriksen, 2023; Modgil *et al.* 2022). These mechanisms improve pre-disruption awareness and support informed positioning under geopolitical uncertainty.

Once disruption materialises, responsiveness refers to the ability to adjust operations rapidly within existing supply chain structures. Scalability and substitution mechanisms enable firms to modulate capacity and reallocate inputs in response to sudden supply or demand shocks (Ivanov, 2021). Digital technologies contribute to responsiveness by accelerating disruption detection and information sharing rather than by altering structural configurations. Blockchain-based transparency tools and real-time data integration reduce information delays and coordination frictions (Lohmer *et al.*, 2020; Min, 2019; Suali *et al.*, 2024). Selective buffering, advanced planning systems, and rapid replanning further support short-term operational adjustment and shock absorption (Namdar *et al.*, 2018; Choi *et al.*, 2023; Suryadi & Rau, 2023; Swink *et al.*, 2025).

Under conditions of persistent disruption, repeated reliance on responsiveness alone becomes insufficient, giving rise to resurgence as a distinct post-disruption capability. Resurgence combines the restoration of performance with deliberate structural reconfiguration aimed at improving alignment with new political, regulatory, and cost conditions. Relocation strategies, including reshoring and nearshoring, reduce reliance on volatile regions and strengthen control over production systems (Johnson & Haug, 2021; Kazancoglu *et al.*, 2024). Digital tools developed as part of readiness support resurgence by enabling post-disruption learning and redesign, with digital twins facilitating structural optimisation and artificial intelligence supporting scenario evaluation and longer-term planning. Zheng *et al.* (2025) conceptualise this process as an evolving capability shaped by iterative alignment between risk management and value creation, reflecting a transition from short-term recovery toward sustained strategic adaptation.

Collaboration operates across all disruption phases as a transversal capability enabling coordinated action, shared visibility, and joint problem-solving. Regional partnership structures can reduce external dependencies and reinforce strategic autonomy (Britsche & Fekete, 2024), while digital collaboration ecosystems such as GAIA-X and Catena-X support synchronised decision-making and data sharing across value chains. At the same time, agent-based modelling studies show that dense interdependencies among autonomous actors may amplify systemic vulnerability, underscoring the need for governance mechanisms that balance openness with control (Zhao *et al.*, 2019).

Overall, firm-level mitigation strategies map closely onto the functional logic of SCRES capabilities. Readiness is operationalised through anticipatory analytics, digital modelling, and diversification; responsiveness through substitution, scalability, buffering, and rapid operational adjustment; resurgence through structural redesign and digitally supported reconfiguration; and collaboration through relational and platform-based coordination. Their interaction illustrates how firms build multi-layered resilience capable of addressing both acute disruptions and persistent geopolitical uncertainty.

Integrating resilience capabilities and mitigation strategies across disruption phases

This chapter conceptualises SCRES as a cumulative and path-dependent capability system through which firms adjust to persistent geopolitical constraints. Rather than modelling resilience as a linear sequence of actions, the framework treats it as an emergent outcome generated by the interaction of capabilities deployed across disruption phases under changing institutional, regulatory, and cost conditions. From an economic perspective, resilience reflects firms' ability to preserve coordination, limit adjustment costs, and sustain participation in international production networks when cross-border exchange becomes unstable. At this stage, the framework is deliberately phase-structured but non-causal, serving as an organising device for capability domains prior to empirical analysis.

Building on this logic, the framework integrates four interdependent capability domains: readiness, responsiveness, resurgence, and collaboration. Each domain is primarily associated with a specific disruption phase—pre-disruption, during disruption, and post-disruption—while remaining dynamically interlinked over time. SCRES does not reside in any single capability, but in how these domains are combined, sequenced, and aligned with geopolitical and institutional pressures.

The framework of resilience capability factors and mitigation strategies (Figure 2.1) provides a structured approach for analysing how firms prepare

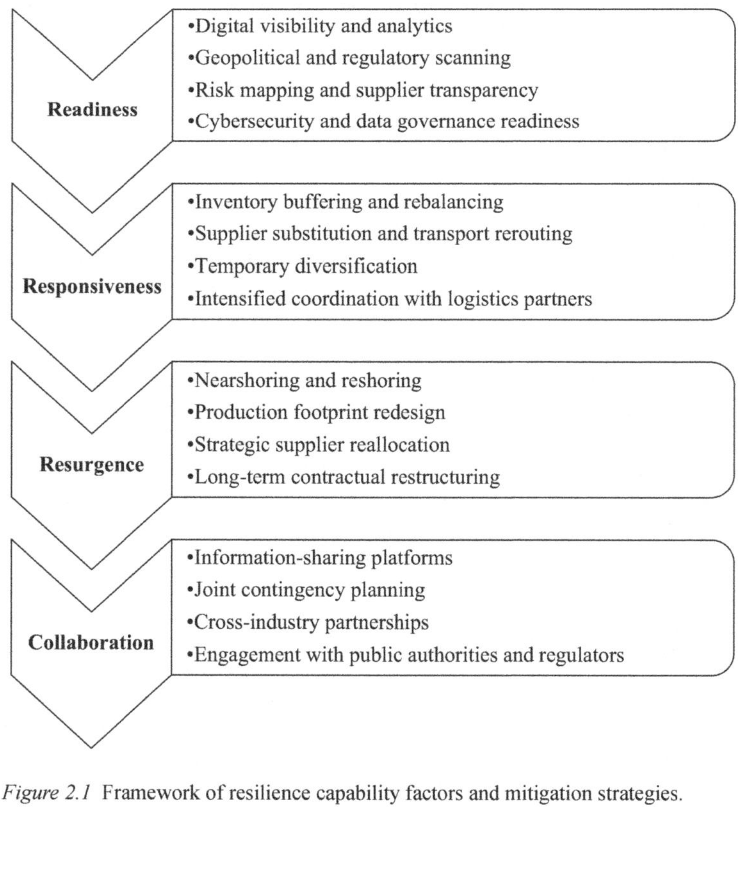

Figure 2.1 Framework of resilience capability factors and mitigation strategies.

for, respond to, and adapt following disruption. It aligns readiness, responsiveness, and resurgence with corresponding mitigation mechanisms across the disruption lifecycle, while treating collaboration as a transversal enabler. This phase-based logic is consistent with the Supply Chain Performance Measurement (SCPM) framework proposed by Han *et al.* (2020), which similarly distinguishes readiness, response, and recovery. The present framework extends SCPM, however, by adopting a decision-oriented perspective that clarifies how resilience capabilities are enacted through concrete organisational actions rather than assessed primarily through performance indicators.

Empirical research further supports this integration. Um and Han (2021) demonstrate that resilience capabilities mediate the relationship between global supply chain risks and firm performance, while mitigation strategies shape disruption severity. Building on these insights, the framework adopts a dynamic capabilities perspective in which resilience emerges from ongoing processes of sensing, seizing, and reconfiguring resources under shifting geopolitical conditions. SCRES is thus conceptualised as an evolving adjustment process shaped through learning and repeated realignment rather than as a static organisational attribute.

Within this perspective, the framework distinguishes three analytically distinct but interrelated disruption phases. Readiness captures anticipatory capabilities related to signal detection, vulnerability assessment, and structural preparedness. Responsiveness reflects short-term adaptive capabilities that stabilise operations and maintain continuity as disruptions unfold. Resurgence focuses on post-disruption renewal and strategic upgrading, transforming disruption experience into longer-term structural improvement. Collaboration underpins all phases by enabling information sharing, coordination, and joint problem-solving across supply networks.

This phased yet systemic orientation reinforces an understanding of resilience that extends beyond isolated practices or short-term recovery. Effective management of geopolitical risk requires coordinated configurations of readiness, responsiveness, and resurgence that are aligned with organisational constraints such as resource availability, process rigidity, and institutional exposure. In line with recent advances in the resilience literature, resilience is therefore understood not merely as the restoration of prior performance, but as the enhancement of long-term adaptive capacity under persistent uncertainty.

The framework contributes to the resilience literature in three main ways. First, it integrates capability development with concrete mitigation mechanisms, strengthening the link between conceptual foundations and operational action. Second, it explicitly embeds geopolitical conditions—such as interventionism, protectionism, and regionalisation—that existing models often treat only indirectly. Third, it incorporates digital and environmental transformation as core elements of resilience formation, recognising their growing influence on the viability of global supply chains.

Readiness constitutes the pre-disruption capability of the system, referring to firms' capacity to anticipate geopolitical disruption through sensing political, regulatory, and technological signals. Economically, readiness reduces uncertainty by improving the timing and quality of information, thereby lowering expected adjustment costs before disruption materialises. Digital technologies enhance this function by increasing visibility and enabling early detection of sanctions exposure, trade policy shifts, regulatory divergence, or infrastructure vulnerability. While readiness does not prevent disruption, it conditions the scope and feasibility of subsequent responses by shaping firms' option sets.

Responsiveness represents the dominant during-disruption capability, capturing firms' ability to stabilise operations through tactical adjustments such as inventory rebalancing, supplier substitution, transport rerouting, and intensified coordination with logistics partners. From an economic standpoint, responsiveness mitigates short-term losses by preserving flows, revenue streams, and contractual continuity under temporary disequilibrium. However, responsiveness remains transitional: without structural adaptation reliance on responsiveness alone increases cumulative adjustment costs under persistent geopolitical disruption.

Resurgence reflects post-disruption structural adaptation through organisational decisions such as nearshoring, reshoring, production footprint redesign, and reallocation of critical activities across jurisdictions. These actions involve sunk costs and irreversible commitments but enable firms to realign supply architectures with new political, regulatory, and security conditions. Economically, resurgence represents a re-optimisation of cost–risk trade-offs under sustained uncertainty, reducing future exposure rather than repeatedly absorbing shocks.

Collaboration operates across all phases as a system-level enabling capability encompassing information sharing, joint contingency planning, platform-based coordination, and engagement with public authorities and industry bodies. Collaboration reduces information asymmetries, distributes adjustment costs, and enables coordinated responses to geopolitical and regulatory constraints that exceed the control of individual firms, particularly in fragmented political environments.

These four capabilities are conceptualised as interrelated components of a cumulative adjustment process unfolding across disruption phases. Readiness conditions the scope and effectiveness of subsequent responses by shaping firms' initial positioning under uncertainty. Responsiveness determines whether operational continuity can be maintained long enough for more substantive adjustment to occur. Resurgence reflects longer-term realignment that alters firms' exposure to future disruptions, while collaboration supports coordination and information exchange across all phases. SCRES outcomes depend on the coherence between these capabilities and the geopolitical and institutional environments in which firms operate; weak alignment increases adjustment costs and constrains adaptive capacity.

The framework is advanced as a theory-building proposition rather than a fully specified causal model. Its capability domains and phase logic provide an organising structure for the analyses conducted in subsequent chapters, where their interactions are examined and refined using bibliometric–systematic literature review, qualitative case studies, and causal modelling techniques. By conceptualising resilience as an economically grounded adjustment process unfolding over time, the framework establishes a coherent analytical foundation for the empirical investigation that follows.

Conceptual implications and research design positioning

This chapter has traced the intellectual evolution of SCRES showing how the field has moved from early recovery-oriented definitions toward multi-theoretical, capability-based explanations of how supply chains anticipate, absorb, respond to, and adapt to disruption. By synthesising foundational perspectives—including the RBV, dynamic capabilities, systems theory, complex adaptive systems, the relational view, OIPT, and panarchy—the chapter demonstrates that resilience is best understood not as a static attribute, but as an emergent outcome of firm-level adjustment shaped by the interaction of resources, organisational structures, coordination mechanisms, and inter-firm relationships under conditions of uncertainty.

A central contribution of the chapter lies in consolidating these theoretical strands into a provisional capability architecture centred on readiness, responsiveness, resurgence, and collaboration. Rather than proposing a validated or empirically integrated model, this structure serves as an analytically grounded orientation that clarifies how distinct capability domains may align with different phases of the disruption lifecycle and how their underlying mechanisms, and interdependencies can be theorised. In doing so, the chapter brings together processes that are often examined separately in the literature—pre-disruption sensing and preparation, concurrent operational adaptation, post-disruption transformation, and network-level coordination—into a coherent conceptual language that facilitates subsequent analysis.

The chapter further advances SCRES theory by embedding geopolitical dynamics directly into the conceptualisation of resilience. Through an examination of trade tensions, regulatory volatility, transportation constraints, and regional instability, alongside a comparative assessment of industrial policy responses in the United States, the European Union, and China, the analysis shows that geopolitical disruption reshapes the economic and institutional space within which firms operate. Industrial policy is therefore positioned as both an enabler and a constraint of firm-level resilience: it may reinforce readiness and resurgence through investment incentives and organisational capacity building, while simultaneously constraining responsiveness and collaboration through tariffs, export controls, and regulatory divergence. This perspective moves beyond treating geopolitics as a purely exogenous shock and instead conceptualises it as a structural condition that influences the formation, deployment, and limits of resilience capabilities.

Collectively, these elements provide more than a descriptive overview of existing theories. They establish a theoretically integrated yet deliberately open foundation for analysing SCRES in an era of geopolitical fragmentation. The conceptual orientation developed in this chapter clarifies the architecture of resilience capabilities, identifies the mechanisms through which geopolitical conditions shape firm-level adjustment, and delineates potential mitigation pathways across different stages of disruption, without presuming their empirical prevalence or causal dominance.

In terms of the book's research design, the chapter does not resolve **RQ1**. Instead, it defines the conceptual categories, theoretical lenses, and capability constructs that are systematically examined in the systematic literature review in Chapter 3. That review assesses how mechanisms related to readiness, responsiveness, resurgence, and collaboration are represented, combined, and contested across the existing body of research. The conceptual orientation developed here also provides the analytical scaffolding for the qualitative investigation in Chapter 4 (**RQ2**), which explores how firms interpret geopolitical risks and activate adjustment mechanisms in practice, and for the causal modelling in Chapter 5 (**RQ3**), which evaluates the relative influence and interdependencies of mitigation strategies under geopolitical conditions. In this way, the chapter establishes a coherent starting point for the cumulative analysis that follows, while reserving full theoretical integration of SCRES for the concluding synthesis of the book.

References

Ahmed, T., Karmaker, C. L., Nasir, S. B., Moktadir, M. A., & Paul, S. K. (2023). Modeling the artificial intelligence-based imperatives of industry 5.0 towards resilient supply chains: A post-COVID-19 pandemic perspective. *Computers & Industrial Engineering*, *177*. https://doi.org/10.1016/j.cie.2023.109055

Aldrighetti, R., Battini, D., Ivanov, D., & Zennaro, I. (2021). Costs of resilience and disruptions in supply chain network design models: A review and future research directions. *International Journal of Production Economics*, *235*. https://doi.org/10.1016/J.IJPE.2021.108103

Alikhani, R., Ranjbar, A., Jamali, A., Torabi, S., & Zobel, C. (2023). Towards increasing synergistic effects of resilience strategies in supply chain network design. *Omega-International Journal of Management Science*, *116*, 21. https://doi.org/10.1016/j.omega.2022.102819

Althaf, S., & Babbitt, C. W. (2021). Disruption risks to material supply chains in the electronics sector. *Resources, Conservation and Recycling*, *167*. https://doi.org/10.1016/j.resconrec.2020.105248

Alvarenga, M., de Oliveira, M., & de Oliveira, T. (2023). The impact of using digital technologies on supply chain resilience and robustness: The role of memory under the COVID-19 outbreak. *Supply Chain Management—An International Journal, 28*, 18. https://doi.org/10.1108/SCM-06-2022-0217

Anderson, P. (1999). Complexity theory and organization science. *Organization Science, 10*(3), 216–232. http://www.jstor.org/stable/2640328

Azadi, M., Saen, R., & Ebrahimnejad, A. (2024). Performance evaluation of supply chain resilience in epidemic crises: An extension of network non-parametric methodology. *Or Spectrum, 42*. https://doi.org/10.1007/s00291-024-00790-y

Barney, J. (1991). Firm resources and sustained competitive advantage. *Journal of Management, 17*(1), 99–120. https://doi.org/10.1177/014920639101700108

BCG. (2022). *Global supply chain realignment: How geopolitics and new priorities are reshaping global manufacturing*. Boston Consulting Group. https://www.bcg.com

Belhadi, A., Kamble, S., Subramanian, N., Singh, R. K., & Venkatesh, M. (2024a). Digital capabilities to manage agri-food supply chain uncertainties and build supply chain resilience during compounding geopolitical disruptions. *International Journal of Operations & Production Management, 44*(11), 1914–1950. https://doi.org/10.1108/IJOPM-11-2022-0737

Belhadi, A., Mani, V., Kamble, S. S., Khan, S. A. R., & Verma, S. (2024b). Artificial intelligence-driven innovation for enhancing supply chain resilience and performance under the effect of supply chain dynamism: An empirical investigation. *Annals of Operations Research, 333*(2), 627–652. https://doi.org/10.1007/s10479-021-03956-x

Bier, T., Lange, A., & Glock, C. (2020). Methods for mitigating disruptions in complex supply chain structures: A systematic literature review. *International Journal of Production Research, 58*, 1835–1856. https://doi.org/10.1080/00207543.2019.1687954

Blackhurst, J., Dunn, K. S., & Craighead, C. W. (2011). An empirically derived framework of global supply resiliency. *Journal of Business Logistics, 32*(4), 374–391. https://doi.org/10.1111/j.0000-0000.2011.01032.x

BlackRock Corporate. (2025). Geopolitical Risk Dashboard.

Bode, C., Wagner, S. M., Petersen, K. J., & Ellram, L. M. (2011). Understanding responses to supply chain disruptions: Insights from information processing and resource dependence perspectives. *Academy of Management Journal, 54*(4), 833–856. https://doi.org/10.5465/amj.2011.64870145

Brandon-Jones, E., Squire, B., Autry, C. W., & Petersen, K. J. (2014). A contingent resource-based perspective of supply chain resilience and robustness. *Journal of Supply Chain Management, 50*(3), 55–73. https://doi.org/10.1111/jscm.12050

Britsche, A., & Fekete, M. (2024). Supply chain resilience in the European automotive industry. *Management Systems in Production Engineering, 32*(3), 380–400. https://doi.org/10.2478/mspe-2024-0036

Brusset, X., & Teller, C. (2017). Supply chain capabilities, risks, and resilience. *International Journal of Production Economics, 184*, 59–68. https://doi.org/10.1016/J.IJPE.2016.09.008

Caldara, D., & Iacoviello, M. (2018). Measuring geopolitical risk. *Political Economy: Government Expenditures & Related Policies eJournal*. https://doi.org/10.17016/IFDP.2018.1222

Caniato, F., & Rice, J. (2003). Building a secure and resilient supply chain. *Supply Chain Management Review, 7*, 22–30.

Choi, T. Y., Dooley, K. J., & Rungtusanatham, M. (2001). Supply networks and complex adaptive systems: Control versus emergence. *Journal of Operations Management, 19*(3), 351–366. https://doi.org/10.1016/S0272-6963(00)00068-1

Choi, T. Y., Netland, T. H., Sanders, N., Sodhi, M. S., & Wagner, S. M. (2023). Just-in-time for supply chains in turbulent times. *Production and Operations Management, 32*(7), 2331–2340. https://doi.org/10.1111/poms.13979

Chowdhury, M. M. H., & Quaddus, M. (2016). Supply chain readiness, response and recovery for resilience. *Supply Chain Management: An International Journal, 21*(6), 709–731. https://doi.org/10.1108/SCM-12-2015-0463

Christopher, M., & Peck, H. (2004). Building the resilient supply chain. *The International Journal of Logistics Management, 15*(2), 1–14. https://doi.org/10.1108/09574090410700275

Contractor, F. J. (2025). Assessing the economic impact of tariffs: Adaptations by multinationals and traders to mitigate tariffs. *Review of International Business and Strategy, 35*, 2–3. https://doi.org/10.1108/RIBS-01-2025-0013

Daghar, A., Alinaghian, L., & Turner, N. (2023). The role of cognitive capital in supply chain resilience: An investigation during the COVID-19 pandemic. *Supply Chain Management-An International Journal, 28*, 22. https://doi.org/10.1108/SCM-09-2021-0457

Deloitte. (2021). Global trade and customs compliance outlook. Deloitte. https://www.deloitte.com/

Dolgui, A., & Ivanov, D. (2021). Ripple effect and supply chain disruption management: New trends and research directions. *International Journal of Production Research, 59*(1), 102–109. https://doi.org/10.1080/00207543.2021.1840148

Dolgui, A., Ivanov, D., & Sokolov, B. (2018). Ripple effect in the supply chain: An analysis and recent literature. *International Journal of Production Research, 56*(1–2), 414–430. https://doi.org/10.1080/00207543.2017.1387680

Dyer, J. H., & Singh, H. (1998). The relational view: Cooperative strategy and sources of interorganizational competitive advantage. *The Academy of Management Review, 23*(4), 660–679. https://doi.org/10.2307/259056

ECB. (2021). *Financial stability review/exchange rate volatility note*. European Central Bank. https://www.ecb.europa.eu/

Echefaj, K., Cherrafi, A., Charkaoui, A., Gruchmann, T., & Ivanov, D. (2024). Firm survivability during long-term disruptions: An adaptation-based view. *Supply Chain Management—An International Journal, 29*, 18. https://doi.org/10.1108/SCM-04-2024-0293

European Union. (2022). *Directive (EU) 2022/2555 of the European parliament and of the council of 14 December 2022 on measures for a high common level of cybersecurity across the union (NIS2 directive). Official Journal of the European Union, L 333*, 80–152.

Fajgelbaum, P. D., & Khandelwal, A. K. (2022). The economic impacts of the U.S.–China trade war. *Annual Review of Economics, 14*, 205–228. http://www.nber.org/papers/w29315

García-Herrero, A., & Schindowski, R. (2024). Unpacking China's industrial policy and its implications for Europe, Working Paper 11/2024, Bruegel. https://www.bruegel.org/working-paper/unpacking-chinas-industrial-policy-and-its-implications-europe

Ghanbarzadeh, A., Mirzazadeh, A., Tavakkoli-Moghaddam, R., & Molamohamadi, Z. (2024). Optimization of a sustainable supply chain for medical device industry under uncertainty and COVID-19 pandemic. *Annals of Operations Research, 37*. https://doi.org/10.1007/s10479-024-06370-1

Główka, C., Gorynia, M., Kania, A., & Mroczek-Dąbrowska, K. (2021). *What drives companies' strategies in the face of Brexit?* In *Brexit and the future of the European Union* (pp. 103–120). Routledge.

Gorynia M., Jankowska B., Mroczek-Dabrowska, K. (2021). Strategies of Polish companies against Brexit: Results of the empirical study. In *Brexit and the future of the European Union* (pp. 121–130). Routledge.

Gunasekaran, A., Lai, K. H., & Cheng, T. C. E. (2008). Responsive supply chain: A competitive strategy in a networked economy, *Omega: The International Journal of Management Science*, *6*, 549–564. https://doi.org/10.1016/j.omega.2006.12.002

Han, Y., Chong, W. K., & Li, D. (2020). A systematic literature review of the capabilities and performance metrics of supply chain resilience. *International Journal of Production Research, 58*(15), 4541–4566. https://doi.org/10.1080/00207543.2020.1785034

Hendriksen, C. (2023). Artificial intelligence for supply chain management: Disruptive innovation or innovative disruption? *Journal of Supply Chain Management, 59*(3), 65–76. https://doi.org/10.1111/jscm.12304

Holland, J. H. (1992). Complex adaptive systems. *Daedalus, 121*(1), 17–30.

Holling, C. S. (1973). Resilience and stability of ecological systems. *Annual Review of Ecology and Systematics, 4,* 1–23. https://doi.org/10.1146/annurev.es.04.110173.000245

Hollnagel, E., Woods, D. D., & Leveson, N. (2006). *Resilience engineering: Concepts and precepts*. Ashgate Publishing.

Huq, F., Pawar, K. S., & Subramanian, N. (2021). Disturbances to the supply chains of high-value manufacturing firms: Comparison of the perceptions of product managers and supply chain managers. *International Journal of Production Research, 59*(13), 3916–3934. https://doi.org/10.1080/00207543.2020.1756505

IBM Security. (2022). *Cost of a data breach report*. IBM and Ponemon Institute. https://www.ibm.com/security/data-breach

ILO. (2022). *World employment and social outlook/labour disruptions note*. International Labour Organization. https://www.ilo.org/

IMF. (2022). *World economic outlook/trade fragmentation note*. International Monetary Fund. https://www.imf.org/

Ivanov, D. (2021). Supply chain viability and the COVID-19 pandemic: A conceptual and formal generalisation of four major adaptation strategies. *International Journal of Production Research, 59*(12), 3535–3552. https://doi.org/10.1080/00207543.2021.1890852

Ivanov, D., Dolgui, A., & Sokolov, B. (2019). The impact of digital technology and Industry 4.0 on the ripple effect and supply chain risk analytics. *International Journal of Production Research, 57*(3), 829–846. https://doi.org/10.1080/00207543.2018.1488086

Jiang, B., Rigobon, D., & Rigobon, R. (2022). From just-in-time, to just-in-case, to just-in-worst-case: Simple models of a global supply chain under uncertain aggregate shocks. *IMF Economic Review, 70*(1), 141–184. https://doi.org/10.1057/s41308-021-00148-2

Johnson, J. E., & Haug, P. (2021). Modifications to global supply chain management strategies resulting from recent trade disruptions: An exploratory study. *Journal of Global Operations and Strategic Sourcing, 14*(4), 701–722. https://doi.org/10.1108/JGOSS-12-2020-0074

Jüttner, U., & Maklan, S. (2011). Supply chain resilience in the global financial crisis: An empirical study. *Supply Chain Management*, 16, 246–259. https://doi.org/10.1108/13598541111139062

Kampton, T., Murphy, K., Mandhana, V., & Verma, V. (2023). *Strategies for resiliency: Working capital index report*. JPMorgan Chase.

Kano, L., & Verbeke, A. (2015). The three faces of bounded reliability: Alfred chandler and the micro-foundations of management theory. *California Management Review*, *58*(1), 97–122. https://doi.org/10.1525/cmr.2015.58.1.97

Katsaliaki, K., Galetsi, P., & Kumar, S. (2022). Supply chain disruptions and resilience: A major review and future research agenda. *Annals of Operations Research*, *319*(1), 965–1002. https://doi.org/10.1007/s10479-020-03912-1

Katz, D., & Kahn, R. L. (1978). *The social psychology of organizations*. Wiley.

Kazancoglu, Y., Lafci, C., Berberoglu, Y., Upadhyay, A., Rocha-Lona, L., & Kumar, V. (2024). The effects of globalization on supply chain resilience: Outsourcing techniques as interventionism, protectionism, and regionalization strategies. *Operations Management Research*, *17*(2), 505–522. https://doi.org/10.1007/s12063-023-00429-1

Kim, Y., Choi, T. Y., Yan, T., & Dooley, K. (2011). Structural investigation of supply networks: A social network analysis approach. *Journal of Operations Management*, *29*(3), 194–211. https://doi.org/10.1016/j.jom.2010.11.001

Knoben, J. (2008). Localized inter-organizational linkages, agglomeration effects, and the innovative performance of firms. *The Annals of Regional Science*, *43*(3), 757–779. https://doi.org/10.1007/s00168-008-0229-8

Kotcharin, S., & Maneenop, S. (2020). Geopolitical risk and shipping firms' capital structure decisions in belt and road initiative countries. *International Journal of Logistics Research and Applications*, *23*(6), 544–560. https://doi.org/10.1080/13675567.2020.1766003

Küffner, C., Münch, C., Hähner, S., & Hartmann, E. (2022). Getting back into the swing of things: The adaptive path of purchasing and supply management in enhancing supply chain resilience. *Journal of Purchasinga and Supply Management*, *28*, 12. https://doi.org/10.1016/j.pursup.2022.100802

Lawrence, P., & Lorsch, J. (1967) Differentiation and integration in complex organizations. *Administrative Science Quarterly*, *12*, 1–30. https://doi.org/10.2307/2391211

Lohmer, J., Bugert, N., & Lasch, R. (2020). Analysis of resilience strategies and ripple effect in blockchain-coordinated supply chains: An agent-based simulation study. *International Journal of Production Economics*, *228*. https://doi.org/10.1016/j.ijpe.2020.107882

Luo, Y., & Van Assche, A. (2023). The rise of techno-geopolitical uncertainty: Implications of the United States CHIPS and Science Act. *Journal of International Business Studies*, *54*(8), 1423–1440. https://doi.org/10.1057/s41267-023-00620-3

Luthar, S. S., Cicchetti, D., & Becker, B. (2000). The construct of resilience: A critical evaluation and guidelines for future work. *Child Development*, *71*(3), 543–562. https://doi.org/10.1111/1467-8624.00164

Manuj, I., & Mentzer, J. T. (2008). Global supply chain risk management strategies. *International Journal of Physical Distribution & Logistics Management*, *38*(3), 192–223. https://doi.org/10.1108/09600030810866986

Manyena, S. B. (2006). The concept of resilience revisited. *Disasters*, *30*(4), 433–450. https://doi.org/10.1111/j.0361-3666.2006.00331.x

Matysek, A., Mroczek-Dąbrowska, K., & Kania, A. (2024). Beyond the COVID-19 pandemic: What *builds organizational resilience capacity? International Journal of Emerging Markets, 19*(10), 3272–3302. https://doi.org/10.1108/IJOEM-06-2022-0948

McEvily, B., & Zaheer, A. (1999). Bridging ties: A source of firm heterogeneity in competitive capabilities. *Strategic Management Journal, 20*(12), 1133–1156. https://doi.org/10.1002/(SICI)1097-0266(199912)20:12<1133::AID-SMJ74>3.0.CO;2-7

McKinsey & Company. (2020, March). *Economic conditions outlook 2024*. McKinsey & Company. https://www.mckinsey.com/capabilities/strategy-and-corporate-finance/our-insights/economic-conditions-outlook-2024

McKinsey & Company. (2023). *Supply chain diversification and concentration risk report*. McKinsey & Company. https://www.mckinsey.com/

Melnyk, S. A., Closs, D. J., Griffis, S. E., Zobel, C. W., & Macdonald, J. R. (2014). Understanding supply chain resilience. *Supply Chain Management Review, 18*(1), 34–41.

Min, H. (2019). Blockchain technology for enhancing supply chain resilience. *Business Horizons, 62*(1), 35–45. https://doi.org/10.1016/j.bushor.2018.08.012

Modgil, S., Singh, R. K., & Hannibal, C. (2022). Artificial intelligence for supply chain resilience: Learning from COVID-19. *The International Journal of Logistics Management, 33*(4), 1246–1268. https://doi.org/10.1108/IJLM-02-2021-0094

Moosavi, J., Fathollahi-Fard, A. M., & Dulebenets, M. A. (2022). Supply chain disruption during the COVID-19 pandemic: Recognizing potential disruption management strategies. *International Journal of Disaster Risk Reduction, 75*. https://doi.org/10.1016/j.ijdrr.2022.102983

Moradlou, H., Reefke, H., Skipworth, H., & Roscoe, S. (2021). Geopolitical disruptions and the manufacturing location decision in multinational company supply chains: A Delphi study on Brexit. *International Journal of Operations & Production Management, 41*, 102–130. https://doi.org/10.1108/IJOPM-07-2020-0465

Nakandala, D., Yang, R., Lau, H., & Weerabahu, S. (2023). Industry 4.0 technology capabilities, resilience and incremental innovation in Australian manufacturing firms: A serial mediation model. *Supply Chain Management—An International Journal, 13*. https://doi.org/10.1108/SCM-08-2022-0325

Namdar, J., Li, X., Sawhney, R., & Pradhan, N. (2018). Supply chain resilience for single and multiple sourcing in the presence of disruption risks. *International Journal of Production Research, 56*(6), 2339–2360. https://doi.org/10.1080/00207543.2017.1370149

Nelson, R. R., & Winter, S. G. (1982). *An evolutionary theory of economic change*. Belknap Press of Harvard University.

Nikookar, E., Stevenson, M., & Varsei, M. (2024). Building an antifragile supply chain: A capability blueprint for resilience and post-disruption growth. *Journal of Supply Chain Management*. https://doi.org/10.1111/jscm.12313

OECD. (2023). *Trade policy implications of global economic fragmentation*. Organisation for Economic Co-operation and Development. https://www.oecd.org/

Penrose, E. (1959). *The theory of the growth of the firm*. Basil Blackwell.

Pessot, E., Zangiacomi, A., Marchiori, I., & Fornasiero, R. (2023). Empowering supply chains with Industry 4.0 technologies to face megatrends. *Journal of Business Logistics, 44*(4), 609–640. https://doi.org/10.1111/jbl.12360

Pettit, T. J., Croxton, K. L., & Fiksel, J. (2013). Ensuring supply chain resilience: Development and implementation of an assessment tool. *Journal of Business Logistics, 34*(1), 46–76. https://doi.org/10.1111/jbl.12009

Pettit, T. J., Fiksel, J., & Croxton, K. L. (2010). Ensuring supply chain resilience: Development of a conceptual framework. *Journal of Business Logistics*, *31*(1), 1–21. https://doi.org/10.1002/j.2158-1592.2010.tb00125.x

Ponis, S. T., & Koronis, E. (2012). Supply chain resilience: Definition of concept and its formative elements. *Journal of Applied Business Research (JABR)*, *28*(5), 921–930. https://doi.org/10.19030/jabr.v28i5.723

Ponomarov, S. Y., & Holcomb, M. C. (2009). Understanding the concept of supply chain resilience. *The International Journal of Logistics Management*, *20*(1), 124–143. https://doi.org/10.1108/09574090910954873

Prahalad, C. K., & Hamel, G. (1990). The core competence of the corporation. *Harvard Business Review*, *68*(3), 79–91.

PwC. (2022). *Geopolitical risk and trade strategy: Business impacts*. Pricewaterhouse-Coopers. https://www.pwc.com/

Ratajczak-Mrozek, M. (2017). *Network embeddedness. Examining the effect on business performance and internationalization*. Palgrave Macmillan. https://doi.org/10.1007/978-3-319-56511-8

Roscoe, S., Skipworth, H., Aktas, E., & Habib, F. (2020). Managing supply chain uncertainty arising from geopolitical disruptions: Evidence from the pharmaceutical industry and Brexit. *International Journal of Operations & Production Management*, *40*, 9. https://doi.org/10.1108/IJOPM-10-2019-0668

Schleifenheimer, M., & Ivanov, D. (2024). Pharmaceutical retail supply chain responses to the COVID-19 pandemic. *Annals of Operations Research*, 26. https://doi.org/10.1007/s10479-024-05866-0

Scholten, K., van Donk, D. P., & Boscari, S. (2025). What options do we have? The supply chain resilience funnel. *The Journal of Supply Chain Management/Institute for Supply Management*, *61*(2), 74–105. https://doi.org/10.1111/jscm.12342

Schumpeter, J. A. (1942). *Capitalism, socialism and democracy* (3rd ed.). Harper & Row.

Seidl, T., & Schmitz, L. (2024). Moving on to not fall behind? Technological sovereignty and the 'geo-dirigiste' turn in EU industrial policy. *Journal of European Public Policy*, *31*(8), 2147–2174. https://doi.org/10.1080/13501763.2023.2248204

Sheffi, Y., & Rice, B. J. (2005). A supply chain view of the resilient enterprise. *MIT Sloan Management Review*, *47*(1), 41–48. https://sloanreview.mit.edu/article/a-supply-chain-view-of-the-resilient-enterprise/

Shivakumar, S., Wessner, C., & Howell, T. (2024). *Balancing the ledger: Export controls on U.S. chip technology to China*. Center for Strategic and International Studies (CSIS). https://www.csis.org/analysis/balancing-ledger-export-controls-us-chip-technology-china

Simon, H. A. (1990). Bounded rationality. In W. J. Eatwell, M. Milgate, & P. Newman (Eds.), *Utility and probability*. Palgrave Macmillan. https://doi.org/10.1007/978-1-349-20568-4_5

Suali, A., Srai, J., & Tsolakis, N. (2024). The role of digital platforms in e-commerce food supply chain resilience under exogenous disruptions. *Supply Chain Management—An International Journal*, *29*, 3. https://doi.org/10.1108/SCM-02-2023-0064

Suryadi, A., & Rau, H. (2023). Considering region risks and mitigation strategies in the supplier selection process for improving supply chain resilience. *Computers & Industrial Engineering*, *181*. https://doi.org/10.1016/j.cie.2023.109288

Swink, M., Kovach, J. J., & Roh, J. (2025). Inventory and supply chain planning systems as drivers of supply chain resilience: Analyses of firm performance through the

COVID-19 pandemic. *Production and Operations Management, 34*, 8. https://doi.org/10.1177/10591478251320528

Tang, C. S. (2006). Robust strategies for mitigating supply chain disruptions. *International Journal of Logistics Research and Applications, 9*(1), 33–45. https://doi.org/10.1080/13675560500405584

Teece, D. J. (2014). The foundations of enterprise performance: Dynamic and ordinary capabilities in an (economic) theory of firms. *Academy of Management Perspectives, 28*(4), 328–352. https://doi.org/10.5465/amp.2013.0116

Teece, D. J., Pisano, G., & Shuen, A. (1997). Dynamic capabilities and strategic management. *Strategic Management Journal, 18*(7), 509–533. https://www.jstor.org/stable/3088148

Um, J., & Han, N. (2021). Understanding the relationships between global supply chain risk and supply chain resilience: The role of mitigating strategies. *Supply Chain Management: An International Journal, 26*(2), 240–255. https://doi.org/10.1108/SCM-06-2020-0248

UNCTAD. (2023). *Global trade and development report*. United Nations Conference on Trade and Development. https://unctad.org/

Vural, C., Balci, G., Balci, E., & Gocer, A. (2024). Looking inside the panarchy: Reorganisation capabilities for food supply chain resilience against geopolitical crises. *Supply Chain Management—An International Journal, 30*, 19. https://doi.org/10.1108/SCM-02-2024-0121

Wieland, A., & Wallenburg, C. M. (2013). The influence of relational competencies on supply chain resilience: A relational view. *International Journal of Physical Distribution & Logistics Management, 43*(4), 300–320. https://doi.org/10.1108/IJPDLM-08-2012-0243

Williamson, O. E. (1989). Transaction cost economics. In R. Schmalensee & R. Willig (Eds.), *Handbook of industrial organization* (Vol. 1, pp. 135–182). Elsevier.

World Bank. (2023). *Logistics performance index report 2023*. The World Bank. https://www.worldbank.org/

World Economic Forum (WEF). (2023). *Global cybersecurity outlook 2023*. World Economic Forum. https://www.weforum.org/

World Trade Organization (WTO). (2023). *World trade report 2023: Re-globalization for resilient supply chains*. World Trade Organization. https://www.wto.org/

Zhao, K., Zuo, Z., & Blackhurst, J. V. (2019). Modelling supply chain adaptation for disruptions: An empirically grounded complex adaptive systems approach. *Journal of Operations Management, 65*(2), 190–212. https://doi.org/10.1002/joom.1009

Zheng, L. J., Islam, N., Zhang, J. Z., Behl, A., Wang, X., & Papadopoulos, T. (2025). Aligning risk and value creation: A process model of supply chain risk management in geopolitical disruptions. *International Journal of Operations & Production Management, 45*, 5. https://doi.org/10.1108/IJOPM-03-2024-0271

Zhou, J., Hu, L., Yu, Y., Zhang, J. Z., & Zheng, L. J. (2024). Impacts of IT capability and supply chain collaboration on supply chain resilience: Empirical evidence from China in COVID-19 pandemic. *Journal of Enterprise Information Management, 37*(2), 777–803. https://doi.org/10.1108/JEIM-03-2022-0091

3 Navigating supply chain resilience in times of geopolitical disruptions

Bibliometric-systematic literature review

Introduction

Systematic literature reviews (SLRs) have become an increasingly prominent method in SCRES research, reflecting the rapid expansion and diversification of the field (e.g. Colicchia & Strozzi, 2012; Ali & Gölgeci, 2019; Ali *et al.*, 2017; Bednarski *et al.*, 2024; Castillo, 2023; Durach *et al.*, 2017; Ergun *et al.*, 2023; Hohenstein *et al.*, 2015; Kamalahmadi & Parast, 2016; Kochan & Nowicki, 2018; Naimi *et al.*, 2021; Poo *et al.*, 2024; Shi *et al.*, 2024; Sienkiewicz-Małyjurek & Szymczak, 2024; Tukamuhabwa *et al.*, 2015). Early reviews document substantial variation in how resilience is conceptualised, ranging from reactive responses activated after disruption to proactive approaches emphasising preparedness and anticipation. While this diversity reflects the growing scope of SCRES research, it has also contributed to conceptual fragmentation and inconsistent operationalisation.

Despite the increasing relevance of geopolitical risk, research explicitly addressing geopolitical disruptions remains limited (Bednarski *et al.*, 2024). Existing SLRs have primarily focused on terrorism (Barnes & Oloruntoba, 2005; Khan *et al.*, 2018), economic crises (Jüttner & Maklan, 2011), natural disasters (Katsaliaki *et al.*, 2022; Kochan & Nowicki, 2018), and pandemic-related shocks. These studies examine both supply-side disruptions, such as supplier failures and sourcing constraints, and demand-side disturbances, including volatility and the bullwhip effect. Consequently, operational risks have been analysed extensively, whereas the implications of geopolitical tensions—trade wars, sanctions, regulatory shifts, political realignments, and armed conflict—remain comparatively underexplored, despite their profound effects on institutions, resource access, and uncertainty.

Within the existing literature, a limited number of SLRs come closest to the focus of the present study, including Chowdhury *et al.* (2021), Dolgui and Ivanov (2021), Spieske and Birkel (2021), Agrawal and Jain (2022), Bednarski *et al.* (2024), and Roshani *et al.* (2024). As summarised in Table 3.1, these reviews collectively examine a wide range of disruption types and mitigation

DOI: 10.4324/9781003733089-3

Table 3.1 Existing relevant systematic literature review articles

References	*Types of disruptions*	*Mitigation strategies*	*Timespan*
Chowdhury *et al.* (2021)	Natural disruptions, man-made and discrete events, system failures, financial disruptions	Collaboration and relationship management, redundancy and flexibility, agility in responses, information sharing, technological solutions, public stakeholder engagement	2020
Dolgui and Ivanov (2021)	Ripple effect	Green logistics, closed-loop SCs, readiness, flexibility, responsiveness	2012–2020
Spieske and Birkel (2021)	Disruptions intensified by the COVID-19 pandemic, including: supply, operational, demand	Big Data Analytics (BDA), internet of things (IoT), artificial intelligence (AI), blockchain (BC), cloud computing (CC, cyber-physical systems (CPS), additive manufacturing (AM)	2011–2021
Agrawal and Jain (2022)	Customer, supply, internal, external	Flexibility, reserve capacity, integration, redundancy, agility, efficiency, ambidexterity, collaboration, information sharing, data analytics	…–2019
Bednarski *et al.* (2024)	Geopolitical (Brexit, U.S.–China trade war, BRI, COVID-19)	Regionalisation and back-shoring, increased stock levels, adopting new technologies, dynamic capability framework	2016–2022
Roshani *et al.* (2024)	Local, regional, global	Proactive, reactive, supply chain design quality	2001–2024
Proposed study	*Geopolitical (Brexit, U.S.–China trade war, COVID-19, armed conflict in Ukraine, cyber security)*	…	*…–2024*

Source: Own elaboration based on Chowdhury *et al.* (2021), Dolgui and Ivanov (2021), Spieske and Birkel (2021), Agrawal and Jain (2022), Bednarski *et al.* (2024), and Roshani *et al.* (2024).

strategies, highlighting themes such as collaboration, redundancy, agility, flexibility, digital technologies, and supply chain design quality.

Several consistent insights emerge across these reviews. First, resilience is increasingly treated as a multi-dimensional construct encompassing structural, relational, and technological elements (Agrawal & Jain, 2022; Chowdhury *et al.*, 2021). Second, the role of digital technologies—particularly

Big Data Analytics, artificial intelligence, blockchain, and additive manufacturing—is emphasised as a key enabler of visibility, speed, and coordination under disruption (Spieske & Birkel, 2021). Third, systemic perspectives such as the ripple effect highlight how disruptions propagate across interconnected networks, reinforcing the importance of readiness, flexibility, and responsiveness (Dolgui & Ivanov, 2021).

Among the reviewed studies, Bednarski *et al.* (2024) most explicitly centre geopolitical disruptions, examining events such as Brexit, the U.S.–China trade conflict, the Belt and Road Initiative, and COVID-19. Their findings highlight regionalisation, reshoring, inventory buffering, technological upgrading, and dynamic capabilities as key mitigation strategies. However, even this review captures geopolitical dynamics primarily through discrete events and policy episodes, offering only partial coverage of more recent developments such as prolonged armed conflict, intensified great-power rivalry, and escalating cyber and technological contestation. Other reviews address geopolitical factors indirectly or treat them as episodic shocks rather than as persistent structural conditions shaping supply chain evolution.

Collectively, existing SLRs demonstrate substantial progress in understanding resilience under operational, natural, and pandemic-related disruptions, while revealing important limitations in the treatment of geopolitical disruption. The structural and systemic implications of sustained geopolitical turbulence for supply chain design, capability development, and organisational behaviour remain fragmented and unevenly theorised. Much of the literature continues to focus on short-term impacts or incorporates political factors peripherally, an approach that is increasingly misaligned with contemporary conditions in which geopolitical uncertainty constitutes a persistent feature of the global economy, reshaping trade relations, production geographies, and corporate risk assessments. The present study responds to this limitation by positioning geopolitical disruption as a distinct and analytically coherent dimension within SCRES research.

The following section outlines the systematic methodology employed in this study, detailing the bibliometric procedures, selection criteria, and analytical techniques used to map the literature, identify thematic developments, and clarify how geopolitical disruptions have been addressed within SCRES research.

Review framework and analytical logic

This chapter adopts a bibliometric-systematic literature review (B-SLR) framework to examine how scholarly understanding of the relationship between geopolitical disruptions and SCRES has evolved over time. SLRs provide transparent and replicable procedures for identifying, evaluating, and synthesising existing research, addressing limitations of narrative reviews related to implicit selection criteria and incomplete coverage (Tranfield *et al.*,

2003). Within rapidly expanding and fragmented research domains such as SCRES these properties are essential for producing analytically robust syntheses.

The B-SLR approach combines established systematic review procedures with quantitative bibliometric analysis, strengthening analytical rigour by complementing qualitative synthesis with objective mapping of the intellectual structure of the field. Bibliometric techniques enhance systematic reviews by revealing citation structures, thematic clusters, and the temporal evolution of research streams through tools such as citation analysis, co-citation, bibliographic coupling, and keyword co-occurrence (Zupic & Čater, 2015). Following the framework proposed by Marzi *et al.* (2024), the review builds on recognised review protocols, including PRISMA (Page *et al.*, 2021) and AMSTAR 2 (Shea *et al.*, 2017), ensuring transparency, replicability, and methodological consistency.

To support systematic and scalable analysis of the literature corpus, the study employs Biblioshiny, an interface based on the Bibliometrix package (Aria & Cuccurullo, 2017), for data cleaning, descriptive statistics, and initial bibliometric mapping. VOSviewer (van Eck & Waltman, 2010) is subsequently used to construct and visualise bibliometric networks, including co-citation, bibliographic coupling, and keyword co-occurrence maps, enabling identification of thematic clusters and the relational positioning of geopolitical disruption within the broader SCRES research landscape. The combined use of these tools facilitates transparent exploration of large and heterogeneous bodies of literature while preserving interpretive depth through qualitative synthesis.

Analytically, the review moves beyond descriptive aggregation of prior findings. It maps dominant conceptual and methodological trajectories within the SCRES literature, examines how geopolitical factors are incorporated into resilience research, and identifies persistent empirical and theoretical blind spots in the treatment of politically induced uncertainty. Bibliometric techniques are used to analyse temporal developments, relational structures, and thematic proximities, while the identification and interpretation of research streams rely on inductive synthesis informed by close reading of the underlying publications. This logic supports theory development by clarifying the boundaries of existing knowledge and motivating the need for more integrated, geopolitically grounded resilience frameworks.

While the B-SLR provides a rigorous foundation for evidence synthesis, potential sources of bias cannot be fully eliminated. Distortions may arise during literature retrieval, study selection, and interpretation, including retrieval bias, publication bias, evidence selection bias, and the influence of competing interests (Adams *et al.*, 2017; Durach *et al.*, 2017; Kraus *et al.*, 2020; Le Clercq, 2024; Williams *et al.*, 2020; Xiao & Watson, 2017). These risks are mitigated through comprehensive multi-database search strategies, transparent inclusion and exclusion criteria, and collective interpretation within the research process. Explicit acknowledgement of these limitations is essential for maintaining analytical credibility and situating the review's findings within their methodological boundaries.

STEP 1. Research question and boundaries of the study

Building on the conceptual foundations developed in Chapter 2, the review examines scholarly work at the intersection of geopolitical disruptions and SCRES. The analysis is organised around one overarching research question and three interrelated sub-questions, which together structure the bibliometric and thematic analyses undertaken in this chapter.

RQ1. *How has scholarly understanding of the relationship between geopolitical disruptions and SCRES evolved over time, and what thematic developments and knowledge gaps characterise this field?*

To operationalise this overarching question, the following sub-questions are addressed:

- **RQ1.1.** *How has the literature evolved in terms of publication dynamics, dominant concepts, and thematic structures over time?*
- **RQ1.2.** *What is the intellectual and geographical structure of the field, as reflected in influential authors, journals, institutions, collaboration networks, and country-level contributions?*
- **RQ1.3.** *What conceptual gaps, underexplored linkages, and emerging research trajectories can be identified within the existing literature?*

To ensure transparency in a systematic review, it is essential to use explicit selection criteria to assess the relevance of each paper in relation to the review question (Denyer & Tranfield, 2009; Marzi *et al.*, 2024). Therefore, the author applied a list of criteria to screen for inclusion and exclusion (cf. Table 3.2).

STEP 2. Search query definition

The search strategy was developed through an iterative, concept-driven process to capture research at the intersection of SCRES and geopolitical disruption. Keyword selection began with identifying major geopolitical events that have materially affected supply chain functioning over the past decade. These events were established through consultation of reputable news sources and industry reports.

Consistent with the conceptualisation adopted in Chapters 1 and 2, geopolitical disruptions are understood as risks arising from wars, terrorist acts,

Table 3.2 List of criteria for inclusion and exclusion

Inclusion criteria	*Exclusion criteria*	*Rationale*
Articles published in English	Articles published not in English	English language dominates the studied academic field.
Papers published in CABS rank 3–4* journals.	Topically relevant articles, but published outside of rank 3–4* CABS journals were excluded.	The Chartered Association of Business Schools (CABS) list, which includes 1823 journal titles, is recognised as a benchmark for quality among peer-reviewed journals in the fields of economics and management.
At least one of the focuses of the paper is the impact of geopolitical disruptions on supply chains.	Studies on geopolitical disruptions pertaining to financial flows, and terrorism were excluded. It is also equally applicable to articles relating solely to SCRES without taking into consideration geopolitical factors.	The purpose of this review is to comprehend how geopolitical disruptions affect the SCRES.

Source: Own elaboration.

and tensions between state actors that interfere with the normal conduct of international relations (Caldara & Iacoviello, 2018, p. 2). When this definition is applied to the supply chain context, several events emerge as particularly relevant in shaping contemporary geopolitical risk exposure. Brexit, the U.S.–China trade tensions, and the armed conflict in Ukraine figure prominently in the literature as structural sources of disruption affecting trade relations, regulatory alignment, and production geographies. In parallel, state-linked cyber threats and cyber-enabled interference have gained importance as instruments of geopolitical contestation, disrupting digital infrastructure, logistics systems, and cross-border data flows that underpin modern supply chains. The COVID-19 pandemic is also included, as it is increasingly interpreted not only as a public health crisis but as a geopolitical shock that reshaped international cooperation, exposed strategic dependencies, and altered global power dynamics (European Parliament, 2020; Roscoe *et al.*, 2022).

Based on these thematic anchors, the search strings reported in Table 3.3 were constructed. The term "supply chain design" was included due to its foundational role in resilience, despite limited integration of design quality into resilience research (Roshani *et al.*, 2024). Boolean operators (AND, OR) and wildcard symbols (*) were applied to capture conceptual synonyms and linguistic variations. The search covered research categories spanning

Table 3.3 Keywords, search strings, and research categories

Construct	*Keywords*	*Search string*	*Research categories*
SCRES amid geopolitical disruptions	supply chain resilienc*, resilient supply chain, supply chain design, geopolitic*, Brexit, COVID, trade war, Ukraine, war, cyber-attack	("supply chain resilienc*" OR resilient supply chain" OR "supply chain design") AND (geopolitic* OR Brexit OR COVID OR "trade war" OR Ukraine OR war OR "cyber-attack")	Economics or Management or Business or Operations Research Management Science or International Relations or Business Finance

Source: Own elaboration.

Economics, Management, Business, Operations Research and Management Science, International Relations, and Business Finance.

Keywords were retained only when they contributed additional relevant records and removed when they generated excessive noise or no incremental results. The iterative refinement process concluded once further adjustments failed to expand the set of relevant publications.

STEP 3. Database selection

The initial stage of the review involved testing the search strategy across two major academic databases. This comparison indicated that Web of Science (WoS) provided broader and more detailed coverage than Scopus for research on SCRES and geopolitical disruption. The decision to rely exclusively on WoS was further supported by evidence that the two databases often return substantially different results and bibliographic formats, making dataset integration technically challenging in bibliometric analysis due to the absence of reliable harmonisation tools (Kasaraneni & Rosaline, 2024).

WoS was also selected for its full compatibility with the analytical tools employed in this study, namely VOSviewer and Biblioshiny. In addition, WoS indexes a substantial share of established and highly cited contributions in the SCRES literature, including foundational studies by Ali *et al.* (2017) and Hohenstein *et al.* (2015), which aligns well with the objectives of the review. Institutional access further reinforced the choice of WoS as the sole data source.

Google Scholar was deliberately excluded. The review focuses exclusively on peer-reviewed journal articles in order to ensure quality control, transparency, and consistency in evidence selection. Given the heterogeneous nature of grey literature and the lack of standardised indexing in Google Scholar, restricting the analysis to a single, curated database was deemed necessary to uphold methodological rigour.

STEP 4. Data screening

The screening process was restricted to peer-reviewed journal articles published in English, reflecting the dominant language of scholarly communication in SCRES and geopolitical risk research (cf. Table 3.2). The search was further limited to selected WoS subject categories listed in Table 3.3. WoS offers both broad research areas and a more granular subject category classification system, the latter comprising 252 categories across major disciplinary domains (Pranckutė, 2021; Wang & Waltman, 2016). The subject category system is widely regarded as more suitable for systematic reviews due to its finer resolution and stronger alignment with disciplinary structures (Waltman & van Eck, 2013; Wang & Waltman, 2016).

Although limitations of both WoS and Scopus classification schemes are well documented, comparative analyses indicate that WoS classifications perform more reliably, particularly in terms of journal assignment accuracy (Wang & Waltman, 2016). This finding further supports the exclusive use of WoS in the present study.

A staged search strategy was applied. An initial comprehensive search was conducted in mid-2023 to support the empirical components of the project, including the development of interview protocols, case study research carried out between July and September 2023, and the DEMATEL data collection undertaken in September 2023. This phase established the conceptual boundaries of the study and ensured alignment between the literature base and empirical design.

Given the rapid expansion of research following post-pandemic disruptions and escalating geopolitical tensions, an updated and extended search was conducted at a later stage. The final full-text search was completed on 31 December 2024, enabling the bibliometric and systematic review components to incorporate the most recent contributions while maintaining coherence with the earlier conceptual scoping.

No publication time restriction was imposed. Although relevant publications began appearing in 2014, contributions from the period 2014–2019 represent only a small fraction of the retrieved literature. Imposing a narrow temporal window would therefore not have materially altered the results or enhanced analytical value. The staged screening process yielded a final dataset of 290 records.

STEP 5. Data cleaning

Following the WoS search, all retrieved records were imported into Biblioshiny via EndNote. The automated screening flagged 26 records as ineligible, after which the remaining dataset was exported to Excel for manual cleaning.

A journal quality filter was then applied. Only articles published in journals ranked 3–4* in the Academic Journal Guide (AJG) 2024 were retained

(Chartered Association of Business Schools, 2024). The AJG covers over 1,800 journals across 22 disciplinary areas and is widely used as a benchmark for identifying internationally significant and methodologically rigorous research. Although journal rankings remain contested, the AJG combines bibliometric indicators with expert assessment and is frequently recommended for systematic field mapping and theory development (Brookes, 1969; Rabetino *et al.*, 2021; Hiebl, 2023). This approach is also consistent with Bradford's Law (Bradford, 1934), which suggests that a relatively small set of core journals accounts for a disproportionate share of foundational contributions.

Based on the 2024 AJG classification, 84 articles were retained for detailed screening. A manual cross-check between the WoS export and the AJG list was conducted to minimise selection errors. Duplicate records were removed using Excel, followed by title, abstract, and full-text screening. Articles were excluded when search terms appeared only in reference lists rather than in the substantive content of the paper.

To be included, articles had to (i) examine geopolitical disruptions in relation to SCRES and (ii) contain the terms "supply chain resilienc*" and "geopolitic*", or equivalent variants, within the main text. This screening excluded 20 papers, resulting in 64 articles. Two additional papers were removed due to lack of institutional access. A backward reference search did not yield any additional eligible studies.

At the final stage, literature reviews were excluded to avoid inflating bibliometric linkages and to maintain focus on original empirical contributions. Review articles typically synthesise existing knowledge and may distort co-citation and keyword analyses due to extensive reference lists. The final dataset therefore comprised 59 articles.

To visualise the data-cleaning process, the PRISMA flow diagram (Page *et al.*, 2021), a core component of the B-SLR framework, is presented in Figure 3.1.

STEP 6. Bibliometric analysis approach

In line with the B-SLR framework proposed by Marzi *et al.* (2024), this step applies quantitative bibliometric techniques to complement and structure the subsequent qualitative synthesis. Bibliometric analysis is used here as an exploratory and descriptive tool to map the intellectual structure of the field and to provide a structured basis for the subsequent identification and interpretation of dominant research streams through qualitative synthesis.

Following the PRISMA-guided screening procedure, the final dataset comprised all publications retained for analysis. For each document, bibliographic metadata were systematically collected, including titles, authors, journal outlets, abstracts, publication years, and cited references. The dataset was managed in EndNote to ensure consistency, transparency, and traceability across

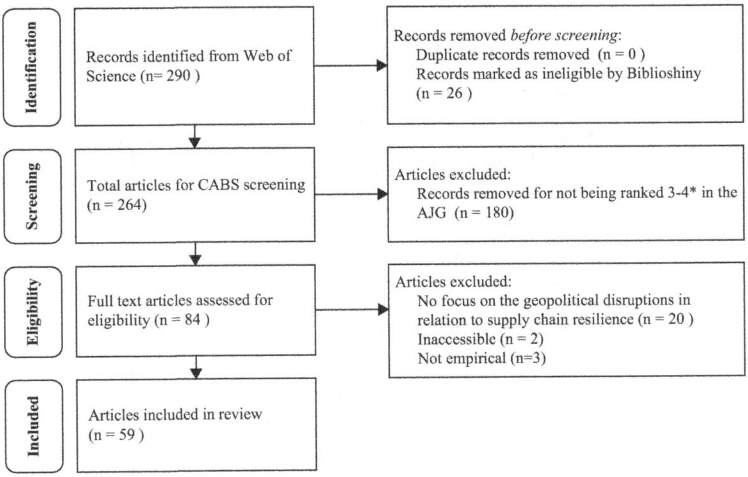

Figure 3.1 Detailed PRISMA flowchart for document selection.

successive analytical stages. Building on established B-SLR practices (Marzi et al., 2024), the bibliometric analysis combines performance indicators with science mapping techniques to provide an objective overview of publication dynamics, scholarly influence, and the thematic configuration of the field.

To operationalise this analytical logic, two complementary tools were employed. Biblioshiny was used to compute descriptive statistics and performance indicators, while VOSviewer was applied to construct and visualise bibliometric networks. This tool combination enabled both an aggregate assessment of the literature and a relational analysis of its underlying intellectual structure, in line with best practice in B-SLRs.

STEP 6a. Bibliometric indicators

Bibliometric performance indicators provided an overview of the scope, growth, and maturity of research on SCRES under geopolitical disruption. Table 3.4 reports the descriptive statistics for the publications included in the analysis, covering the period 2014–2024. The final sample comprises 59 journal articles published in 16 peer-reviewed outlets, reflecting the outcome of a multi-stage screening process focusing on studies explicitly addressing geopolitical disruptions and SCRES.

Overall, the indicators point to a rapidly expanding research domain. This expansion is reflected in a high annual publication growth rate and a low average document age, suggesting that the field has gained momentum only recently. Despite its relatively short history, the literature already exhibits

Table 3.4 Descriptive statistics about the publications extracted between 2014 and 2024

Description	*Results*
Timespan	2014–2024
Sources (Journals, Books, etc)	16
Documents	59
Annual growth rate %	31.95
Document average age	2.51
Average citations per doc	57.9
References	3485
Authors	191
Authors of single-authored docs	2
Co-authors per doc	3.56
International co-authorships %	54.24

Source: Own elaboration with use of Biblioshiny.

substantial scholarly impact, as indicated by high average citation counts. Authorship patterns further reveal a strong collaborative orientation, with a high average number of co-authors per article and a significant share of international co-authorships.

To further contextualise publication patterns within the field, Table 3.5 presents the most relevant journal outlets contributing to this body of research. The distribution of publications is concentrated in leading supply chain and

Table 3.5 Most relevant sources

Sources	*Articles*
INTERNATIONAL JOURNAL OF OPERATIONS & PRODUCTION MANAGEMENT	14
SUPPLY CHAIN MANAGEMENT—AN INTERNATIONAL JOURNAL	13
ANNALS OF OPERATIONS RESEARCH	6
OMEGA-INTERNATIONAL JOURNAL OF MANAGEMENT SCIENCE	5
JOURNAL OF PURCHASING AND SUPPLY MANAGEMENT	4
JOURNAL OF BUSINESS RESEARCH	3
JOURNAL OF OPERATIONS MANAGEMENT	3
TECHNOLOGICAL FORECASTING AND SOCIAL CHANGE	3
DECISION SCIENCES	1
EUROPEAN JOURNAL OF OPERATIONAL RESEARCH	1
INDUSTRIAL MARKETING MANAGEMENT	1
INTERNATIONAL MARKETING REVIEW	1
JOURNAL OF INTERNATIONAL FINANCIAL MARKETS INSTITUTIONS & MONEY	1
JOURNAL OF INTERNATIONAL MANAGEMENT	1
JOURNAL OF SUPPLY CHAIN MANAGEMENT	1
OR SPECTRUM	1

Source: Own elaboration with use of Biblioshiny.

Figure 3.2 Word cloud of keywords.

operations journals, complemented by contributions from operations research and management journals. This pattern underscores the interdisciplinary positioning of the topic at the intersection of supply chain management, operations, and coordination and allocation decision-making.

Beyond publication outlets, keyword frequency analysis was conducted to identify the conceptual core of the literature. Figure 3.2 presents a word cloud of the most frequently used author keywords. The size of each word represents its frequency of occurrence, with larger words indicating higher usage. The prominence of terms related to SCRES and disruption confirms the central focus of the field, while the visibility of COVID-19 reflects the role of pandemic-related shocks in shaping recent research trajectories. At the same time, the presence of dynamic capabilities, digital readiness, and sustainability points to a gradual broadening of theoretical and empirical scope.

The temporal evolution of publication output is illustrated in Figure 3.3. Publication activity remained limited prior to 2019 but increased sharply

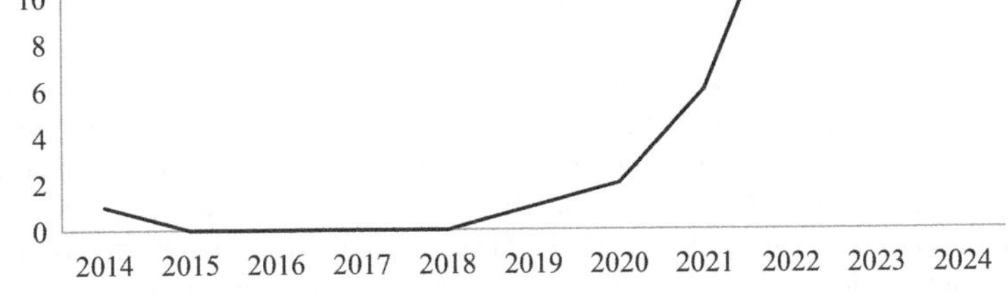

Figure 3.3 Publications on geopolitical disruptions and supply chain resilience (per year).

Table 3.6 Top authors in terms of publications

Author	*Articles*
IVANOV, DMITRY	5
AKTAS, EMEL	2
BELHADI, AMINE	2
BIRKEL, HENDRIK	2
E. L. BAZ, JAMAL	2
GEBHARDT, MAXIMILIAN	2
HENDRY, LINDA CAROLINE	2
KAMBLE, SACHIN	2
KAZANCOGLU, YIGIT	2
KOPYTO, MATTHIAS	2
ROSCOE, SAMUEL	2
RUEL, SALOMEE	2
SILVA, MINELLE E.	2
SPIESKE, ALEXANDER	2
VAN HOEK, REMKO	2
VENKATESH, MANI	2

Source: Own elaboration with use of Biblioshiny.

thereafter. This acceleration coincides with major global disruptions, including the COVID-19 pandemic, escalating trade tensions, and the armed conflict in Ukraine. The observed pattern suggests a shift from marginal scholarly attention towards sustained research engagement with geopolitical disruption as a structural condition affecting supply chains.

In addition to publication dynamics, authorship patterns provide insight into the structure of the research community. Author productivity is highly skewed, with a small number of scholars accounting for multiple publications and the majority contributing a single study. Table 3.6 identifies the most prolific authors in the dataset, with Ivanov emerging as the leading contributor, followed by a group of authors with two publications each.

This distribution reflects a pattern commonly observed in research fields at an early stage of consolidation. In line with Lotka's Law (Lotka, 1926), the dominance of single-publication authors indicates an expanding research community, while the presence of a small, highly productive group suggests the emergence of recognised reference points shaping the coherence and direction of the field.

The geographical distribution of publications is presented in Figure 3.4. Research output is concentrated in Europe and North America, with strong representation from the United Kingdom, the United States, and Germany, alongside meaningful contributions from Asia-Pacific economies. This pattern reflects both the global exposure of supply chains to geopolitical risk and the internationalisation of scholarly responses to these challenges.

To integrate these dimensions, a three-field plot analysis using a Sankey diagram illustrates how research flows across countries, authors, and keywords.

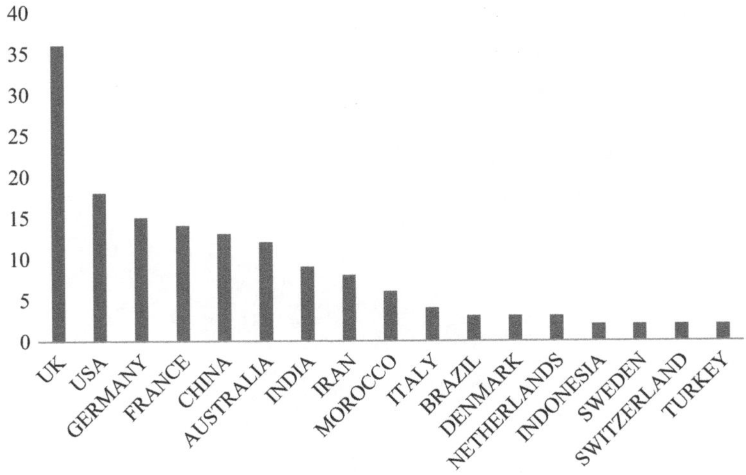

Figure 3.4 Top countries in terms of publications.

The widths of the connecting lines indicate the intensity of linkages, revealing which countries are associated with particular authors and thematic emphases. SCRES emerges as the dominant research theme, while countries such as the United Kingdom, France, and Germany appear as leading contributors. The United States shows a particularly strong association with COVID-19-related studies. Figure 3.5 visualises these relationships and underscores the global academic engagement with resilience under geopolitical pressure.

These findings directly address **RQ1.1** by illustrating how scholarship on SCRES under geopolitical disruption has evolved and which themes have gained prominence. They also respond to **RQ1.2** by identifying influential authors and countries contributing to this literature. The observed diversity of geographical participation suggests that resilience under geopolitical uncertainty has become a shared research concern across both advanced and emerging economies.

STEP 6b. Science mapping

Following Marzi *et al.* (2024), science mapping techniques are employed to uncover relational structures within the literature that extend beyond publication counts and citation volumes. Science mapping focuses on the interconnections among authors, documents, and concepts, enabling the visualisation of thematic proximities and intellectual linkages that inform subsequent cluster interpretation (Moral-Munoz *et al.*, 2019; van Eck & Waltman, 2010).

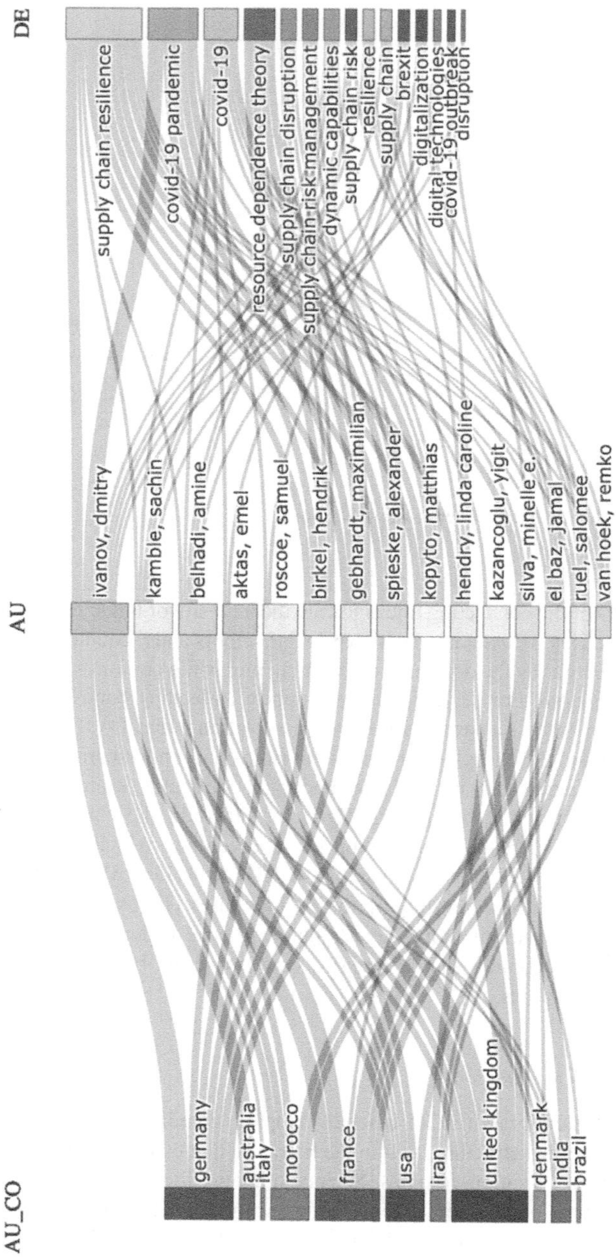

Figure 3.5 Sankey diagram (three-field plot).

The core author method offers a structured approach to examining collaborative dynamics and author contributions within research on geopolitical disruptions and resilient supply chains. Using VOSviewer, authors were grouped into clusters according to their co-authorship patterns, with cluster colours indicating distinct collaboration communities. The network displayed in Figure 3.6 includes authors with the highest total link strength who have published at least three papers in the dataset.

The collaboration network reveals several small clusters with varying levels of internal cohesion. One of the most central and densely interconnected groups consists of Birkel and Kopyto, whose repeated co-authorship signals a sustained partnership and a focused research trajectory. Their cluster includes additional co-authors, suggesting a small but active research group contributing jointly to the field.

Ivanov appears as the largest node in the network, reflecting both a high publication output and broad collaborative activity. Despite this prominence, his positioning indicates limited repeated co-authorship with the same collaborators, which creates a more distributed and less clustered pattern around his work.

Other identifiable pairs include Belhadi and Venkatesh, who have collaborated on multiple publications, as well as Ruel and El Baz, whose dyadic relationship indicates a similarly close partnership. Yanadori and Nikookar

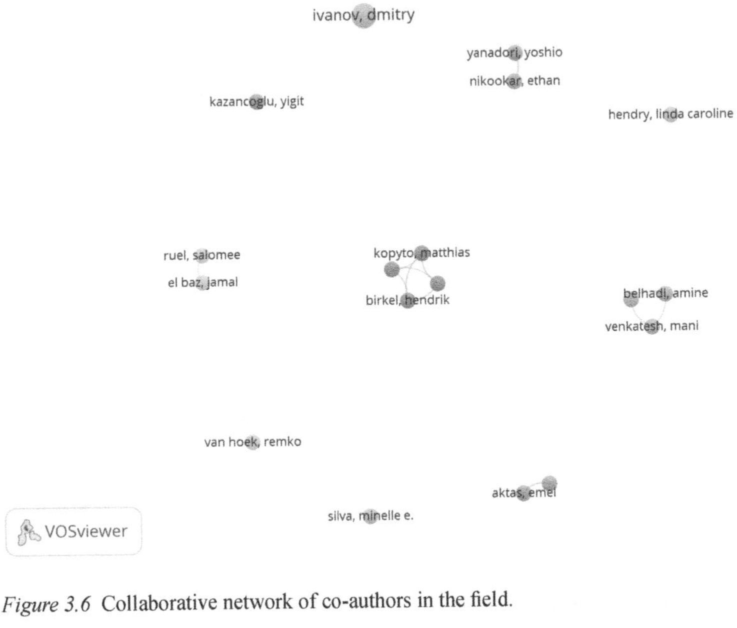

Figure 3.6 Collaborative network of co-authors in the field.

form another small subgroup with internal ties. Authors such as Kazancoglu, van Hoek, Hendry, and Silva show limited connectivity within the visible network, reflecting either independent contributions or collaborations with authors beyond the threshold for inclusion.

The overall structure of the network illustrates fragmentation, with several small, cohesive clusters instead of a unified co-authorship community. This fragmentation suggests that research in this domain is pursued across multiple parallel groups rather than through large-scale collective efforts. Expanding collaboration across clusters may support deeper integration of perspectives and strengthen the cumulative development of the field.

The bibliographic coupling map presented in Figure 3.7 complements this perspective by showing how documents are linked based on shared reference lists. Authors whose papers cite similar bodies of work cluster together, even if they do not collaborate directly. This pattern reveals intellectual proximity that is not visible in the co-authorship network. For instance, papers by Ivanov, Hendry, and Belhadi exhibit strong coupling patterns, indicating alignment in conceptual foundations and methodological choices despite differing collaboration structures. Such coupling suggests that knowledge in this field advances through both collaborative ties and shared theoretical anchors, reinforcing the thematic coherence of research on geopolitical disruptions and SCRES.

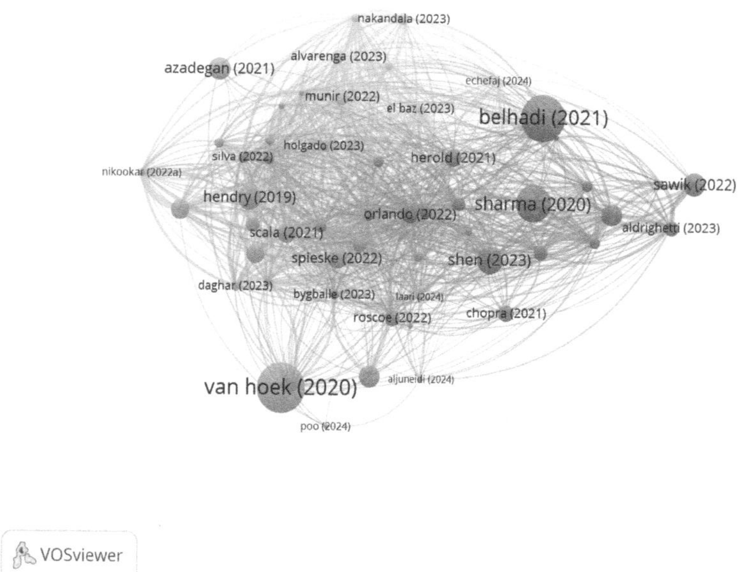

Figure 3.7 Bibliographic coupling.

Table 3.7 Highly cited research papers in the field

Paper	*Total citations (TC)*	*TC per year*
Van Hoek, R., 2020, International Journal of Operations & Production Management	534	89.00
Belhadi, A., 2021, Technological Forecasting and Social Change	465	93.00
Sharma, A., 2022, Journal of Business Research	297	49.50
Shen, Z. M., 2023, Journal of Operations Management	160	53.33
Hendry, L. C., 2019, International Journal of Operations & Production Management	131	18.71
Azadegan, A., 2021, Journal of Supply Chain Management	117	23.40
Sawik, T., 2022, Omega - International Journal of Management Science	107	26.75
Rozhkov, M., 2022, Omega - The International Journal of Management Science	106	26.50
Urciuoli, L., 2014, Supply Chain Management	102	8,50
Scala, B., 2021, Supply Chain Management	84	16.80
Spieske, A., 2022, Journal Of Purchasing And Supply Management	82	20.50
Nikookar, E., 2022, International Journal of Operations and Production Management	81	20.25
Chen, L. J., 2023, Journal of Operations Management	79	26.33
Herold, D. M., 2021, Supply Chain Management	72	14.40
Orlando, B., 2022, J INT MANAG	66	16.50

Source: Own elaboration with use of Biblioshiny.

Citation and co-citation analyses further clarify patterns of intellectual influence. Table 3.7 lists the most highly cited publications, while Figures 3.8 and 3.9 visualise citation and co-citation networks.

To explore the structure of intellectual influence within this research domain, VOSviewer was used to generate a citation network. Applying a threshold of at least 10 citations per document resulted in a network of 43 publications grouped into nine clusters (Figure 3.8). Each node in the network represents a paper, with node size reflecting citation frequency. Cluster colours indicate groups of publications that frequently cite one another, signalling shared themes or methodological approaches. Central and highly cited works, such as van Hoek (2020), Belhadi *et al.* (2021), and Sharma *et al.* (2022), appear prominently and function as intellectual anchors of the field. Their central placement suggests that these studies shape multiple thematic directions, particularly those related to resilience strategies and pandemic-induced disruptions. More recent papers, including Silva *et al.* (2023), Browning *et al.* (2023), and Aldrighetti *et al.* (2023), begin to form peripheral but emerging nodes, indicating early stages of influence and integration into the network.

A complementary co-citation map (Figure 3.9) illustrates how often pairs of documents are cited together across the dataset. Node size represents

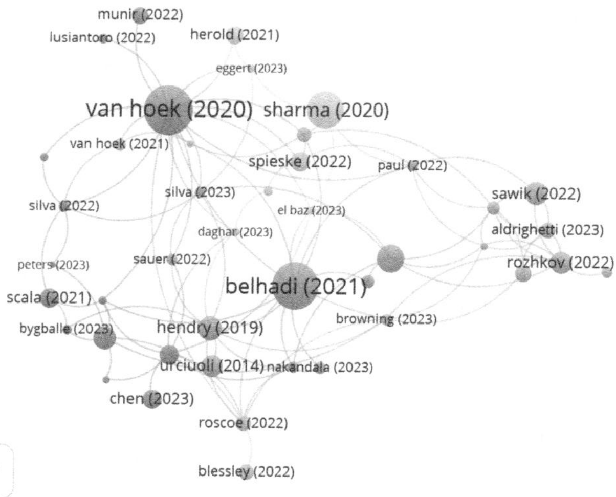

Figure 3.8 The citation network.

co-citation frequency, while cluster colours reflect groups of papers that jointly underpin specific research streams. The first cluster comprises foundational works in supply chain management and resilience, including Christopher and Peck (2004), Sheffi and Rice (2005), Jüttner and Maklan (2011), and Wieland and Wallenburg (2013). These studies provide the theoretical

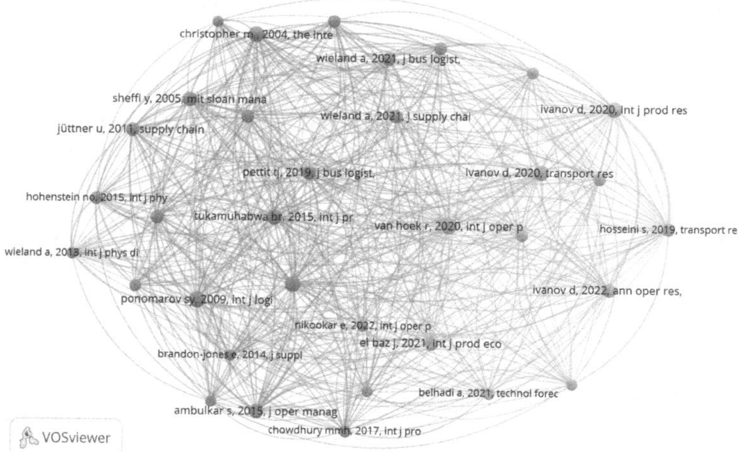

Figure 3.9 The co-citation network.

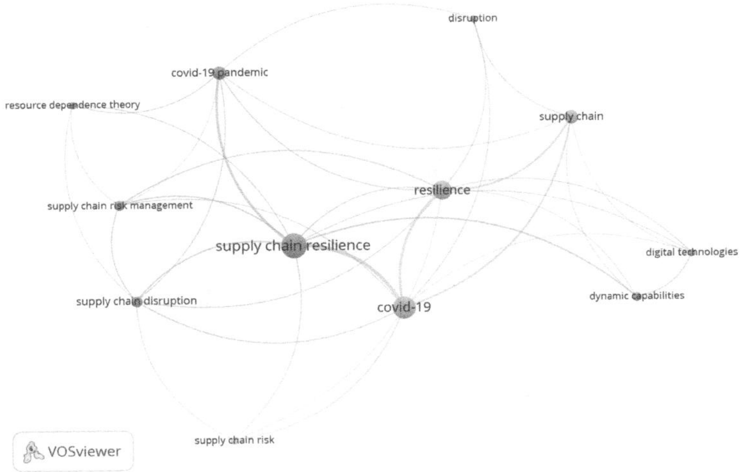

Figure 3.10 Keywords co-occurrence visualisation.

grounding for much of the field's conceptual development. The next cluster contains more recent and application-oriented work, particularly on digital resilience and supply chain design. Ivanov *et al.* (2019a, 2021, 2022) appears prominently, together with Hosseini *et al.* (2019, 2022) and Belhadi *et al.* (2021, 2024), indicating shared methodological approaches and a common focus on analytical modelling. The last cluster bridges these two areas and includes authors such as Wieland and Durach (2021), El Baz and Ruel (2021), and Belhadi *et al.* (2021), whose contributions integrate insights from both foundational theory and contemporary empirical challenges.

Furthermore, the keyword co-occurrence analysis conducted in VOSviewer reveals four main conceptual clusters (Figure 3.10). SCRES stands at the centre of the network, acting as the dominant linking term across studies. COVID-19 emerges as a key contextual factor, closely connected with themes such as uncertainty, disruption, and risk, illustrating how pandemic-related shocks have shaped recent research. Digitalisation appears as a smaller but clearly identifiable node, pointing to a growing interest in technology-enabled resilience strategies. Dynamic capabilities feature in the network with lower frequency, yet their presence signals an emerging connection between resilience and firms' adaptive capability development.

The thematic map (Figure 3.11) further clarifies the structure of the field by plotting themes according to their relevance and degree of development. SCRES and supply chain appear as motor themes, confirming their central position and conceptual maturity. SCRES related to COVID-19 is located in the basic themes quadrant, reflecting its high relevance but ongoing consolidation.

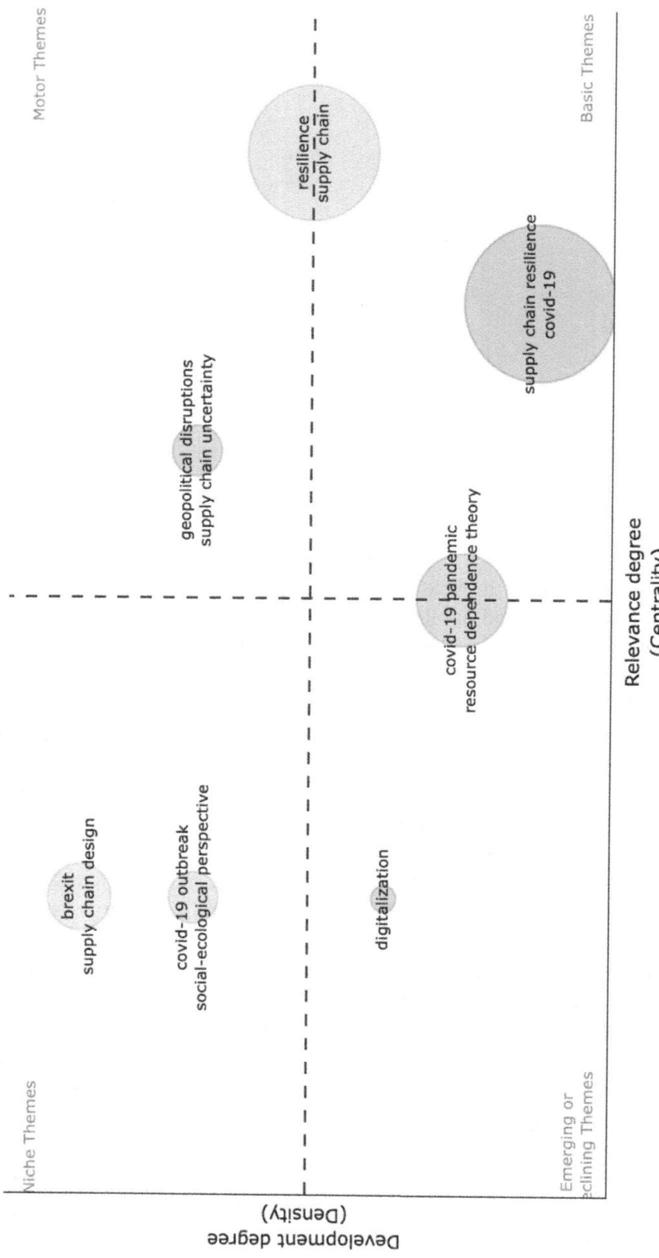

Figure 3.11 Thematic map.

Geopolitical disruptions and supply chain uncertainty occupy an intermediate position, suggesting that these topics are becoming increasingly integrated into mainstream research. Digitalisation appears among emerging themes, indicating that technological aspects of resilience are still developing. Dynamic capabilities do not meet the threshold to form a separate mapped theme, but their presence in the co-occurrence network aligns them conceptually with this emerging cluster. This pattern suggests that while scholars increasingly acknowledge the role of capability-building in resilience, explicit theorisation remains limited.

These combined visualisations respond directly to **RQ1.3** by highlighting both emerging trends and unresolved gaps. The dominance of COVID-19-related terms indicates that pandemic-driven disruptions still heavily influence research trajectories, which may overshadow other forms of geopolitical shock. The transitional positioning of geopolitical disruptions and uncertainty signals that these themes are rising in importance but remain underdeveloped. The limited visibility of digitalisation and dynamic capabilities points to a notable gap: technology adoption is increasingly studied, yet its integration into broader capability-based frameworks is still incomplete. These insights point to several avenues for future research, including expanding the analytical lens beyond pandemic disruptions, deepening exploration of geopolitical risk mechanisms, and examining more systematically how digital tools contribute to the development of dynamic capabilities that underpin SCRES.

Collectively, the bibliometric performance analysis and science mapping provide a structured empirical foundation for identifying thematic clusters and ordering the literature. This prepares the ground for cluster identification and qualitative synthesis undertaken in STEPs 7–9, in line with the staged logic of the B-SLR framework proposed by Marzi *et al.* (2024).

STEP 7. Clusters' topic identification

Evidence from bibliometric analyses provides a structured mapping of the research landscape on SCRES under geopolitical disruption. The thematic clusters discussed in this study were subsequently refined through qualitative interpretation of the reviewed literature, drawing on close reading of the selected publications. Accordingly, the four clusters represent an inductive synthesis developed by the author through the integration of quantitative bibliometric patterns and qualitative interpretation, rather than categories derived solely from algorithmic procedures.

The first cluster, labelled *operational resilience*, reflects a mature and well-established stream within the literature. The associated body of research concentrates on operational continuity and short-term recovery following disruption. Qualitative synthesis indicates that resilience in this stream is predominantly framed as the capacity to maintain or rapidly restore operational performance. Empirical work emphasises mitigation strategies, continuity planning, response speed, and short-term recovery, with evidence largely drawn from pandemic-related contexts (Hendry *et al.*, 2019; van Hoek, 2020; Sharma *et al.*, 2022; Nikookar & Yanadori, 2021; Spieske *et al.*, 2022).

The second cluster, referred to as *strategic reconfiguration*, captures research focused on longer-term structural adjustment of supply networks under prolonged or systemic disruption. Although less consolidated than operational resilience, this stream exhibits a coherent orientation towards questions of network design, robustness, and adaptability. Interpretation of the underlying studies shows a strong prevalence of modelling and simulation approaches examining trade-offs between efficiency, redundancy, and resilience under sustained disruption (Ivanov, 2021; Rozhkov *et al.*, 2022; Sawik, 2022; Zeng *et al.*, 2024; Aldrighetti *et al.*, 2023).

The third cluster, labelled *collaborative ecosystem*, encompasses research that conceptualises resilience as a relational and collective outcome. This stream emphasises coordination, information sharing, governance, and inter-organisational dependencies as central mechanisms shaping resilience outcomes. Qualitative synthesis suggests that resilience is framed as a negotiated process influenced by power asymmetries and constrained access to critical resources across supply networks (Hassan *et al.*, 2024; Peters *et al.*, 2023; Roscoe *et al.*, 2022; Scala & Lindsay, 2021; van Hoek, 2020).

The fourth cluster, labelled *digital readiness*, corresponds to an emerging research stream examining the role of digital tools and infrastructures in supporting resilience. While scholarly attention to this area is increasing, conceptual integration remains limited. Qualitative synthesis indicates that digitalisation is often treated as a technical enabler of sensing, monitoring, and decision-making, rather than as a context-dependent capability shaped by geopolitical and institutional constraints (Belhadi *et al.*, 2021; El Baz & Ruel, 2024; Hosseini *et al.*, 2019; Ivanov *et al.*, 2019b).

These clusters depict a research landscape characterised by strong consolidation around operational resilience and more fragmented development of strategic reconfiguration, collaborative, and digital streams. This pattern highlights unresolved gaps in the literature, particularly the limited treatment of geopolitical disruption as a persistent structural condition rather than a temporary shock.

STEP 8. Sample ordering and selection

This step links the bibliometric analyses with the qualitative synthesis by structuring the final corpus of studies included in the SLR. Although all documents retained after the screening process were included, ordering the sample was necessary to guide the sequencing, depth, and analytical emphasis of the qualitative synthesis undertaken in Step 9.

Following cluster identification, studies were first grouped by cluster membership to ensure that each thematic stream was examined as a coherent body of knowledge. Within clusters, documents were ordered using a combination of qualitative judgement and bibliometric indicators. Bibliometric criteria included citation counts, network centrality, and link strength derived from citation, co-citation, and bibliographic coupling analyses conducted in VOSviewer. These indicators were used to identify influential and representative publications, particularly those occupying central or bridging positions within the networks.

As the total sample size remained suitable for in-depth qualitative review, no further subsampling was applied. The ordering procedure therefore served an analytical rather than exclusionary purpose. Highly influential studies were prioritised in the narrative synthesis, while more recent or peripheral contributions were used to capture emerging perspectives and thematic diversification within clusters. Bibliometric ordering was complemented by qualitative assessment based on field-specific expertise, including re-examination of abstracts and selected full texts to ensure conceptual relevance and alignment with the research questions.

The outcome of this step was an ordered and thematically structured corpus of literature organised by analytical prominence within each cluster. This corpus provided the foundation for the systematic qualitative synthesis presented in Step 9.

STEP 9. Systematic literature review

This step moves from thematic identification to interpretive synthesis, examining how the literature conceptualises SCRES as a process of economic adjustment under geopolitical constraint. Rather than reiterating cluster characteristics, the qualitative review focuses on the dominant logics, assumptions, and limitations through which resilience is theorised, as well as on how firms and supply networks are understood to reallocate resources, restructure production, and renegotiate inter-organisational relations in politically charged environments. Through this interpretive synthesis, the review clarifies how existing research frames resilience under sustained geopolitical disruption and addresses the gaps identified in **RQ1.3**.

Across the literature concerned with *operational responses*, resilience is predominantly framed in terms of short-term stabilisation. The reviewed studies emphasise continuity of flows, buffering against volatility, and rapid restoration of operational performance, often linking resilience to cost containment and service reliability. Contributions by Hendry *et al.* (2019), van Hoek (2020), Sharma *et al.* (2020), Nikookar and Yanadori (2021), and Spieske *et al.* (2022) provide detailed insight into managing acute disruption. However, the qualitative synthesis indicates that geopolitical pressures are usually treated as external shocks rather than as persistent structural conditions. This framing implicitly assumes a return to equilibrium and limits the explanatory capacity of operational resilience in contexts shaped by enduring sanctions, trade fragmentation, or regulatory divergence.

In comparison, work addressing *structural adaptation* adopts a longer temporal horizon and interprets resilience as the outcome of strategic reconfiguration. Modelling- and simulation-based studies analyse how firms redesign supply networks through diversification, redundancy, and geographic reallocation in order to rebalance cost–risk trade-offs under sustained uncertainty. Research by Ivanov (2021), Rozhkov *et al.* (2022), Sawik (2022), Zeng *et al.* (2024), and Aldrighetti *et al.* (2023) conceptualises these adjustments as economically rational responses to systemic disruption. At the same time, the synthesis reveals that organisational decision-making, managerial interpretation of geopolitical risk, and institutional constraint are only weakly integrated into these models. As a result, strategic reconfiguration is frequently analysed as a technical optimisation problem, abstracted from the political and organisational processes through which adjustment unfolds in practice.

In turn, *relational perspectives* interpret resilience as an outcome of negotiated coordination under conditions of constrained choice. The literature highlights the role of trust, information sharing, and governance arrangements in managing inter-organisational dependencies and power asymmetries. The use of resource dependence theory provides a political-economy lens, framing collaboration as a reconfiguration response to asymmetric access to critical resources, and regulatory pressure. Studies by van Hoek (2020), Scala and Lindsay (2021), Roscoe *et al.* (2022), Peters *et al.* (2023), and Hassan *et al.* (2024) demonstrate that resilience often emerges through collective adjustment rather than unilateral firm action, particularly in regulated or geopolitically exposed sectors. Nonetheless, the synthesis indicates that collaboration under adversarial geopolitical conditions—such as forced decoupling, politically constrained partner selection, or state-driven realignment—remains weakly theorised.

Finally, research on *digital readiness* interprets resilience-enhancing technologies primarily through their effects on information and coordination. The qualitative synthesis indicates that analytics, visibility tools, platforms, and advanced technologies reduce information asymmetries, improve monitoring, and support decision-making under uncertainty, thereby lowering transaction costs. Contributions by Ivanov *et al.* (2019a), Hosseini *et al.* (2019), Belhadi *et al.* (2021), Stentoft *et al.* (2023), and El Baz and Ruel (2024) suggest that digital readiness improves resilience outcomes indirectly, through its interaction with organisational capabilities such as absorptive capacity, organisational memory, and social capital. However, digital readiness is largely treated as a technical efficiency enhancer, with limited attention to how its effectiveness is shaped by geopolitical regulation, data sovereignty, and institutional control.

Overall, the qualitative synthesis reveals a literature that increasingly acknowledges geopolitical disruption but remains uneven in its incorporation of political-economy mechanisms. Short-term stabilisation dominates operational accounts, while longer-term structural, relational, and technological adjustments are only partially theorised as responses to persistent geopolitical constraint. By interpreting resilience as an ongoing process of economic adjustment shaped by institutional pressures and power relations, this step provides the analytical bridge between the bibliometric mapping and the integrative interpretation developed in the subsequent chapter.

STEP 10. Developing a theoretical contribution

The thematic synthesis of the literature indicates that mitigation mechanisms addressing geopolitical disruption are conceptualised differently across research streams, particularly with respect to their temporal scope, unit of analysis, and treatment of political constraints. When interpreted through the integrated framework of resilience capabilities developed in Chapter 2, these differences can be understood not as inconsistencies, but as literature-level manifestations of phase-dominant adjustment logics operating within a cumulative resilience process (Dolgui *et al.*, 2018; Pettit *et al.*, 2010; Ponomarov & Holcomb, 2009).

Research clustered around *operational resilience* primarily reflects a responsiveness-oriented logic, emphasising short-term stabilisation through buffering, flexibility, and rapid reallocation of resources (Spieske *et al.*, 2022; van Hoek, 2020). In contrast, studies grouped within the *strategic reconfiguration* cluster foreground longer-term adjustment mechanisms associated with resurgence, such as supplier diversification, geographic dispersion, and network redesign, treated as economically rational responses to sustained uncertainty (Aldrighetti *et al.*, 2023; Ivanov, 2021; Sawik, 2022). While both streams address legitimate dimensions of resilience, the literature rarely theorises how short-term stabilisation evolves into longer-term structural renewal within a single adjustment trajectory.

The *digital readiness* cluster spans multiple disruption phases but is most closely aligned with readiness-oriented capabilities, particularly sensing, visibility, and anticipatory decision support (Belhadi *et al.*, 2021; El Baz & Ruel, 2024; Ivanov *et al.*, 2019a). However, *digital readiness* is seldom theorised as a capability that dynamically links readiness with subsequent responsiveness and resurgence. Similarly, the *collaborative ecosystem* cluster corresponds to a collaboration-oriented capability logic, conceptualising resilience as a collective outcome shaped by inter-organisational dependencies, governance structures, and power asymmetries (Peters *et al.*, 2023; Roscoe *et al.*, 2022). Yet this stream often abstracts from how geopolitical constraints delimit feasible partnership configurations over time.

By integrating these literature-derived clusters within a phase-based capability framework, the model advanced in this chapter reconceptualises supply chain resilience as an ongoing process of economic adjustment under persistent geopolitical constraint. Rather than privileging any single mechanism or phase, the framework explains how readiness, responsiveness, resurgence, and collaboration interact sequentially and cumulatively. The theoretical contribution therefore lies not in proposing new resilience practices, but in offering an integrative, capability-based interpretation that explains why similar strategies yield different outcomes depending on timing, positioning, and institutional context.

Accordingly, the empirical investigations presented in the subsequent chapters are designed and interpreted in line with these assumptions, treating the phase-based resilience capability framework as a structuring device for analysing firm-level adjustment processes under geopolitical constraint.

Synthesis of bibliometric and systematic insights

This chapter addresses the first research question by examining how scholarly understanding of SCRES under geopolitical disruption has evolved, how the field is structured, and where its principal limitations lie. Drawing on an integrated bibliometric and qualitative review, the chapter provides a consolidated assessment of the literature that frames and motivates the subsequent empirical analysis.

Addressing **RQ1.1**, the review shows that research on SCRES has expanded rapidly over the past decade, with particularly strong growth after 2020. Early contributions focused primarily on generic risk exposure and resilience concepts, while more recent work has shifted towards disruption, adaptation, and adjustment processes. Despite this evolution, geopolitical disruption remains unevenly embedded in core conceptual frameworks and is still frequently treated as an episodic shock rather than as a persistent structural condition shaping supply chain organisation over time.

In relation to **RQ1.2**, the analysis clarifies the intellectual and geographical structure of the field. Scholarly influence is concentrated among a limited set of authors, journals, and countries, with research output dominated by Europe and North America and increasing contributions from Asia. Collaboration patterns remain fragmented, suggesting that knowledge development proceeds through parallel thematic streams rather than a cohesive research community, contributing to the persistence of partially disconnected perspectives on resilience.

With respect to **RQ1.3**, the synthesis identifies several research gaps arising from the thematic and temporal imbalances in the literature. Operational resilience is predominantly examined through the lens of short-term stabilisation, offering limited insight into prolonged, politically driven disruptions such as sanctions or regulatory divergence. Research on strategic reconfiguration is largely modelling-oriented, with comparatively limited empirical attention to organisational decision-making and institutional constraints. Collaboration under adversarial geopolitical conditions remains weakly theorised, while digital readiness is often treated as a neutral enabler, with insufficient consideration of geopolitical regulation, data governance, and institutional control.

Overall, the findings indicate that existing research offers a fragmented and phase-specific understanding of SCRES under geopolitical disruption. While individual streams provide valuable insight into operational, structural, relational, and technological mechanisms, their limited integration constrains explanatory depth. By making these gaps explicit, this chapter establishes the need for empirical investigation into how resilience capabilities are interpreted, sequenced, and combined over time under persistent geopolitical constraint, directly informing the design of the subsequent empirical chapters.

References

Adams, R. J., Smart, P., & Huff, A. S. (2017). Shades of grey: Guidelines for working with the grey literature in systematic reviews for management and organizational studies. *International Journal of Management Reviews*, *19*(4), 432–454. https://doi.org/10.1111/ijmr.12102

Agrawal, N., & Jain, R. K. (2022). Insights from systematic literature review of supply chain resilience and disruption. *Benchmarking: An International Journal*, *29*(8), 2495–2526. https://doi.org/10.1108/BIJ-02-2021-0084

Aldrighetti, R., Battini, D., & Ivanov, D. (2023). Efficient resilience portfolio design in the supply chain with consideration of preparedness and recovery investments. *Omega-International Journal of Management Science*, 117, 21. https://doi.org/10.1016/j.omega.2023.102841

Ali, A., & Gölgeci, I. (2019). Where is supply chain resilience research heading? A systematic and co-evolutionary analysis. *International Journal of Physical Distribution & Logistics Management*, *49*(8), 793–815. https://doi.org/10.1108/IJPDLM-02-2019-0038

Ali, A., Mahfouz, A., & Arisha, A. (2017). Analysing supply chain resilience: Integrating the constructs in a concept mapping framework via a systematic literature review. *Supply Chain Management: An International Journal*, *22*(1), 16–39. https://doi.org/10.1108/SCM-06-2016-0197

Aria, M., & Cuccurullo, C. (2017). Bibliometrix: An R-tool for comprehensive science mapping analysis. *Journal of Informetrics*, *11*(4), 959–975. https://doi.org/10.1016/j.joi.2017.08.007

Barnes, P., & Oloruntoba, R. (2005). Assurance of security in maritime supply chains: Conceptual issues of vulnerability and crisis management. *Journal of International Management*, *11*(4), 519–540. https://doi.org/10.1016/j.intman.2005.09.008

Bednarski, L., Roscoe, S., Blome, C., & Schleper, M. C. (2024). Geopolitical disruptions in global supply chains: A state-of-the-art literature review. *Production Planning & Control*, *36*(4), 536–562. https://doi.org/10.1080/09537287.2023.2286283

Belhadi, A., Kamble, S., Jabbour, C. J. C., Gunasekaran, A., Ndubisi, N. O., & Venkatesh, M. (2021). Manufacturing and service supply chain resilience to the COVID-19 outbreak: Lessons learned from the automobile and airline industries. *Technological Forecasting and Social Change, 163*. https://doi.org/10.1016/j.techfore.2020.120447

Belhadi, A., Kamble, S., Subramanian, N., Singh, R. K., & Venkatesh, M. (2024). Digital capabilities to manage agri-food supply chain uncertainties and build supply chain resilience during compounding geopolitical disruptions. *International Journal of Operations & Production Management, 44*(11), 1914–1950. https://doi.org/10.1108/IJOPM-11-2022-0737

Bradford, S. C. (1934). Sources of information on specific subjects. *Engineering, 26*, 85–86.

Brookes, B. C. (1969). Bradford's law and the bibliography of science. *Nature, 224*, 953–956. https://doi.org/10.1038/224953a0

Browning, T., Kumar, M., Sanders, N., Sodhi, M. S., Thürer, M., & Tortorella, G. L. (2023). From supply chain risk to system-wide disruptions: Research opportunities in forecasting, risk management and product design. *International Journal of Operations & Production Management, 43*(12), 1841–1858. https://doi.org/10.1108/IJOPM-09-2022-0573

Caldara, D., & Iacoviello, M. (2018). Measuring geopolitical risk. *Political Economy: Government Expenditures & Related Policies eJournal*. https://doi.org/10.17016/IFDP.2018.1222

Castillo, C. (2023). Is there a theory of supply chain resilience? A bibliometric analysis of the literature. *International Journal of Operations & Production Management, 43*(1), 22–47. https://doi.org/10.1108/IJOPM-02-2022-0136

Chartered Association of Business Schools. (2024). *Academic Journal Guide 2024*. https://charteredabs.org/academic-journal-guide/academic-journal-guide-2024

Chowdhury, P., Paul, S., Kaisar, S., & Moktadir, M. (2021). COVID-19 pandemic related supply chain studies: A systematic review. *Transportation Research. Part E, Logistics and Transportation Review, 148*, 102271–102271. https://doi.org/10.1016/j.tre.2021.102271

Christopher, M., & Peck, H. (2004). Building the resilient supply chain. *The International Journal of Logistics Management, 15*(2), 1–14. https://doi.org/10.1108/09574090410700275

Colicchia, C., & Strozzi, F. (2012). Supply chain risk management: A new methodology for a systematic literature review. *Supply Chain Management, 17*, 403–418. https://doi.org/10.1108/13598541211246558

Denyer, D., & Tranfield, D. (2009). Producing a systematic review. In D. A. Buchanan & A. Bryman (Eds.), *The Sage handbook of organizational research methods* (pp. 671–689). Sage Publications Ltd.

Dolgui, A., & Ivanov, D. (2021). Ripple effect and supply chain disruption management: New trends and research directions. *International Journal of Production Research, 59*(1), 102–109. https://doi.org/10.1080/00207543.2021.1840148

Dolgui, A., Ivanov, D., & Sokolov, B. (2018). Ripple effect in the supply chain: An analysis and recent literature. *International Journal of Production Research, 56*(1–2), 414–430. https://doi.org/10.1080/00207543.2017.1387680

Durach, C., Kembro, J., & Wieland, A. (2017). A new paradigm for systematic literature reviews in supply chain management. *Journal of Supply Chain Management*, 53, 67–85. https://doi.org/10.1111/JSCM.12145

El Baz, J., & Ruel, S. (2021). Can supply chain risk management practices mitigate the disruption impacts on supply chains' resilience and robustness? Evidence from an empirical survey in a COVID-19 outbreak era. *International Journal of Production Economics*, 233, 107972. https://doi.org/10.1016/j.ijpe.2020.107972

El Baz, J., & Ruel, S. (2024). Achieving social performance through digitalization and supply chain resilience in the COVID-19 disruption era: An empirical examination based on a stakeholder dynamic capabilities view. *Technological Forecasting and Social Change*, 201, 123209. https://doi.org/10.1016/j.techfore.2024.123209

Ergun, O., Hopp, W. J., & Keskinocak, P. (2023). A structured overview of insights and opportunities for enhancing supply chain resilience. *IISE Transactions*, *55*(1), 57–74. https://doi.org/10.1080/24725854.2022.2080892

European Parliament. (2020). *The geopolitical implications of the COVID-19 pandemic*. https://www.europarl.europa.eu/RegData/etudes/STUD/2020/603511/EXPO_STU%282020%29603511_EN.pdf

Hassan, J., Chugh, R., Ren, M., & Gao, H. (2024). Situational control and strategic choices during supply chain disruptions: Case studies of SME exporters. *International Marketing Review*, 41, 39. https://doi.org/10.1108/IMR-07-2023-0161

Hendry, L., Stevenson, M., Macbryde, J., Ball, P., Sayed, M., & Liu, L. (2019). Local food supply chain resilience to constitutional change: The Brexit effect. *International Journal of Operations & Production Management, 39*. https://doi.org/10.1108/IJOPM-03-2018-0184

Hiebl, M. R. (2023). Sample selection in systematic literature reviews of management research. *Organizational Research Methods*, *26*(2), 229–261. https://doi.org/10.1177/1094428120986851

Hohenstein, N. O., Feisel, E., Hartmann, E., & Giunipero, L. (2015). Research on the phenomenon of supply chain resilience: A systematic review and paths for further investigation. *International Journal of Physical Distribution & Logistics Management*, *45*(1-2), 90–117. https://doi.org/10.1108/IJPDLM-05-2013-0128

Hosseini, S., & Ivanov, D. (2022). A new resilience measure for supply networks with the ripple effect considerations: A Bayesian network approach. *Annals of Operations Research, 319*(1), 581–607. https://doi.org/10.1007/s10479-019-03350-8

Hosseini, S., Ivanov, D., & Dolgui, A. (2019). Review of quantitative methods for supply chain resilience analysis. *Transportation Research Part E: Logistics and Transportation Review*. 125, 258–307. https://doi.org/10.1016/J.TRE.2019.03.001

Ivanov, D. (2021). Supply chain viability and the COVID-19 pandemic: A conceptual and formal generalisation of four major adaptation strategies. *International Journal of Production Research*, *59*(12), 3535–3552. https://doi.org/10.1080/00207543.2021.1890852

Ivanov, D., Dolgui, A., & Sokolov, B. (2019a). The impact of digital technology and Industry 4.0 on the ripple effect and supply chain risk analytics. *International Journal of Production Research*, *57*(3), 829–846. https://doi.org/10.1080/00207543.2018.1488086

Ivanov, D., Tsipoulanidis, A., & Schönberger, J. (2019b). *Global supply chain and operations management* (2nd ed.). Springer.

Jüttner, U., & Maklan, S. (2011). Supply chain resilience in the global financial crisis: An empirical study. *Supply Chain Management*, 16, 246–259. https://doi.org/10.1108/13598541111139062

Kamalahmadi, M., & Parast, M. M. (2016). A review of the literature on the principles of enterprise and supply chain resilience: Major findings and directions for future research. *International Journal of Production Economics, 171*, 116–133. https://doi.org/10.1016/j.ijpe.2015.10.023

Kasaraneni, H., & Rosaline, S. (2024). Automatic merging of scopus and web of science data for simplified and effective bibliometric analysis. *Annals of Data Science, 11*(3), 785–802. https://doi.org/10.1007/s40745-022-00438-0

Katsaliaki, K., Galetsi, P., & Kumar, S. (2022). Supply chain disruptions and resilience: A major review and future research agenda. *Annals of Operations Research, 319*(1), 965–1002. https://doi.org/10.1007/s10479-020-03912-1

Khan, M. N., Akhtar, P., & Merali, Y. (2018). Strategies and effective decision-making against terrorism affecting supply chain risk management and security: A novel combination of triangulated methods. *Industrial Management & Data Systems, 118*(7), 1528–1546. https://doi.org/10.1108/IMDS-09-2017-0449

Kochan, C., & Nowicki, D. (2018). Supply chain resilience: A systematic literature review and typological framework. *International Journal of Physical Distribution & Logistics Management, 48*. https://doi.org/10.1108/IJPDLM-02-2017-0099

Kraus, S., Breier, M., & Dasí-Rodríguez, S. (2020). The art of crafting a systematic literature review in entrepreneurship research. *International Entrepreneurship and Management Journal*, 1–20. https://doi.org/10.1007/s11365-020-00635-4

Le Clercq, L. S. (2024). ABCal: A Python package for author bias computation and scientometric plotting for reviews and meta-analyses. *Scientometrics, 129*(1), 581–600. https://doi.org/10.1007/s11192-023-04880-6

Lotka, A. J. (1926). *The frequency distribution of scientific productivity. Journal of the Washington Academy of Sciences, 16*(12), 317–323.

Marzi, G., Balzano, M., Caputo, A., & Pellegrini, M. M. (2024). Guidelines for bibliometric-systematic literature reviews: 10 steps to combine analysis, synthesis, and theory development. *International Journal of Management Reviews, 27*(1), 81–103. https://doi.org/10.1111/ijmr.12381

Moral-Munoz, J. A., López-Herrera, A. G., Herrera-Viedma, E., & Cobo, M. J. (2019). *Science mapping analysis software tools: A review*. In Glänzel, W., Moed, H. F., Schmoch, U., Thelwall, M. (eds.), *Springer handbook of science and technology indicators*. Springer Handbooks. Springer. https://doi.org/10.1007/978-3-030-02511-3_7

Naimi, M., Faisal, M., Sobh, R., & Sabir, L. (2021). A systematic mapping review exploring 10 years of research on supply chain resilience and reconfiguration. *International Journal of Logistics Research and Applications*, 25, 1191–1218. https://doi.org/10.1080/13675567.2021.1893288

Nikookar, E., & Yanadori, Y. (2022). Preparing supply chain for the next disruption beyond COVID-19: Managerial antecedents of supply chain resilience. *International Journal of Operations & Production Management*. https://doi.org/10.1108/ijopm-04-2021-0272

Page, M. J., McKenzie, J. E., Bossuyt, P. M., Boutron, I., Hoffmann, T. C., Mulrow, C. D., Shamseer, L., Tetzlaff, J. M., Akl, E. A., Brennan, S. E., Chou, R., Glanville, J., Grimshaw, J. M., Hróbjartsson, A., Lalu, M. M., Li, T., Loder, E. W., Mayo-Wilson, E., McDonald, S., …, & Moher, D. (2021). The PRISMA 2020 statement: An updated guideline for reporting systematic reviews. *BMJ, 372*. https://doi.org/10.1136/bmj.n71

Peters, E., Knight, L., Boersma, K., & Uenk, N. (2023). Organizing for supply chain resilience: A high reliability network perspective. *International Journal Of Operations & Production Management*, 43, 22. https://doi.org/10.1108/IJOPM-03-2022-0167

Pettit, T. J., Fiksel, J., & Croxton, K. L. (2010). Ensuring supply chain resilience: Development of a conceptual framework. *Journal of Business Logistics*, *31*(1), 1–21. https://doi.org/10.1002/j.2158-1592.2010.tb00125.x

Ponomarov, S. Y., & Holcomb, M. C. (2009). Understanding the concept of supply chain resilience. *The International Journal of Logistics Management*, *20*(1), 124–143. https://doi.org/10.1108/09574090910954873

Poo, M., Wang, T., & Yang, Z. (2024). Global food supply chain resilience assessment: A case in the United Kingdom. *Transportation Research Part A-Policy and Practice*, 181, 19. https://doi.org/10.1016/j.tra.2024.104018

Pranckutė, R. (2021). Web of Science (WoS) and Scopus: The titans of bibliographic information in today's academic world. *Publications*, *9*(1), 12. https://doi.org/10.3390/publications9010012

Rabetino, R., Kohtamäki, M., & Federico, J. S. (2021). A (re) view of the philosophical foundations of strategic management. *International Journal of Management Reviews*, *23*(2), 151–190.

Roscoe, S., Aktas, E., Petersen, K. J., Skipworth, H. D., Handfield, R. B., & Habib, F. (2022). Redesigning global supply chains during compounding geopolitical disruptions: The role of supply chain logics. *International Journal of Operations & Production Management*, *42*(9), 1407–1434. https://doi.org/10.1108/IJOPM-12-2021-0777

Roshani, A., Walker-Davies, P., & Parry, G. (2024). Designing resilient supply chain networks: A systematic literature review of mitigation strategies. *Annals of Operations Research*, *341*(2), 1267–1332. https://doi.org/10.1007/s10479-024-06228-6

Rozhkov, M., Ivanov, D., Blackhurst, J., & Nair, A. (2022). Adapting supply chain operations in anticipation of and during the COVID-19 pandemic. *Omega-International Journal of Management Science*, *110*, 17. https://doi.org/10.1016/j.omega.2022.102635

Sawik, T. (2022). Stochastic optimization of supply chain resilience under ripple effect: A COVID-19 pandemic related study. *Omega*, *109*, 102596. https://doi.org/10.1016/j.omega.2022.102596

Scala, B., & Lindsay, C. (2021). Supply chain resilience during pandemic disruption: Evidence from healthcare. *Supply Chain Management-An International Journal*, 26, 17. https://doi.org/10.1108/SCM-09-2020-0434

Sharma, A., Kumar, V., Borah, S. B., & Adhikary, A. (2022). Complexity in a multinational enterprise's global supply chain and its international business performance: A bane or a boon?. *Journal of International Business Studies*, 53(5), 850–878. https://doi.org/10.1057/s41267-021-00497-0

Shea, B. J., Reeves, B. C., Wells, G., Thuku, M., Hamel, C., Moran, J., & Henry, D. A. (2017). AMSTAR 2: A critical appraisal tool for systematic reviews that include randomised or non-randomised studies of healthcare interventions, or both. *BMJ*, *358*. https://doi.org/10.1136/bmj.j4008

Sheffi, Y., & Rice, B. J. (2005). A supply chain view of the resilient enterprise. *MIT Sloan Management Review*. 47, 1, 41–48. https://sloanreview.mit.edu/article/a-supply-chain-view-of-the-resilient-enterprise/

Shi, X., Liu, W., & Lim, M. K. (2024). Supply chain resilience: New challenges and opportunities. *International Journal of Logistics Research and Applications*, *27*(12), 2485–2512. https://doi.org/10.1080/13675567.2023.2262396

Sienkiewicz-Małyjurek, K., & Szymczak, M. (2024). Understanding public service supply chain management: A systematic literature review. *Management Review Quarterly*, *74*(3), 1879–1943. https://doi.org/10.1007/s11301-023-00350-8

Silva, M. E., Pereira, M. M., & Hendry, L. C. (2023). Embracing change in tandem: Resilience and sustainability together transforming supply chains. *International Journal of Operations & Production Management, 43*(1), 166–196. https://doi.org/10.1108/IJOPM-09-2022-0625

Spieske, A., & Birkel, H. (2021). Improving supply chain resilience through industry 4.0: A systematic literature review under the impressions of the COVID-19 pandemic. *Computers & Industrial Engineering,* 158. https://doi.org/10.1016/j.cie.2021.107452

Spieske, A., Gebhardt, M., Kopyto, M., & Birkel, H. (2022). Improving resilience of the healthcare supply chain in a pandemic: Evidence from Europe during the COVID-19 crisis. *Journal of Purchasing and Supply Management*, 28, 19. https://doi.org/10.1016/j.pursup.2022.100748

Stentoft, J., Mikkelsen, O., & Wickstrom, K. (2023). Supply chain resilience and absorptive capacity: Crisis mitigation and performance effects during COVID-19. *Supply Chain Management-An International Journal*, 28, 18. https://doi.org/10.1108/SCM-10-2022-0384

Tranfield, D., Denyer, D., & Smart, P. (2003). Towards a methodology for developing evidence-informed management knowledge by means of systematic review. *British Journal of Management, 14*(3), 207–222. https://doi.org/10.1111/1467-8551.00375

Tukamuhabwa, B. R., Stevenson, M., Busby, J., & Zorzini, M. (2015). Supply chain resilience: Definition, review and theoretical foundations for further study. *International Journal of Production Research, 53*(18), 5592–5623. https://doi.org/10.1080/00207543.2015.1037934

van Eck, N. J., & Waltman, L. (2010). Software survey: VOSviewer, a computer program for bibliometric mapping. *Scientometrics, 84*(2), 523–538. https://doi.org/10.1007/s11192-009-0146-3

van Hoek, R. (2020). Research opportunities for a more resilient post-COVID-19 supply chain – Closing the gap between research findings and industry practice. *International Journal of Operations & Production Management, 40*(4), 341–355. https://doi.org/10.1108/IJOPM-03-2020-0165

Waltman, L., & van Eck, N. J. (2013). Source normalized indicators of citation impact: An overview of different approaches and an empirical comparison. *Scientometrics, 96*(3), 699–716. https://doi.org/10.1007/s11192-012-0913-4

Wang, Q., & Waltman, L. (2016). Large-scale analysis of the accuracy of the journal classification systems of Seb of Science and Scopus. *Journal of Informetrics, 10*(2), 347–364. https://doi.org/10.1016/j.joi.2016.02.003

Wieland, A., & Durach, C. F. (2021). Two perspectives on supply chain resilience. *Journal of Business Logistics, 42*(3), 315–322. https://doi.org/10.1111/jbl.12271

Wieland, A., & Wallenburg, C. M. (2013). The influence of relational competencies on supply chain resilience: A relational view. *International Journal of Physical Distribution & Logistics Management, 43*(4), 300–320. https://doi.org/10.1108/IJPDLM-08-2012-0243

Williams, R., Clark, L., Clark, W., & Raffo, D. (2020). Re-examining systematic literature review in management research: Additional benefits and execution protocols. *European Management Journal*, 39, 4. https://doi.org/10.1016/J.EMJ.2020.09.007

Xiao, Y., & Watson, M. (2017). Guidance on conducting a systematic literature review. *Journal of Planning Education and Research*, 39, 112–93. https://doi.org/10.1177/0739456X17723971

Zeng, L., Chen, H., Chen, M., & Zhao, X. (2024). Resilience assessment of the aircraft manufacturing core products supply chain: The international trade network perspective. *Annals of Operations Research*, 39. https://doi.org/10.1007/s10479-024-06359-w

Zupic, I., & Čater, T. (2015). Bibliometric methods in management and organization. *Organizational Research Methods*, *18*(3), 429–472. https://doi.org/10.1177/1094428114562629

4 Supply chain resilience in Central and Eastern Europe

Case studies and lessons learned

Introduction

As established in earlier chapters, SCRES does not follow a universal model but is shaped by institutional, sectoral, and geopolitical context (Seuring *et al.*, 2022). The systematic literature review presented in Chapter 3 demonstrates that empirical research on SCRES remains geographically concentrated, with a strong emphasis on North America, China, and Western Europe. This concentration limits understanding of how resilience forms in economies that are highly integrated into global production networks but lack the structural insulation, market power, or policy autonomy characteristic of core economies. To address this limitation, this chapter examines firm-level responses to geopolitical disruption in Poland.

Poland represents a boundary case for the study of SCRES under contemporary geopolitical constraint. As one of the largest economies in Central and Eastern Europe, it is deeply embedded in European and global value chains while occupying a structurally exposed position at the intersection of economic integration and geopolitical confrontation. Firms operating in Poland are subject to European Union regulatory frameworks and NATO-aligned security architectures and are geographically proximate to active conflict zones to the east. At the same time, they remain dependent on global sourcing networks extending to Asia and other regions. This combination places Poland neither at the core nor at the periphery of the global economy, but in an intermediate position where geopolitical shocks are transmitted rapidly and with limited buffering capacity.

Recent political conflicts and wars have intensified these conditions. Russia's invasion of Ukraine has transformed the security, energy, and logistics environment of Central and Eastern Europe, positioning the region simultaneously as a frontline and a logistical hub. CEE economies have become critical transit corridors for military aid, humanitarian supplies, and reconfigured trade flows, while absorbing spillover effects in the form of energy price volatility, labour-market disruptions, sanctions compliance costs, and heightened uncertainty in cross-border contracting.

DOI: 10.4324/9781003733089-4

In this sense, firms in the region are not passive recipients of geopolitical shocks but active nodes within restructured political, security, and production networks.

Until the early twenty-first century, geopolitical considerations played a relatively limited role in firm-level decision-making in Poland, where integration into European and global markets was primarily associated with efficiency gains, market expansion, and cost advantages (Banaszyk *et al.*, 2025; Mroczek-Dąbrowska & Kania, 2020; Rutkowski, 2015). Over the past decade, however, shifts in global political alignments, trade fragmentation, and regulatory divergence have fundamentally altered the economic environment in which firms operate. Earlier developments, including the U.S.–China trade conflict, had already contributed to trade fragmentation, regulatory divergence, and growing uncertainty in global sourcing networks, thereby reshaping firms' baseline exposure to geopolitical risk prior to the escalation of regional security shocks in Europe. As a result, geopolitical risk has become a material factor in decisions concerning input sourcing, energy dependence, logistics routing, and market participation. In 2024, experts contributing to the European Financial Congress identified escalating geopolitical conflict as the most significant external threat to the Polish economy, underscoring the exposure of domestic firms to politically induced supply disruptions (Mrowiec & Penczar, 2024).

These pressures are cumulative and interacting. Brexit introduced additional transaction costs and regulatory frictions in EU–UK trade, while Russia's invasion of Ukraine disrupted access to key raw materials and intermediates, generated sharp volatility in energy prices, and imposed sanctions-related constraints on trade with eastern markets. At the same time, conflict- and crisis-induced migration flows have altered labour availability, wage pressures, and skill compositions across host economies, introducing further adjustment challenges for firms operating within tightly coordinated and labour-dependent supply chain systems (Gaweł *et al.*, 2024, 2025). Heightened geopolitical tension has also increased the incidence and perceived risk of cyberattacks, affecting operational continuity and data security. Recent disruptions along major international transport corridors such as the Red Sea and the Suez Canal underscore how geopolitical tensions external to Europe can quickly translate into logistics bottlenecks, cost escalation, and delivery delays for firms embedded in global sourcing networks (Mrowiec & Penczar, 2024; Politico, 2024).

Corporate disclosures reflect this structural shift. Evidence reported by Ernst & Young indicates a marked increase in references to geopolitical risk in company filings from 2022 onward, with elevated levels persisting through 2023 (Ernst & Young, 2024). From an economic perspective, these developments alter relative prices, increase coordination costs, and reduce the predictability of cross-border exchange. Firms operating in Poland and the wider CEE region are therefore compelled to reassess established supply chain configurations, revise governance arrangements, and rebalance efficiency considerations against heightened security and regulatory constraints.

Against this background, the chapter examines how multinational enterprises operating in Poland interpret geopolitical risk and adjust their supply chain structures over time. By analysing firm-level adjustment processes in an economy characterised by deep value-chain integration and heightened geopolitical exposure, the chapter advances a process-oriented understanding of SCRES as an adaptive response to persistent external constraint. The findings provide empirically grounded insight into the sequencing of adjustment mechanisms and establish a contextual foundation for the causal analysis developed in the subsequent chapter.

Qualitative research design and data collection

Although geopolitical shocks are widely documented at the macroeconomic level, considerably less is known about how firms operating under heightened geopolitical exposure interpret such disturbances and translate them into concrete economic adjustment decisions. Aggregate indicators of geopolitical risk capture shifts in volatility and uncertainty but offer limited insight into the organisational mechanisms through which firms absorb shocks, reallocate resources, and adapt supply chain structures under changing institutional, regulatory, and cost conditions (Caldara & Iacoviello, 2018). Given the simultaneity of shocks affecting Central and Eastern Europe—including armed conflict, sanctions, transport disruptions, and cyber threats—an in-depth firm-level perspective is required to explain how SCRES emerges as an economic outcome in practice.

The contemporary geopolitical environment has introduced persistent and interacting forms of uncertainty for firms engaged in cross-border production and trade. Armed conflict, trade disputes, cyber-security risks, and regulatory divergence increasingly disrupt supply flows, alter relative prices, and constrain market access. The COVID-19 pandemic and the subsequent war in Ukraine intensified these pressures, exposing structural vulnerabilities in global value chains and underscoring the sensitivity of the CEE region to externally generated shocks (Kania, 2023). Firms operating in this environment have been compelled to reassess sourcing strategies, reconsider the geographic allocation of production, and revise coordination and governance arrangements in response to shifting cost–risk trade-offs.

The present study examines how firms interpret and respond to geopolitical disruptions affecting their supply chains. To address this objective, a qualitative research design was adopted, combining in-depth semi-structured interviews with senior managers and industry experts and analysis of internal corporate documentation. The empirical focus is on multinational and regional firms whose supply chain operations include Poland and the wider CEE region, while their sourcing, production, and governance arrangements extend across multiple geographic areas. This design enables close examination of firm-level decision processes and provides a robust basis for addressing the following research question:

RQ2: *How do firms operating in Central and Eastern Europe interpret geopolitical disruptions, what mitigation mechanisms do they activate in response, and what outcomes do these mechanisms generate for SCRES?*

Case studies are employed to identify and explain the adjustment mechanisms through which geopolitical disruption translates into changes in sourcing, production, and governance structures, rather than to achieve statistical generalisation.

A realist evaluation framework was applied to analyse how manufacturing firms operating from or through the CEE region navigate geopolitical risk and reconfigure their supply networks. Realist evaluation focuses on identifying Context–Mechanism–Outcome (CMO) configurations, enabling explanation of how specific contextual conditions activate underlying mechanisms that generate differentiated economic outcomes (Pawson & Tilley, 1997). This approach is particularly suitable where the objective is to explain why and under what conditions certain adjustment mechanisms are effective, rather than whether they are effective on average.

This mechanism-oriented perspective is well suited to the analysis of geopolitical disruption, where shocks such as sanctions, armed conflict, regulatory divergence, and trade realignment are structural and context-dependent. Under such conditions, similar firm-level actions may produce different outcomes across countries, sectors, and institutional environments. The realist perspective adopted here aligns with dynamic capabilities reasoning by emphasising how firms sense environmental change, seize adjustment opportunities, and reconfigure resources in response to external shocks (Teece *et al.*, 1997). It also complements systems-oriented perspectives that conceptualise supply chains as adaptive economic systems shaped by interdependencies and feedback effects (Choi *et al.*, 2001; Senge, 1990; Wieland *et al.*, 2023).

Data collection centred on semi-structured interviews with senior managers and supply chain specialists from seven multinational and regional manufacturing firms operating in sectors including automotive, medical technology, and metals processing. The firms were headquartered in advanced economies and maintained production or sourcing operations in Poland as well as in locations outside Europe. All firms experienced heightened geopolitical volatility between 2020 and 2023.

Interview data were triangulated with internal corporate documentation, industry reports, and relevant policy materials, enhancing analytical robustness. The coding and analysis focused on identifying contextual conditions, including geopolitical tensions, regulatory change, and regional conflict; mechanisms such as supplier diversification, localisation, digital readiness, and scenario-based planning; and outcomes reflected in operational continuity, resilience formation, and economic trade-offs.

Seven case studies were selected following established case study logic balancing analytical depth and theoretical generalisation (Eisenhardt, 1989). Interviews were conducted in Polish between July and September 2023 and typically lasted 50–60 minutes. Internal documentation covered the period 2020–2023. To ensure candour and reduce response bias, all participants were guaranteed anonymity and confidentiality. Ethical approval was granted by the Committee on the Ethics of Scientific Research Involving Humans at the Poznan University of Economics and Business (Resolution No. 11/2023). Table 4.1 summarises the characteristics of the firms included in the study.

During the interviews, participants were asked to identify anticipated supply chain risks in light of current geopolitical tensions, including the Russia–Ukraine armed conflict, the U.S.–China trade dispute, and increasing instability in East Asia. This enabled examination of how evolving geopolitical conditions are perceived and interpreted by firms operating from or through the CEE region, addressing the first analytical dimension of **RQ2**. Subsequent interview sections examined the mitigation strategies firms had implemented or were considering in response to these risks. For the purposes of this study, mitigation strategies are understood as organisational initiatives and capability-based adjustments through which firms seek to maintain or enhance SCRES under geopolitical uncertainty. Analysis of these strategies informs the remaining analytical dimensions of **RQ2** concerning mechanism activation and resilience outcomes.

Empirical findings: resilience mechanisms in practice

The empirical material collected from the seven participating firms reveals how organisations operating in Poland and the wider CEE region have navigated overlapping shocks linked to the pandemic, the armed conflict

Table 4.1 Case studies—overview

Case	*Industry*	*Country of headquarters*	*Company age*
A	Medical equipment	Germany	31 years
B	Metal processing	Poland	15 years
C	Automotive	Germany	23 years
D	Medical equipment	Germany	8 years
E	Medical equipment	Sweden	34 years
F	Automotive	Sweden	24 years
G	Metal processing	Poland	34 years

Source: Own elaboration.

in Ukraine, rising geopolitical tensions in Asia, and recurrent disruptions in global transport corridors. Although the companies differ in size, sector, and international reach, their experiences point to several common patterns: heightened sensitivity to supply chain fragility, accelerated digital readiness and automation, growing interest in dual-sourcing and regionalisation, and a marked increase in risk awareness related to China and Taiwan. The interviews also show how firms interpret, prioritise, and operationalise resilience measures in practice, offering insight into both the strategic and operational consequences of geopolitical turbulence. The following subsections present summary of findings for each company, highlighting sector-specific vulnerabilities and the capability-building responses that emerged in this volatile environment.

Company A

Company A has developed into a major producer in the medical device sector, offering a portfolio of more than 4,800 types of surgical instruments used in general surgery, orthopaedics, neurosurgery, cardiology, dentistry, and veterinary medicine. Its product range also includes infusion pumps, suture materials, container systems, and disinfection products. Beyond final assembly, the company operates a forging plant producing several million hot and semi-hot forgings annually and has developed cold precision forging technologies. An in-house tool shop supports both the production and regeneration of specialised tooling, reflecting a high degree of vertical integration and process control.

The COVID-19 pandemic triggered an abrupt surge in global demand for essential medical supplies, accompanied by the introduction of export restrictions in several countries; Belgium, for instance, temporarily limited glove exports. These developments exposed vulnerabilities within the firm's supply base and accelerated efforts to strengthen digital readiness. To improve visibility and coordination across geographically dispersed operations, the company expanded its reliance on cloud-based platforms and data-driven planning tools. These solutions were intended to support real-time monitoring, cross-site coordination, and faster decision-making under conditions of heightened uncertainty.

However, differences in national regulatory frameworks and compliance requirements constrained the pace at which these digital solutions could be implemented uniformly across subsidiaries. In particular, divergent approaches to data protection, cybersecurity obligations, and system validation between countries—most notably Poland and Germany—necessitated separate approval procedures and the localisation of digital workflows. Interviewees noted that emerging cybersecurity and data-governance expectations, anticipated to become more stringent under forthcoming EU-level regulation, further increased uncertainty around standardisation and reinforced a cautious, incremental approach to digital deployment across sites.

Logistics disruptions added an additional layer of complexity. Security incidents in the Red Sea and the effective disruption of the Suez Canal route forced shipping companies to reroute vessels via longer maritime corridors, substantially extending delivery times for components sourced from Asia. These delays reduced planning reliability and amplified the cost and time penalties associated with long-distance sourcing, reinforcing managerial concerns about exposure to geographically distant shocks.

Supply disruptions also prompted structural adjustments to the company's geographic footprint. Parts of production previously located in Asia were relocated to Europe in order to reduce lead times and enhance supply flexibility. Recurrent shortages—most notably of semiconductor components—subsequently intensified managerial attention to geopolitical risk, particularly in relation to Taiwan. In response, the firm began evaluating second-sourcing arrangements for critical inputs and considering the regionalisation of selected processes where feasible, including the potential internalisation of activities previously sourced externally.

As the interviewee explained, these developments reflect a broader shift in organisational logic driven by expectations of persistent geopolitical instability:

> *Geopolitical uncertainties and resulting supply chain instability will heavily influence our strategic decisions in the coming years. We are already actively exploring second sourcing options for semiconductor chips manufactured in Taiwan, ideally closer to our region. There is even the possibility that we could become that second source ourselves, by relocating or adapting certain processes locally. These conversations began during the pandemic, which exposed the fragility of global supply chains. While the most urgent disruptions have been contained, the ripple effects persist—particularly around ongoing supply shortages.*

Company B

Company B specialises in the design, production, and installation of steel structures and mechanical systems, primarily for the automotive and construction industries. Established in 2010, the firm has expanded its operations to reach a production capacity of approximately 500 tons of steel structures per month. Its activities cover the full project lifecycle, including conceptual design and engineering, manufacturing, transportation, installation, and post-installation technical support. The company's product portfolio comprises steel structures, insulated panels, high-temperature furnaces, and a range of mechanical components such as conveyors, lift stations, roller beds, hangers, and tanks.

During the COVID-19 pandemic, the company faced significant challenges related to employee transportation, which disrupted day-to-day operations. In response, it introduced remote communication tools to sustain coordination and operational continuity. Both the pandemic and the subsequent armed conflict in Ukraine had a pronounced impact on the firm's cost structure, particularly through sharp increases in steel prices and disruptions in the availability of key production materials. Seeking to mitigate efficiency pressures, the company piloted the use of a welding robot, which resulted in measurable productivity improvements. At the same time, access to public grants and digitalisation support remains uneven, with funding schemes disproportionately favouring larger enterprises, creating additional constraints for mid-sized firms such as Company B.

The firm operates internationally, with active projects in the United States, Turkey, and South Africa, and previous operations in Russia and Belgium. Cooperation with Chinese partners continues, but is increasingly perceived as high risk due to geopolitical tensions and the possibility of regional conflict. As the interviewed manager noted:

> *Another pressing concern is the increasing presence of Chinese partners in global outsourcing. Many of them fail to meet contractual obligations, yet they seem to have virtually unlimited financial resources. While payment isn't usually an issue, doing business with them raises a serious question: should we take the risk of signing contracts with them, especially considering the threat of war in Taiwan? Traditional insurance—whether through Coface, Allianz, or others—cannot cover war-related risks. If conflict breaks out, insurance becomes meaningless.*

Company C

Company C specialises in advanced mobility solutions for passenger cars, commercial vehicles, and industrial applications. Its activities include the production of components for driveline, chassis, and safety systems, as well as the development of technologies related to automated driving and electromobility.

During the COVID-19 pandemic, the company was required to adapt to rapidly fluctuating order volumes and the introduction of hybrid work arrangements. Factory shutdowns in China led to global delays in semiconductor deliveries, intensifying supply chain pressures across multiple production sites. In response, the firm accelerated automation efforts through the deployment of collaborative robots within its manufacturing processes. At the same time, digitalisation initiatives were subject to strict investment criteria, with implementation contingent on clearly defined returns on investment, often assessed through short payback periods. This requirement constrained the scope and pace of broader digital transformation.

Throughout the pandemic, order volumes from key markets, including Europe and China, exhibited pronounced volatility. These experiences heightened managerial awareness of concentration risk in critical inputs, particularly semiconductors. To mitigate future exposure, the company has begun pursuing dual-sourcing strategies aimed at reducing reliance on suppliers located in China and Taiwan.

As the interviewee explained:

> *First and foremost, we are focusing on dual sourcing. This means that whenever we work with suppliers from Asia, we also establish or renew partnerships with suppliers from other regions to ensure supply chain diversification. Additionally, a semiconductor production facility is being developed in Europe, and our company has entered into a cooperation agreement with this initiative. As a result, within the next few years, we expect to achieve partial independence from suppliers in China and Taiwan.*

Company D

Company D is a global leader in medical technology, specialising in diagnostic imaging, laboratory diagnostics, and advanced therapeutic solutions. Its portfolio includes MRI scanners, CT scanners, X-ray systems, and ultrasound devices, alongside laboratory diagnostic equipment and digital healthcare services. The company positions digitalisation as a central element of its strategy, aiming to support healthcare providers in advancing precision medicine, transforming care delivery, and improving patient experiences.

During the COVID-19 pandemic, demand for diagnostic imaging equipment—particularly computed tomography and X-ray systems—increased sharply. This surge coincided with the outbreak of the armed conflict in Ukraine, which further compounded supply-side pressures. Production capacity was constrained by disruptions in the availability of key inputs, most notably helium and electronic components, while rising prices for these materials intensified cost pressures and limited device availability. The pandemic and the war exposed the firm to upstream vulnerabilities extending well beyond its immediate operational control.

As the interviewee explained:

> *Take, for example, MRI scanners, which require helium for cooling. Helium is a rare and highly sought-after resource, not only for medical imaging but across various industries. Its price has surged significantly, both during the pandemic and following the outbreak of armed conflict in Ukraine. The same applies to electronics, where component shortages and supply chain disruptions continue to impact product availability. These upstream issues sometimes lead to limitations in delivering our own products.*

At the same time, the crisis accelerated the development and adoption of artificial intelligence in radiology, improving the efficiency of doctors and technicians and supporting workflow optimisation. However, the absence of clear legal and reimbursement frameworks for AI-based medical solutions continues to constrain the large-scale implementation of these technologies. Operating primarily in Poland, the company is particularly exposed to global supply chain disruptions and regulatory developments that shape both technology adoption and market access.

Company E

Company E specialises in the production and supply of medical equipment and solutions supporting the care of individuals with limited mobility. Its product portfolio includes medical beds, lifting systems, hygiene and disinfection devices, therapeutic mattresses, and systems designed to prevent pressure sores and thrombosis. In addition to supplying equipment, the company cooperates closely with healthcare facilities by providing training and technical support for medical personnel.

During the COVID-19 pandemic, the company experienced a sharp increase in demand for its products. At the same time, supplier shutdowns—particularly in China—disrupted the availability of raw materials, while port blockades in Chinese logistics hubs led to rising transportation costs and prolonged lead times. In response, the firm strengthened its internal processes by improving acceptance and quality-control procedures and expanding in-house capabilities through the recruitment of specialists in software development. The company's primary export markets include the United States, the United Kingdom, France, Canada, and Germany. In parallel, the firm faced workforce-related challenges linked to the employment of workers from Ukraine following the outbreak of the armed conflict, requiring it to navigate disruptions related to labour availability, mobility constraints, and the broader humanitarian implications of the war.

Reflecting on these developments, the interviewee emphasised a perceived structural shift in global sourcing strategies:

> *We are observing a clear shift in the global supply chain landscape—from globalisation to regionalisation. While in the past there was a strong emphasis on outsourcing production and sourcing globally, today there is a growing tendency to relocate activities to 'safe' regions, including within Europe. Although we haven't taken direct actions yet, we are exploring various Asian markets. China is becoming less attractive, not only due to geopolitical tensions but also because of rising costs. Countries like India, Vietnam, and others in the region are becoming more appealing alternatives, especially as our components are complex and require reliable sourcing.*

Company F

Company F operates a bus manufacturing plant in Poland and is responsible for the sales of buses, trucks, and construction equipment across multiple European markets. In addition to manufacturing and sales, the firm manages global service centres that provide shared services in information technology, finance, and human resources. This organisational configuration reflects a high degree of functional integration across borders and a strong dependence on coordinated supply, production, and service planning.

The company has experienced the effects of geopolitical developments primarily through indirect yet persistent supply-side pressures. Rising geopolitical tensions—most notably the armed conflict in Ukraine and the deterioration of EU–China relations—disrupted the availability of critical inputs, including electronic components and batteries used in electric buses. These disruptions were accompanied by escalating input prices, higher logistics costs, and extended lead times, collectively increasing production uncertainty and compressing margins. Although none of these shocks led to a complete halt in production, their cumulative impact altered the firm's cost structure and reduced predictability in procurement and delivery schedules.

In response, the company intensified efforts to simplify product architectures, standardise components, and reduce production complexity in order to strengthen cost control and operational flexibility. These operational adjustments coincided with a broader strategic reassessment of the firm's European manufacturing footprint. The decision to close the production facility in Wrocław and relocate manufacturing activities to Spain was formally justified on the grounds of efficiency and cost optimisation. However, industry commentary and internal assessments suggest that geopolitical considerations—particularly proximity to the armed conflict in Ukraine, exposure to regional instability, and heightened perceptions of investment risk in Central and Eastern Europe—also played a role in shaping evaluations of long-term location viability.

Company G

Company G was founded in 1991 as a manufacturer of license plates for the Polish market. Over time, the firm has evolved into a technologically advanced and largely self-sufficient enterprise that not only produces license plates but also designs and supplies the equipment used in their manufacture. Since 2001, machines for license plate production have been developed and manufactured in-house, enabling the company to offer a comprehensive solution ranging from machine design and construction, through customisation, to the delivery of finished license plates.

In recent years, geopolitical tensions—particularly those involving China—have disrupted access to selected components and materials critical to the company's production processes. In response, the firm has begun transitioning towards more reliable and geographically proximate suppliers in order to strengthen SCRES and reduce dependence on high-risk regions. Supplier evaluation practices have become more stringent, with greater emphasis placed not only on current cost and availability but also on long-term reliability and the strategic implications of supplier relationships. These considerations have emerged as a significant concern for the company's leadership.

As the interviewee noted:

> *The world is increasingly divided into distinct geopolitical blocs—with China and India on one side, and the Western world, including the United States, Europe, Japan, and South Korea, on the other. This growing divide creates tangible challenges, especially in sourcing components from China.*

A particularly acute challenge concerns the decision of a major American corporation to cease production of reflective license plate film, which had previously accounted for nearly half of global supply. In the short term, the company has relied on Chinese reflective film to sustain production, but actively seeks alternative solutions given the strategic importance of this input. To mitigate future dependency, Company G has initiated cooperation with a major domestic industry player, encouraging the accelerated development of effective locally produced reflective films.

Similar adjustments are evident in the sourcing of electronic and electrical components. Despite higher prices and ongoing supply constraints, the firm increasingly prioritises dependable suppliers based in Europe, such as Siemens in Germany. This shift reflects a broader strategic orientation towards reducing exposure to unstable supply chains and prioritising quality, reliability, and long-term continuity over short-term cost considerations.

Interpretation of findings across cases

The case data structured through the CMO framework contributes directly to answering **RQ2** by empirically illustrating how firms operating in Central and Eastern Europe interpret, respond to, and adapt to geopolitical disruptions. The analysis reveals how contextual shocks shape firms' perceptions of exposure, how mitigation mechanisms are activated within their supply chain systems, and how these mechanisms give rise to distinct resilience outcomes (c.f. Table 4.2).

Table 4.2 CMO framework—SCRES in CEE under geopolitical risks

Case	*Context*	*Mechanism*	*Outcome*
A	Pandemic-driven surge in global demand for medical supplies combined with export restrictions and logistics disruptions	Expansion of digital readiness through cloud-based platforms and data-driven planning; localisation of digital workflows due to regulatory divergence; production relocation from Asia to Europe; evaluation of second sourcing for semiconductors	Improved visibility and coordination under uncertainty; slower digital standardisation across subsidiaries; reduced lead times and exposure to distant shocks; increased strategic awareness of Taiwan-related geopolitical risk
B	Pandemic-related labour mobility constraints and war-induced input price volatility	Introduction of remote coordination tools; piloting of automation (welding robot); cautious continuation of cooperation with Chinese partners despite rising geopolitical risk	Maintenance of operational continuity despite workforce disruptions; productivity gains from automation; persistent exposure to uninsured geopolitical risks and constrained access to public digitalisation support
C	Semiconductor shortages caused by factory shutdowns in China and volatile global demand	Deployment of collaborative robots; strict ROI-based screening of digital investments; adoption of dual-sourcing strategies and participation in European semiconductor initiatives	Enhanced short-term operational flexibility; slower pace of digital transformation; gradual reduction of dependency on China and Taiwan for critical inputs
D	Simultaneous pandemic shock and armed conflict in Ukraine affecting energy and component markets	Acceleration of AI adoption in radiology workflows; operational coping with helium and electronics shortages; reliance on regulatory compliance within national healthcare systems	Improved clinical efficiency and workflow optimisation; constrained scaling of AI solutions due to reimbursement and legal uncertainty; continued vulnerability to upstream geopolitical shocks

(*Continued*)

Table 4.2 (Continued)

Case	*Context*	*Mechanism*	*Outcome*
E	Pandemic-related demand surge combined with supplier shutdowns, port blockades, and war-related labour disruptions	Strengthening of internal quality-control and acceptance processes; recruitment of in-house software specialists; exploration of alternative Asian sourcing locations beyond China	Increased internal process robustness; partial mitigation of logistics delays; growing strategic orientation towards regionalisation and "safe-region" sourcing
F	War in Ukraine and deterioration of EU–China relations affecting critical components and batteries	Simplification of product architectures; standardisation of components; strategic reassessment of manufacturing footprint including relocation from Poland to Spain	Improved cost control and operational flexibility; altered European production geography; implicit reduction of exposure to regional geopolitical instability in CEE
G	Geopolitical bloc formation and withdrawal of key global suppliers	Transition towards local and European suppliers; intensified supplier screening; cooperation with domestic partners to develop critical inputs; substitution of electronics suppliers with reliable Western firms	Reduced dependency on high-risk regions; short-term reliance on Chinese inputs combined with long-term local capability building; prioritisation of reliability over cost efficiency

Source: Own elaboration.

The cases demonstrate that firms operating in the CEE region are exposed to multiple, overlapping sources of geopolitical risk that differ in origin, scope, and temporal persistence. Pandemic-related shocks with geopolitical spillovers shape exposure through export restrictions, material shortages, and transport disruptions (Cases A, B, and E). Tensions involving China and Taiwan primarily affect access to semiconductors and critical components, increasing dependency risks in technology-intensive supply chains (Cases A, B, and C). Region-specific shocks, most notably the war in Ukraine, generate workforce instability (Case E), heightened perceptions of investment risk (Case F), and uncertainty regarding the long-term viability of CEE-based operations. In parallel, sector-specific regulatory regimes—particularly in medical technology and digital systems (Cases A and D)—add an institutional layer of constraint that interacts with these external shocks. Rather than acting independently, these pressures accumulate and intersect, reshaping firms' operating conditions across sourcing, production, and coordination activities.

In response, firms deploy a set of adaptation mechanisms that vary in depth and temporal orientation. Structural responses dominate where exposure is persistent or strategically salient. These include partial reshoring (Case A), incremental regionalisation (Case E), relocation of production capacity (Case F), and diversification of supplier geographies (Cases C and G). Such measures reflect deliberate efforts to reduce dependence on vulnerable nodes rather than short-term disruption management. Supplier diversification plays a central role in this process, taking the form of second sourcing (Case A), dual sourcing (Case C), or forward-looking reassessment of supplier reliability based on geopolitical alignment (Case G).

Technological and organisational adjustments operate alongside these structural measures. Automation and collaborative robotics (Cases B and C), digital coordination platforms and analytics (Case A), and AI-supported diagnostic systems (Case D) are used to stabilise operations and maintain continuity under volatile conditions. These interventions primarily target internal processes—decision cycles, coordination routines, and capacity utilisation—rather than network structure itself. Organisational changes reinforce these efforts through revised contracting practices (Case B), internal capability development in software and quality-control functions (Case E), and formalisation of supplier selection criteria incorporating geopolitical risk considerations (Case G).

The resulting resilience outcomes are heterogeneous. Some firms achieve greater robustness by reducing exposure to high-risk regions and inputs (Cases A, C, and G). Others rely more heavily on operational and technological stabilisation mechanisms, such as automation, remote coordination, or AI deployment, to sustain performance under uncertainty (Cases B and D). Gradual capability accumulation combined with selective regional sourcing supports longer-term adjustment trajectories (Case E), while relocation decisions (Case F) lower exposure to regional shocks but alter firms' embeddedness within the CEE industrial landscape. Across cases, constraints remain visible: regulatory requirements slow digital deployment, return-on-investment thresholds limit automation scale, and footprint reconfiguration introduces new organisational and spatial trade-offs.

Differences across cases reflect sectoral and organisational conditions rather than uniform exposure. Firms facing critical-input dependencies or logistical chokepoints pursue regionalisation more actively (Cases A, E, and F), whereas globally integrated firms with scale advantages (Cases C and D) retain international footprints and mitigate risk through sourcing diversification or technological upgrading. Automation is prioritised in labour-intensive and demand-volatile industries (Cases B and C), while firms in highly regulated medical sectors (Cases A and D) focus on digital coordination, traceability, and efficiency gains within constrained compliance frameworks. These contrasts indicate that resilience pathways are shaped as much by sectoral and institutional context as by the nature of geopolitical disruption itself.

Industrial policy constitutes an additional layer influencing these trajectories. European initiatives targeting semiconductors, electric mobility, and advanced manufacturing expand the adjustment space for firms in strategically prioritised sectors (Cases C and F), facilitating dual sourcing and partial regionalisation. By contrast, mid-sized firms in metal processing and specialised medical equipment (Cases B and E) report limited access to digital readiness funding and automation support, reinforcing asymmetries in capability development. Regulatory regimes further mediate these effects: stringent compliance requirements in medical technology (Case D) constrain the pace of digital and AI adoption, while more permissive frameworks in automotive and metal-processing sectors enable faster experimentation. Industrial policy thus actively shapes which resilience strategies are feasible, rather than merely conditioning their effectiveness.

The cross-case evidence follows a consistent CMO pattern. Geopolitical disruptions alter firms' external operating conditions (context), prompting structural, technological, and organisational adjustments (mechanisms) that reshape supply continuity, operational stability, and network configuration (outcomes). This configuration explains why firms facing comparable geopolitical pressures nonetheless exhibit differentiated resilience trajectories, reflecting variation in sectoral constraints, institutional positioning, and access to policy support within the CEE region.

Linking empirical mechanisms to resilience theory

The empirical evidence from firms operating in Central and Eastern Europe supports an economic interpretation of SCRES that directly addresses the limitations identified in the systematic literature review presented in Chapter 3. While prior research has frequently examined operational, structural, relational, or digital aspects of resilience in isolation, the case evidence demonstrates that these dimensions interact as components of a broader adjustment process shaped by persistent geopolitical constraint rather than episodic disruption.

From an institutional perspective, geopolitical disruption represents a transformation of the formal and informal rules governing cross-border exchange. In line with North (1990), shifts in sanctions regimes, export controls, regulatory requirements, and enforcement practices alter firms' incentives, expectations, and feasible courses of action. These changes redefine the institutional environment in which supply chains are organised, converting geopolitical risk into a structural condition that conditions coordination, governance, and investment decisions over time.

Within this altered institutional context, firm-level adjustment can be explained through transaction cost reasoning. Building on Coase's (1937) analysis of the firm as a response to market coordination costs and Williamson's (1989) governance framework, the empirical findings show how heightened uncertainty, increased asset specificity, and stronger safeguarding requirements prompt firms to reassess existing sourcing and coordination arrangements. Rather than converging towards a single organisational form, firms selectively reconfigure market, hybrid, and hierarchical relationships in response to changing transaction costs and increased exposure to opportunistic behaviour arising from contractual incompleteness and weakened enforcement under geopolitical disruption.

Decisions to reshore selected activities, diversify suppliers, regionalise production, or invest in digital coordination mechanisms thus emerge as economically rational responses to rising adjustment and coordination costs. These responses reflect attempts to manage contract incompleteness, enforcement risk, and coordination failure while preserving the efficiency benefits associated with participation in international production networks. Geopolitical disruption therefore does not simply interrupt supply chains; it reshapes the institutional and governance logic underpinning supply chain design.

This mechanism is most clearly illuminated through a global value chain perspective. Across the cases, firms do not withdraw from international production networks in response to geopolitical disruption; instead, they adapt by repositioning within them. Partial reshoring, supplier diversification, dual sourcing, and selective internalisation of critical activities reflect adjustments in governance structures and inter-firm coordination rather than disengagement from global production. Institutional change alters the conditions of participation (context), firms modify sourcing relationships and coordination mechanisms to manage dependency and risk (mechanism), and resilience outcomes vary according to firms' capacity to recalibrate their position within value chains (outcome). This pattern aligns with Gereffi's account of global value chain governance, in which firms respond to shifting institutional and power configurations by adjusting coordination and upgrading trajectories rather than abandoning global production altogether (Gereffi *et al.*, 2005).

Viewed from a realist perspective, this adaptive sequence can be formalised as a CMO configuration. Geopolitical disruption alters the institutional context within which exchange takes place; governance, coordination, and sourcing adjustments constitute the operative mechanisms; and differentiated resilience trajectories across firms, sectors, and regions emerge as observable outcomes. This framing clarifies why adjustment strategies that appear similar at a surface level generate heterogeneous effects depending on institutional setting, sectoral constraints, and position within global production networks—an issue that remains insufficiently theorised in much of the existing resilience literature.

These empirical regularities can be coherently integrated using the preliminary integrated framework of SCRES introduced earlier in the monograph.

Readiness is reflected in enhanced sensing of geopolitical and institutional change, including monitoring exposure to high-risk regions and investing in digital visibility. Responsiveness captures short-term operational adjustments aimed at stabilising activities under acute disruption. Resurgence denotes longer-term governance and structural reconfiguration undertaken to restore viability under altered cost, risk, and regulatory conditions. Collaboration reflects reliance on hybrid and relational arrangements to manage interdependence, uncertainty, and coordination within constrained networks.

Overall, the findings indicate that SCRES under sustained geopolitical uncertainty emerges as a cumulative and path-dependent process of economic adjustment. Firms revise sourcing decisions, governance structures, and coordination mechanisms incrementally in response to institutional change, rather than converging towards a universally optimal configuration. By integrating fragmented insights from the systematic literature review into a mechanism-based explanation grounded in institutional theory, transaction cost economics, and global value chain analysis, this chapter advances a coherent theoretical interpretation of resilience formation in geopolitically exposed supply chains.

Key insights and implications

This chapter examined how recent crises—including the COVID-19 pandemic, the armed conflict in Ukraine, and rising geopolitical tensions in Asia—have reshaped the economic and institutional conditions under which firms operating in Central and Eastern Europe organise their supply chains. Given its geographic proximity to active conflict zones and its deep integration into trade with the European Union, China, and the United States, the region constitutes a high-exposure environment in which geopolitical developments directly affect firms' risk profiles, cost structures, and feasible adjustment options.

The empirical evidence shows that firms respond through differentiated and selective adjustment rather than a single dominant strategy. Supplier diversification has emerged as a central response, with firms reducing reliance on single-source suppliers—particularly in Asia—through dual sourcing and broader regional portfolios. Digital investments, including cloud-based coordination tools, data analytics, robotics, and artificial intelligence, support visibility and responsiveness across dispersed operations and frequently accompany localisation or regionalisation decisions such as selective nearshoring or reshoring.

Geopolitical risk is increasingly incorporated into procurement, contracting, and investment decisions. In some sectors, firm-level adjustment intersects with public policy and industrial strategies, although access to state support remains uneven. As a result, digital upgrading, supply network restructuring, and capability development proceed at different speeds across firms, reflecting variation in sectoral exposure, regulatory environments, and policy eligibility.

The economic effects of these adjustments are mixed. Firms report improved flexibility and reduced dependence on high-risk regions, but these gains are offset by higher coordination costs, increased organisational complexity, and exposure to multiple regulatory regimes. While such changes contribute to resilience, they have not resulted in widespread reshoring or a fundamental redesign of global production systems. Financial constraints, technological dependencies, and sunk investments continue to limit the scope of reconfiguration.

Evidence from the automotive, medical technology, and metals processing sectors indicates that most firms remain embedded in globally dispersed production networks. Where reconfiguration occurs, it is typically incremental, sector-specific, and often shaped by state-led initiatives in strategically sensitive areas such as semiconductors, energy systems, and electric mobility. These patterns reveal an enduring tension between reducing vulnerability and maintaining cost competitiveness.

Overall, the findings suggest that global supply chains are not fragmenting into closed regional blocs but are undergoing gradual, politically mediated adjustment. Resilience is increasingly achieved through targeted mechanisms—supplier diversification, selective localisation, and capability upgrading—sometimes reinforced by industrial policy. This trajectory points to hybrid supply chain configurations that combine global reach with regionally anchored capacities rather than a retreat from globalisation.

The main contribution of this chapter is to demonstrate, using firm-level evidence from a high-exposure region, that geopolitical disruption leads to incremental and selective reconfiguration within global value chains rather than deglobalisation or isolated resilience practices. In doing so, the chapter addresses **RQ2** by showing how firms in the CEE region interpret geopolitical disruption, activate portfolios of structural, technological, and organisational mechanisms, and generate differentiated resilience outcomes shaped by sectoral and institutional conditions. The following chapter turns to **RQ3** and examines how these mechanisms interact systemically through causal modelling.

References

Banaszyk, P., Budner, W., & Lewandowska-Ciszek, A. (2025). *Ewolucja przestrzennej konfiguracji międzynarodowych łańcuchów dostaw. U podstaw geologistyki.* Wydawnictwo Uniwersytetu Ekonomicznego w Poznaniu. https://doi.org/10.18559/978-83-8211-280-1

Caldara, D., & Iacoviello, M. (2018). Measuring geopolitical risk. *Political Economy: Government Expenditures & Related Policies eJournal.* https://doi.org/10.17016/IFDP.2018.1222.

Choi, T. Y., Dooley, K. J., & Rungtusanatham, M. (2001). Supply networks and complex adaptive systems: Control versus emergence. *Journal of Operations Management*, *19*(3), 351–366. https://doi.org/10.1016/S0272-6963(00)00068-1

Coase, R. H. (1937). *The nature of the firm. Economica*, *4*(16), 386–405.

Eisenhardt, K. M. (1989), Building theories from case study research. *The Academy of Management Review*, *14*(4), https://doi.org/10.2307/258557.

Ernst & Young. (2024). Geopolitical risk in corporate reporting: Global trends and implications. EY Global. https://www.ey.com

Gaweł, A., Mroczek-Dabrowska, K., Kania, A., & Bednar, R. (2025). *Drivers of entrepreneurial activities among new-coming Ukrainian female forced migrants in Poland. Population, Space and Place*, *31*, 5. https://doi.org/10.1002/psp.70059

Gaweł, A., Mroczek-Dabrowska, K., Marcinkowski, B., & Kania, A. (2024). The local solidarity network in the reception of female Ukrainian Refugees' Influx of 2022. *Journal of Immigrant & Refugee Studies*, 1–15. https://doi.org/10.1080/15562948.2024.2403074

Gereffi, G., Humphrey, J., & Sturgeon, T. (2005). The governance of global value chains. *Review of International Political Economy*, *12*(1), 78–104. https://doi.org/10.1080/09692290500049805

Kania, A. (2023). *Companies' exposure to the COVID-19 pandemic*. In Mroczek-Dąbrowska, K., Kania, A., & Matysek-Jędrych, A. (Eds.). *Economic policy, COVID-19 and corporations. Perspectives from Central and Eastern Europe*. Routledge. https://doi.org/10.4324/9781003345428-8

Mroczek-Dąbrowska, K., & Kania, A. (2020). *Poland's competitive position between 2005 and 2017 – A road to success*. In Visvizi, A., Matysek-Jędrych, A., & Mroczek-Dąbrowska, K. (Eds.). *Poland in the single market: Politics, economics, the euro*. Routledge. https://doi.org/10.4324/9780429285301-4

Mrowiec, M., & Penczar, M. (2024). The most important threats to economic policy, financial system stability and PLN credibility – Results of the 12th edition of the forecast consensus of the European financial congress. *Bezpieczny Bank*, (4), 7–28. https://repozytorium.bg.ug.edu.pl/info/article/UOG40a20fcd978d4e48ac59d9a4b65ef363/.

North, D. C. (1990). *Institutions, Institutional change and economic performance*. Cambridge University Press.

Pawson, R., & Tilley, N. (1997). *Realistic evaluation*. Sage Publications.

Politico. (2024). *Houthi rebels and the EU make your coffee more expensive*. Politico. https://www.politico.eu/article/coffee-trade-espresso-europe-covid-global-supply/

Rutkowski, K. (2015). Rekonfiguracja międzynarodowych łańcuchów dostaw jako narzędzie zapobiegania zagrożeniom kryzysowym – szansa dla Polski. In Rutkowski, K. (Ed.). *Strategie i logistyka w warunkach kryzysu*, 92–104. Wydawnictwo Uniwersytetu Ekonomicznego we Wrocławiu.

Senge, P. M. (1990). *The fifth discipline: The art and practice of the learning organization*. Doubleday/Currency.

Seuring, S., Brandenburg, M., Sauer, P. C., Schünemann, D. S., Warasthe, R., Aman, S., Qian, C., Petljak, K., Neutzling, D. M., Land, A., & Khalid, R. U. (2022). Comparing regions globally: Impacts of COVID-19 on supply chains – A Delphi study. *International Journal of Operations & Production Management*, *42*(8), 1077–1108. https://doi.org/10.1108/IJOPM-10-2021-0675

Teece, D. J., Pisano, G., & Shuen, A. (1997). Dynamic capabilities and strategic management. *Strategic Management Journal*, *18*(7), 509–533. https://doi.org/10.1002/(SICI)1097-0266(199708)18:7<509::AID-SMJ882>3.0.CO;2-Z

Wieland, A., Stevenson, M., Melnyk, S. A., Davoudi, S., & Schultz, L. (2023). Thinking differently about supply chain resilience: What we can learn from social-ecological systems thinking. *International Journal of Operations & Production Management*, *43*(1), 1–21. https://doi.org/10.1108/IJOPM-10-2022-0645

Williamson, O. E. (1989). *Transaction cost Economics, handbook of industrial organization*. Elsevier, Cham, 135–182.

5 Causal analysis of resilience strategies amid geopolitical disruptions

Introduction

The Decision-Making Trial and Evaluation Laboratory method is a structured analytical approach designed to examine complex systems by identifying the direction and strength of causal relationships among interdependent factors. Its principal advantage lies in its capacity to move beyond correlation-based analysis and to reveal how specific mechanisms operate as causal drivers or dependent outcomes within systems characterised by feedback effects and non-linear interactions. This makes DEMATEL particularly suitable for analysing SCRES, where firm-level adjustment mechanisms interact cumulatively under conditions of uncertainty and institutional constraint.

This chapter employs DEMATEL to address **RQ3**, which examines the structure and relative strength of causal relationships among mitigation mechanisms that enhance SCRES under conditions of geopolitical disruption. Empirical attention is directed to firms operating in Central and Eastern Europe, where heightened geopolitical exposure, intermediate positioning within global value chains, and reliance on extra-regional inputs increase the analytical importance of causal sequencing and interdependence among resilience mechanisms.

Rather than evaluating individual strategies in isolation, the analysis models how adjustment mechanisms influence one another, identifying which mechanisms function as primary causal drivers and which emerge as dependent or downstream effects within the resilience system. By shifting analytical attention from discrete actions to causal architecture, the chapter advances a systems-oriented understanding of resilience formation.

Building on the conceptual foundations established for **RQ1** and the firm-level evidence developed for **RQ2**, this chapter addresses **RQ3** by identifying the causal structure and relative influence of interdependent resilience mechanisms, integrating prior conceptual and qualitative insights into a system-level explanation of how SCRES emerges under geopolitical constraint.

DOI: 10.4324/9781003733089-5

In contrast to prescriptive resilience frameworks, the chapter does not assess whether particular strategies should be adopted. Instead, it offers an explanatory account of how mitigation mechanisms are causally linked and how influence propagates across the resilience architecture under given institutional and cost conditions. The methodological procedures underpinning the DEMATEL analysis are presented in the sections that follow.

DEMATEL applications in supply chain resilience research

Originally developed at the Battelle Memorial Institute in Geneva, DEMATEL offers a structured approach for analysing and visualising causal relationships among criteria within complex decision environments (Fontela & Gabus, 1976). Unlike traditional multi-criteria decision-making techniques, which typically assume independence among criteria, DEMATEL explicitly incorporates interdependence, reciprocal influence, and feedback loops among variables (Alam *et al.*, 2021; Kouhizadeh *et al.*, 2021; Si *et al.*, 2018). This feature makes it particularly well suited to resilience research, where systemic effects and cascading disruptions are prevalent (Scheibe & Blackhurst, 2018).

In contrast to econometric approaches, which infer causality from statistical variation across observations, DEMATEL captures causal structure in the sense of directional influence among mechanisms, as assessed through expert judgement within a system. Econometric methods are effective for estimating average effects under assumptions of exogeneity and separability, but they are less suited to settings in which causal relationships are simultaneous, recursive, and shaped by institutional and organisational interaction. DEMATEL does not estimate behavioural parameters; instead, it distinguishes between driving and dependent mechanisms, revealing how influence propagates through a complex adjustment system.

Reflecting these properties, DEMATEL has been increasingly applied in recent supply chain research, particularly in response to the growing complexity and vulnerability of global production networks. Existing studies use the method to analyse interdependencies among challenges and enablers, identify critical drivers and barriers, and structure complex decision problems under conditions of uncertainty (cf. Table 5.1).

As outlined in Table 5.1, DEMATEL and its extensions have become widely used tools for modelling complex interdependencies among supply chain factors. Prior to the COVID-19 pandemic, applications focused primarily on sustainability and digital transformation, with studies such as Luthra *et al.* (2020) using Grey-DEMATEL to assess Industry 4.0 drivers and highlighting the central role of government support and inter-firm collaboration.

Table 5.1 Applications of DEMATEL technique reported in the recent supply chain literature

Study	*Application area*	*DEMATEL contribution*
Luthra *et al.* (2020)	Industry 4.0 and sustainability in emerging-economy supply chains	Identified causal drivers of I4.0 adoption, highlighting policy and transparency as key enablers.
Paul *et al.* (2021)	Post-COVID recovery of the Bangladeshi RMG supply chain	Mapped causal recovery challenges to prioritise intervention areas.
Alam *et al.* (2021)	COVID-19 vaccine supply chains	Classified pandemic-related challenges to support prioritisation aligned with sustainable development goals (SDGs).
Kouhizadeh *et al.* (2021)	Blockchain adoption barriers in sustainable supply chains	Distinguished technological and standardisation barriers as primary causal constraints.
Agi and Jha (2022)	Blockchain adoption in French supply chains	Revealed transaction costs, traceability, and regulation as dominant drivers.
Raj *et al.* (2022)	COVID-related supply chain challenges in Indian manufacturing	Distinguished core causal challenges shaping resilience responses.
Zaman *et al.* (2023)	Digital banking and e-commerce supply chain resilience	Identified key adoption drivers through combined DEMATEL and interpretive structural modelling analysis.
Liu *et al.* (2023)	Maritime supply chain resilience during COVID-19	Identified government support and technology as central causal enablers.
Zhong *et al.* (2024)	SCRES capability factors in agri-food supply chains	Classified resilience capabilities into cause–effect groups to reveal system hierarchy.
Sonar *et al.* (2025)	Industry 5.0, resilience, and carbon neutrality	Identified causal challenges shaping sustainable digital readiness.

Source: Own elaboration based on Luthra *et al.* (2020), Alam *et al.* (2021), Kouhizadeh *et al.* (2021), Paul *et al.* (2021), Agi and Jha (2022), Liu *et al.* (2023), Raj *et al.* (2022), Zama *et al.* (2023), Zhong *et al.* (2024), Sonar *et al.* (2025).

During the pandemic, DEMATEL was increasingly applied to analyse disruption and recovery dynamics under conditions of heightened uncertainty. Paul *et al.* (2021) employed a Delphi-based Grey-DEMATEL approach to classify recovery challenges in the Bangladeshi garment sector, while Alam *et al.* (2021) applied Intuitionistic Fuzzy DEMATEL to vaccine supply chain challenges, identifying manufacturing capacity and coordination as key causal elements. These studies demonstrate the method's suitability for contexts characterised by uncertainty in expert judgement and cascading disruption.

Subsequent research extended DEMATEL's application to resilience and technology adoption. Raj *et al.* (2022) examined pandemic-related challenges in Indian manufacturing supply chains, identifying supply inconsistency and labour shortages as dominant drivers, while Liu *et al.* (2023) analysed maritime SCRES and showed the strong influence of government support and redundancy planning. Beyond crisis response, Agi and Jha (2022) and Kouhizadeh *et al.* (2021) applied DEMATEL to blockchain adoption, modelling interdependencies among technological, regulatory, and organisational factors.

More recent studies have broadened the method's scope to digital readiness and Industry 5.0. Zaman *et al.* (2023) combined DEMATEL with interpretive structural modelling to analyse digital banking adoption in e-commerce supply chains, and Sonar *et al.* (2025) used fuzzy Delphi and DEMATEL to examine Industry 5.0 implementation challenges linking digital readiness with resilience and carbon-neutrality objectives. Collectively, this body of work demonstrates DEMATEL's capacity to structure causal relationships among interdependent supply chain mechanisms in environments characterised by complexity and uncertainty.

Research design and expert-based data collection

A central strength of the DEMATEL method is its capacity to formalise expert judgement into an explicit causal structure capturing interdependencies within complex systems. By producing influence matrices and causal diagrams, DEMATEL facilitates the identification of dominant drivers, transmission mechanisms, and leverage points shaping system behaviour. This capability explains its frequent use as a structuring tool in hybrid decision-making frameworks, where it is commonly combined with ranking or optimisation techniques such as TOPSIS or VIKOR in areas including supplier selection, outsourcing decisions, and risk management (Govindan & Sivakumar, 2016).

Notwithstanding these advantages, DEMATEL entails methodological constraints that warrant careful consideration. As causal relationships are derived from expert assessments, the approach is inherently exposed to subjectivity and potential inconsistency in judgements (Zhou *et al.*, 2024). Analytical complexity also increases with the number of evaluated factors, which can result in dense causal structures that are challenging to interpret. Moreover, the application of threshold values to filter weaker relationships introduces an element of discretion, and the method does not generate priority rankings of alternatives, requiring integration with complementary techniques when prioritisation is an analytical objective.

These limitations are amplified in Computer-Assisted Web Interviewing (CAWI) settings. The requirement to assess multiple pairwise causal relations can impose a substantial cognitive burden on respondents, increasing the risk of fatigue and reduced judgement reliability, particularly in the absence of interviewer guidance.

To mitigate these concerns, two design features were incorporated. First, a Delphi-style expert pre-filtering stage was used to reduce the initial pool of mitigation mechanisms to a coherent and theoretically grounded set aligned with the readiness–responsiveness–resurgence–collaboration framework. This step limited the dimensionality of the influence matrix and reduced cognitive burden during the CAWI phase. Second, the online questionnaire was carefully structured to guide respondents through the pairwise assessment process in a clear and sequential manner, using standardised instructions and consistent scaling to ensure uniform interpretation of influence intensity.

Despite these safeguards, sensitivity to subjective judgement remains an unavoidable constraint in DEMATEL-based analysis. To mitigate this limitation, the study applies systematic aggregation and normalisation procedures that attenuate individual bias and stabilise the resulting influence matrices. Analytical robustness is further strengthened by the size and composition of the respondent group. Recent DEMATEL applications increasingly rely on larger practitioner samples—typically ranging from 30 to 100 participants—because broader aggregation reduces idiosyncratic noise and enhances the stability of inferred causal structures (Li & Tzeng, 2009). With 50 experienced managers participating in the assessment, the present study exceeds the scale of traditional expert-only designs and aligns with emerging best practice in practitioner-based causal modelling.

Within these constraints, DEMATEL offers a transparent and well-suited approach for examining causal complexity in environments characterised by dynamic and non-linear interactions. This is particularly pertinent in the context of geopolitical disruption, where mitigation mechanisms operate as interdependent elements rather than isolated responses. By structuring expert judgements into a system of directional influences, the method enables identification of dominant drivers, transmission mechanisms, and dependent factors, thereby addressing **RQ3** through an empirically grounded representation of the causal architecture underlying SCRES under geopolitical uncertainty.

DEMATEL modelling of resilience mechanisms under geopolitical constraint

Building on established applications of DEMATEL in sustainability, technology adoption, and crisis contexts, this study applies the method to examine how mitigation mechanisms interact within supply chains exposed to persistent geopolitical disruption. Rather than treating resilience strategies as independent responses, the analysis conceptualises them as interdependent adjustment mechanisms whose effects depend on their position within a broader causal structure. Geopolitical constraints—by altering relative costs, institutional conditions, and coordination feasibility—make such interdependence analytically salient.

The research design therefore employs DEMATEL as a structuring device that translates qualitative insights developed in Chapters 2–4 into a system-level representation of directional influence. The analysis builds on mitigation mechanisms conceptualised in Chapters 2 and 3 and empirically grounded through realist case studies in Chapter 4, translating these cumulative insights into a causal structure rather than extending the mechanism set. The objective is not to evaluate individual strategies in isolation, but to clarify how combinations of mechanisms shape resilience outcomes under sustained geopolitical pressure.

The empirical analysis follows a four-phase procedure. First, the analytical scope is defined by specifying the set of mitigation mechanisms to be examined and the purpose of the causal analysis. Second, evidence from the literature and prior qualitative findings is combined with expert validation to confirm the relevance and completeness of the selected mechanisms. Third, DEMATEL is applied to construct the direct-relation, normalised, and total-relation matrices, enabling the identification of causal and effect mechanisms within the system. Finally, the resulting influence structure is interpreted to explain how supply chains adjust and reconfigure when geopolitical disruption becomes a persistent operating condition.

PHASE 1. Formulation of objectives

The first phase establishes the analytical purpose of the DEMATEL application. The overarching objective is to identify how mitigation mechanisms shaping SCRES under geopolitical disruption are causally related and which of them exert the strongest influence within the system. In doing so, the analysis directly addresses **RQ3** by determining the directionality and relative strength of influence among resilience-enhancing strategies.

Beyond identifying influential mechanisms, the analysis seeks to construct a hierarchical representation of adjustment processes. This structure supports theoretical interpretation by clarifying how different types of mechanisms—technological, structural, and relational—interact over time, and it provides an analytical basis for understanding why certain configurations of responses generate stronger resilience outcomes under volatile geopolitical conditions.

PHASE 2. Identifying and validating key mitigation strategies

Prior research emphasises the importance of ensuring conceptual clarity and factor stability before applying DEMATEL (Fontela & Gabus, 1976). In line with this guidance, the present study adopts a two-stage mixed-method procedure that integrates qualitative expert validation with subsequent quantitative causal modelling. This phase ensures continuity between the conceptual framework developed in Chapter 2, the systematic literature review in Chapter 3, and the empirical evidence generated through case studies in Chapter 4.

A. Expert screening and refinement

Because DEMATEL requires a coherent, non-redundant, and context-sensitive set of factors, an initial list of mitigation strategies was subjected to expert screening. This list was derived from the integrated resilience framework developed in Chapter 2, refined through the thematic synthesis of the literature in Chapter 3 and case study evidence in Chapter 4.

The screening stage was conducted as part of the first section of the CAWI survey and involved the full sample of 50 senior managers and specialists from manufacturing multinational enterprises operating in Central and Eastern Europe. Respondents were asked to assess the relevance of each proposed strategy under conditions of sustained geopolitical disruption, identify conceptual overlaps, comment on definitional clarity, and indicate whether any empirically significant mechanisms were missing (cf. Appendix A).

This procedure corresponds to a Delphi-style content validation process commonly applied prior to DEMATEL modelling (Tzeng *et al.*, 2007). Aggregating responses across a broad practitioner sample ensured that the final set of mitigation mechanisms reflected shared expert judgement rather than idiosyncratic firm-level perspectives. In addition, this pre-filtering step reduced redundancy within the factor set, thereby limiting potential cognitive burden during the subsequent pairwise comparisons and improving the reliability of causal assessments in Phase 3.

B. Final strategy set for DEMATEL analysis

The mitigation strategies retained through this validation process constitute the analytical input for the DEMATEL modelling conducted in Phase 3. Consistent with the analytical structure developed in Chapter 3, the strategies are organised into four overarching categories: operational resilience, strategic reconfiguration, collaborative ecosystem, and digital readiness. Table 5.2 presents the final set of strategies together with their definitions, coding, and source references.

As synthesised from the preceding chapters, recent research converges on these four categories as the principal domains through which firms adjust their supply chains under geopolitical disruption. They capture the multidimensional and interdependent nature of resilience formation and provide a coherent analytical basis for causal modelling.

Operational resilience refers to firm-level buffering and short-term adjustment mechanisms aimed at maintaining continuity during disruption.

Table 5.2 Key mitigation strategies influencing supply chain resilience

Strategic category	*Capability factor*	*Code*	*Description*	*Source*
Operational resilience	Excess production capacity and inventory	RPR	Transition from a just-in-time (JIT) to a just-in-case approach by building surplus capacity and stock rather than minimising inventory.	Zhang and Doan (2023); Choi *et al.* (2023)
	Production optimisation with supply chain planning	POP	Synchronisation of all elements of the supply chain.	Swink *et al.* (2025)
Strategic reconfiguration	Nearshoring of production	NEAR	Relocating production activities to locations close to the company's headquarters.	Kazancoglu *et al.* (2024)
	Reshoring of production	RESH	Relocating production activities back to the company's headquarters.	Chen *et al.* (2022)
	Diversification of the production network	PND	Diversifying production bases by forming new partnerships or requesting existing partners to supply from different locations.	Jiang *et al.* (2022)
	Supplier diversification by quantity	SDQ	Expanding the supplier portfolio in terms of the number of suppliers.	Tang (2006)
	Supplier diversification by location (multi region supplier)	SDL	Expanding the supplier portfolio in terms of geographic distribution.	Sawik (2022) Suryadi and Rau (2023)
	Multi-sourcing	MULT	Maintaining an existing supplier base by cooperating with multiple suppliers.	Namdar *et al.* (2018) Suryadi and Rau (2023) Mamun (2024)
Collaborative ecosystem	Creation of cross-industry partner networks	CPN	Cooperating with strategic raw material suppliers and external service partners.	Ivanov (2021) Britsche and Fekete (2024)

Digital readiness	Implementation of machine learning (ML), artificial intelligence (AI), and big data	MLBD	Understanding and utilising data to increase efficiency and effectiveness.	Modgil *et al.* (2022) Belhadi *et al.* (2024)
	Technology improvement (e.g. blockchain)	BLCH	Automating processes through improved digitalisation.	Ivanov *et al.* (2019) Min (2019) Lohmer *et al.* (2020)
	Alternative components (e.g. 3D printing)	AC3D	On-demand manufacturing of certain products/components using 3D printing techniques to fill crisis gaps without long-term disruption to normal business processes.	Ivanov *et al.* (2019) Belhadi *et al.* (2022)

Source: Own elaboration based on Namdar *et al.* (2018), Ivanov *et al.* (2019), Min (2019), Lohmer *et al.* (2020), Ivanov (2021), Belhadi *et al.* (2022), Jiang *et al.* (2022), Chen *et al.* (2022), Modgil *et al.* (2022), Sawik (2022), Suryadi and Rau (2023), Zhang and Doan (2023), Belhadi *et al.* (2024), Britsche and Fekete (2024), Kazancoglu *et al.* (2024), Mamun (2024), Swink *et al.* (2025).

These include inventory buffering, excess capacity, production flexibility, and real-time reallocation of resources. From an economic perspective, such forms of operational slack function as shock absorbers that reduce adjustment costs and stabilise performance under volatile demand and supply conditions.

Strategic reconfiguration encompasses longer-term structural adjustments in supply network design. In geopolitically exposed environments, firms increasingly reallocate production and sourcing across locations through nearshoring, reshoring, multi-sourcing, and geographic diversification of production networks. Evidence from both the literature and the case studies in Chapter 4 indicates that partitioning supply structures and developing multi-regional sourcing pathways reduces dependence on single locations or suppliers and lowers exposure to region-specific geopolitical risk.

Collaborative ecosystem development captures inter-firm coordination mechanisms extending beyond bilateral transactions. Networks characterised by information sharing, transparency, and coordinated contingency planning facilitate collective adjustment and reduce coordination failures when disruptions propagate across organisational boundaries. Such arrangements support synchronisation among supply chain actors and enhance network-level stability under geopolitical stress.

Digital readiness comprises investments in advanced technologies such as machine learning, artificial intelligence, big data analytics, blockchain, and additive manufacturing. These technologies enhance visibility, accelerate information processing, and support decision-making under uncertainty. Economically, digital capabilities reduce information asymmetries, improve sensing of geopolitical and market signals, and enable earlier and more informed adjustment responses.

Importantly, these four categories align directly with the readiness–responsiveness–resurgence–collaboration framework introduced in Chapter 2. Digital readiness primarily strengthens readiness by enhancing sensing and information processing; operational resilience supports responsiveness through short-term buffering and adjustment; strategic reconfiguration underpins resurgence by enabling longer-term structural adaptation; and collaborative ecosystem development corresponds to collaboration by coordinating inter-firm responses and stabilising network-level adjustment under geopolitical disruption.

Moreover, the categories closely mirror the mechanisms identified through the Context–Mechanism–Outcome analysis in Chapter 4. Digital readiness mechanisms correspond to technological adjustments observed in Firms A and D; reconfiguration strategies such as nearshoring and multi-sourcing align with responses documented in Firms A, C, and E; and collaborative ecosystem mechanisms reflect coordination patterns identified in Cases B and C. This convergence between literature-based synthesis and firm-level evidence provides methodological triangulation and strengthens the internal validity of the DEMATEL model applied in this chapter.

PHASE 3. Model development

Following the identification and validation of mitigation strategies in Phase 2, Phase 3 develops the DEMATEL-based causal model. This phase operationalises the conceptual framework introduced in Chapter 2, refined through the systematic literature review and case study evidence in Chapters 3 and 4 by quantifying the interdependencies among mitigation mechanisms. The objective is to distinguish between causal (driving) and effect (dependent) mechanisms and to map their relative influence within the resilience system. The first step in this process is the construction of the direct-relation matrix, which constitutes the empirical foundation for all subsequent DEMATEL calculations.

STEP 1. Constructing the direct-relation matrix

Data were collected using a structured CAWI survey (cf. Appendix A). Fifty respondents responsible for procurement, logistics, and supply chain decision-making evaluated the direct influence of each mitigation strategy on every other strategy using a five-point scale ranging from 0 (no influence) to 4 (very high influence). Individual judgements were subsequently aggregated to construct the direct-relation matrix.

Respondents were senior-level managers representing manufacturing sectors classified under Section C of NACE Rev. 2, including automotive, chemicals, machinery, and industrial equipment. To ensure relevance to geopolitical disruption, participating firms were required to meet three criteria: (i) headquarters located in a Central or Eastern European country; (ii) at least one foreign subsidiary or international production activity beyond exporting; and (iii) dependence on supplies originating from geopolitically sensitive regions, including but not limited to Ukraine, Belarus, Russia, Taiwan, or China.

The final sample comprised supply chain directors, heads of procurement, logistics managers, managing directors, and other senior executives (Table 5.3). Respondents' professional experience ranged from 3 to 30 years, with a mean of 16.1 years and a median of 15 years, indicating a highly experienced expert group. The standard deviation of 6.74 years suggests moderate dispersion while confirming substantial accumulated expertise relevant to SCRES and geopolitical risk management.

The diversity of roles and sectors represented in the respondent pool supports the external validity of the analysis across industrial supply chains.

Table 5.3 Overview of experts' portfolio

Characteristics		*N*	*%*
Represented Industry	23—Manufacture of other non-metallic mineral products	6	12%
	25—Manufacture of fabricated metal products, except machinery and equipment		
	24—Manufacture of basic metals	5	10%
	10—Manufacture of food products		
	20—Manufacture of chemicals and chemical products	4	8%
	28—Manufacture of machinery and equipment n.e.c.	3	6%
	27—Manufacture of electrical equipment		
	22—Manufacture of rubber and plastic products		
	17—Manufacture of paper and paper products		
	31—Manufacture of furniture	2	4%
	29—Manufacture of motor vehicles, trailers, and semi-trailers		
	26—Manufacture of computer, electronic, and optical products		
	21—Manufacture of basic pharmaceutical products and pharmaceutical preparations	1	2%
	16—Manufacture of wood and of products of wood and cork, except furniture		
	15—Manufacture of leather and related products		
	14—Manufacture of wearing apparel		
	13—Manufacture of textiles		
	11—Manufacture of beverages		
Job Role	Head of Procurement	14	28%
	Supply Chain Director	10	20%
	Managing Director	8	16%
	Sales Director	7	14%
	Director of Foreign Markets	3	6%
	Supply Chain Specialist	3	6%
	Deputy Managing Director	2	4%
	Director of Development	2	4%
	Financial Director	1	2%

Source: Own elaboration.

Relying on expert judgement allows the study to capture nuanced interdependencies among resilience mechanisms, distinguishing between enabling drivers and downstream, dependent elements within the system. As a result, the DEMATEL model reflects a broad range of operational contexts rather than a single-industry perspective.

Once the data were collected, the first step of the DEMATEL procedure was to construct the initial direct-relation matrix (Table 5.4). Experts assessed pairwise influences among the selected strategies, indicating whether an influence exists and, if so, its intensity. Assessments were made using a five-point Likert scale, where 0 denotes no influence, 1 low influence, 2 medium influence, 3 high influence, and 4 very high influence. The influence of factor i

Table 5.4 Direct-relation matrix A

Code	*RPR*	*POP*	*NEAR*	*RESH*	*PND*	*SDQ*	*SDL*	*MULT*	*CPN*	*MLBD*	*BLCH*	*AC3D*
RPR	0.00	0.40	0.24	0.56	1.96	1.18	0.96	0.78	0.72	0.40	0.48	0.24
POP	0.80	0.00	0.16	0.24	1.28	1.40	1.50	1.42	0.96	0.28	0.30	0.24
NEAR	0.98	1.10	0.00	0.48	0.96	1.50	2.06	0.40	0.46	0.48	0.24	0.24
RESH	0.52	0.66	0.30	0.00	1.28	3.08	1.92	0.88	0.56	0.46	0.38	0.22
PND	1.10	0.92	0.30	0.44	0.00	2.20	1.80	2.36	1.18	0.40	0.22	0.28
SDQ	1.26	1.70	0.30	0.56	2.08	0.00	1.84	1.40	1.32	0.70	0.66	0.20
SDL	1.56	1.84	0.36	0.62	2.50	2.14	0.00	2.50	2.14	1.80	1.90	0.90
MULT	1.58	1.24	0.22	0.52	2.22	2.70	2.64	0.00	1.42	0.72	0.66	0.30
CPN	0.96	1.80	0.30	0.74	2.12	2.56	2.14	2.54	0.00	0.58	0.56	0.34
MLBD	1.86	0.04	0.22	1.06	2.76	2.34	2.08	1.02	1.40	0.00	0.70	0.38
BLCH	0.96	0.46	0.58	1.14	1.84	1.50	1.00	2.98	0.54	0.68	0.00	0.62
AC3D	0.32	0.16	0.20	0.30	0.14	0.06	0.14	0.20	0.22	0.22	0.18	0.00

Source: Own elaboration.

on factor j is denoted as x_{ij}. By definition, diagonal elements are set to 0, as self-influence is not evaluated.

Each expert provided a non-negative n × n matrix. With N = 50 experts, 50 matrices were obtained and aggregated into the initial direct-relation matrix A = [a_{ij}] by taking the arithmetic mean of expert ratings:

$$a_{ij} = \frac{1}{N}\sum_{k=1}^{N} x_{ij}^{k}$$

where k = the number of an expert evaluating the criteria,
N = total number of experts evaluating the criteria.

STEP 2. Developing the normalised and total influence matrix

Following the construction of the direct-relation matrix, the next step involved is normalising A and computing the total-relation matrix. These operations implement the core logic of DEMATEL, which recognises that complex systems contain not only direct causal influences but also indirect effects that propagate through multiple pathways (Fontela & Gabus, 1976; Govindan & Sivakumar, 2016).

First, normalisation is required to ensure comparability across factors and to satisfy the stability condition for the convergence of the series of indirect effects (Table 5.5). In line with standard DEMATEL practice, A was scaled so that the maximum row or column sum equals 1, yielding the normalised direct-relation matrix D, with all elements constrained to the [0,1] interval:

$$D = Z \times m$$

Table 5.5 Normalised matrix D

Code	*RPR*	*POP*	*NEAR*	*RESH*	*PND*	*SDQ*	*SDL*	*MULT*	*CPN*	*MLBD*	*BLCH*	*AC3D*
RPR	0.00	0.02	0.01	0.03	0.09	0.06	0.05	0.04	0.03	0.02	0.02	0.01
POP	0.04	0.00	0.01	0.01	0.06	0.07	0.07	0.07	0.05	0.01	0.01	0.01
NEAR	0.05	0.05	0.00	0.02	0.05	0.07	0.10	0.02	0.02	0.02	0.01	0.01
RESH	0.03	0.03	0.01	0.00	0.06	0.15	0.09	0.04	0.03	0.02	0.02	0.01
PND	0.05	0.04	0.01	0.02	0.00	0.11	0.09	0.11	0.06	0.02	0.01	0.01
SDQ	0.06	0.08	0.01	0.03	0.10	0.00	0.09	0.07	0.06	0.03	0.03	0.01
SDL	0.08	0.09	0.02	0.03	0.12	0.10	0.00	0.12	0.10	0.09	0.09	0.04
MULT	0.08	0.06	0.01	0.03	0.11	0.13	0.13	0.00	0.07	0.03	0.03	0.01
CPN	0.05	0.09	0.01	0.04	0.10	0.12	0.10	0.12	0.00	0.03	0.03	0.02
MLBD	0.09	0.00	0.01	0.05	0.13	0.11	0.10	0.05	0.07	0.00	0.03	0.02
BLCH	0.05	0.02	0.03	0.06	0.09	0.07	0.05	0.14	0.03	0.03	0.00	0.03
AC3D	0.02	0.01	0.01	0.01	0.01	0.00	0.01	0.01	0.01	0.01	0.01	0.00

Source: Own elaboration.

where

$$m = \left[\frac{1}{\max\limits_{1<i<n} \sum_{j=1}^{n} |a_{ij}|}, \frac{1}{\max\limits_{1<j<n} \sum_{i=1}^{n} |a_{ij}|} \right]$$

Once D was obtained, the total-relation matrix W was computed to capture both direct and indirect influences. This is achieved by aggregating influence transmissions across all path lengths, operationalised through matrix inversion:

$$W = D(I - D)^\wedge\{-1\}$$

where I denotes the identity matrix. Each element w_{ij} therefore represents the total influence of factor i on factor j, including both immediate effects and indirect effects mediated through other factors. Table 5.6 reports the total-relation matrix.

For the purposes of graphical representation, a threshold value was applied solely to improve the readability of the digraph by suppressing very weak relationships. In line with common DEMATEL practice (Fontela & Gabus, 1976), the threshold was defined as the mean value of the elements in the total-relation matrix (W). Relationships equal to or exceeding this threshold are highlighted in Table 5.6; all relationships were retained in the underlying calculations and interpretation.

Table 5.6 Total relation matrix W

Code	*RPR*	*POP*	*NEAR*	*RESH*	*PND*	*SDQ*	*SDL*	*MULT*	*CPN*	*MLBD*	*BLCH*	*AC3D*
RPR	0.05	0.07	0.02	0.05	0.17	0.14	0.12	0.11	0.09	0.05	0.05	0.03
POP	0.10	0.06	0.02	0.04	0.15	0.16	0.15	0.15	0.10	0.05	0.05	0.03
NEAR	0.10	0.11	0.01	0.05	0.14	0.16	0.17	0.10	0.08	0.06	0.05	0.03
RESH	0.09	0.10	0.03	0.03	0.17	0.25	0.18	0.14	0.10	0.06	0.06	0.03
PND	0.13	0.12	0.03	0.06	0.12	0.22	0.19	0.21	0.13	0.06	0.06	0.04
SDQ	0.14	0.15	0.03	0.07	0.22	0.13	0.19	0.18	0.14	0.08	0.08	0.04
SDL	0.18	0.19	0.05	0.09	0.29	0.28	0.16	0.27	0.21	0.15	0.15	0.08
MULT	0.16	0.15	0.03	0.07	0.25	0.27	0.25	0.13	0.16	0.09	0.09	0.04
CPN	0.14	0.17	0.04	0.08	0.24	0.27	0.23	0.25	0.10	0.08	0.08	0.05
MLBD	0.17	0.09	0.03	0.09	0.26	0.25	0.22	0.17	0.15	0.05	0.08	0.05
BLCH	0.12	0.09	0.05	0.09	0.20	0.20	0.16	0.24	0.10	0.08	0.04	0.05
AC3D	0.03	0.02	0.01	0.02	0.03	0.03	0.03	0.03	0.02	0.02	0.02	0.00

Note: shaded cells relate to values that are equal to or exceed the threshold of 0.11.
Source: Own elaboration.

STEP 3. Identifying cause-and-effect factors

To interpret the structural properties of the system, the total-relation matrix W was summarised using two indices commonly reported in DEMATEL studies. The first index, denoted as d_i, is obtained as the sum of the *i*-th row of W and represents the total influence exerted by factor *i* on all other factors (dispatch). The second index, denoted as r_i, is calculated as the sum of the *i*-th column of W and captures the total influence received by factor *i* from the rest of the system (receive):

$$d = \left[d_i\right]_{nx1} = \left[\sum_{j=1}^{n} w_{ij}\right]_{nx1}$$

$$r = \left[r_i\right]_{nx1} = \left[\sum_{i=1}^{n} w_{ij}\right]_{nx1}$$

Two composite measures were then derived (Table 5.7). First, $\mathbf{d_i + r_i}$ indicates the *prominence* of a factor, reflecting its overall embeddedness within the network of interdependencies. Second, $\mathbf{d_i - r_i}$ captures the *net causal role* of a factor: when $\mathbf{d_i - r_i > 0}$, the factor is classified as a net cause (driver), whereas $\mathbf{d_i - r_i < 0}$ identifies a net effect (dependent) factor. This interpretation is widely adopted in DEMATEL-based analyses to distinguish leverage points from downstream elements in complex systems (e.g. Luthra *et al.*, 2020; Raj *et al.*, 2022; Zhong *et al.*, 2024).

The results reveal a clear hierarchical ordering among resilience mechanisms. Strategies with the highest positive $\mathbf{(d_i - r_i)}$ values operate as

Table 5.7 Identification of cause and effect factors

Code	*d*	*r*	*di + ri*	$d_i - r_i$	*Comment*
RPR	0.95	2.38	3.33	–1.43	Effect
POP	1.05	1.31	2.36	–0.26	Effect
NEAR	1.06	0.37	1.44	0.69	Cause
RESH	1.25	0.75	2.00	0.49	Cause
PND	1.36	2.23	3.59	–0.87	Effect
SDQ	1.43	2.34	3.77	–0.91	Effect
SDL	2.09	2.07	4.15	0.02	Cause[1]
MULT	1.69	1.97	3.67	–0.28	Effect
CPN	1.73	1.38	3.11	0.36	Cause
MLBD	1.64	0.84	2.48	0.80	Cause
BLCH	1.44	0.80	2.23	0.64	Cause
AC3D	0.25	0.47	0.72	–0.22	Effect

Source: Own elaboration.

principal causal drivers within the system. Digital capabilities related to machine learning, artificial intelligence, and big data analytics (MLBD) exhibit the strongest net causal influence (**d – r = +0.80**), indicating that advanced information-processing capabilities actively condition adjustments across the broader resilience architecture. Blockchain technologies (BLCH) also emerge as a significant driver (**d – r = +0.64**), consistent with their role in enhancing transparency, traceability, and secure data exchange, thereby enabling the activation and coordination of other resilience mechanisms.

Production-location reconfiguration constitutes a second causal layer. Both nearshoring (NEAR; **d – r = +0.69**) and reshoring (RESH; **d – r = +0.49**) are identified as net causes, underscoring the importance of spatial reallocation of production in reducing geopolitical exposure and logistical vulnerability under persistent disruption.

Several mechanisms occupy intermediate positions within the causal structure, displaying modestly positive **(d – r)** values. Collaborative partner networks (CPN; **d – r = +0.35**) and supplier diversification by location (SDL; **d – r = +0.02**) transmit influence across the system, but their effectiveness appears contingent on prior technological and locational reconfiguration. These mechanisms therefore function primarily as channels through which upstream drivers propagate their effects, rather than as independent sources of systemic change.

By contrast, diversification-oriented mechanisms emerge predominantly as effect factors, characterised by negative **(d – r)** values. Supplier diversification by quantity (SDQ; **d – r = –0.91**), production network diversification (PND; **d – r = –0.87**), and multi-sourcing (MULT; **d – r = –0.28**) are largely shaped by upstream causal drivers rather than initiating adjustment themselves. A similar pattern is observed for operational mechanisms such as inventory buffers (RPR; **d − r = −1.43**), production optimisation and planning (POP; **d − r = −0.26**), and the adoption of alternative components (AC3D; **d − r = −0.22**), which function primarily as downstream responses once foundational drivers—particularly digital capabilities and production-location reconfiguration—are in place.

The prominence measure (**$d_i + r_i$**) further highlights the systemic embeddedness of individual mechanisms. SDL exhibits the highest prominence (**d + r = 4.15**), followed by SDQ, multi-sourcing (MULT), and PND. This indicates that diversification mechanisms remain central to the resilience architecture in terms of connectivity and interdependence, even though they are largely shaped by upstream causal forces.

Overall, the DEMATEL results reveal a layered causal structure in which digital and information-processing capabilities and production-location reconfiguration act as primary drivers of system adaptation. Diversification mechanisms constitute the downstream structural response, while collaborative arrangements facilitate the transmission of influence between these layers. This empirically grounded causal ordering provides the analytical foundation for the capability-based sequencing developed in the following section.

Visualisation of causal interdependencies

To facilitate interpretation of the DEMATEL results, very weak influence relationships were suppressed solely for graphical clarity in the visual representation of the causal structure. In line with established DEMATEL practice, a threshold equal to the mean of all non-zero entries in the total-relation matrix was used as a visual filter (Li & Tzeng, 2009). The average influence value across the dataset was 0.11 and was therefore adopted as the threshold for display purposes. Only relationships with influence values equal to or exceeding this level are shown in the digraph, while all relationships were retained in the underlying calculations and analytical interpretation. This approach improves readability without altering the substantive structure of the results.

Figure 5.1 presents a directed cause–effect network derived from the DEMATEL total-relation matrix and visualised using Gephi. Each node represents a mitigation mechanism, while directed edges indicate the direction and strength of influence between mechanisms. Node colour reflects the net causal role derived from DEMATEL (drivers, dependent factors, and near-neutral transmission mechanisms), and node size corresponds to overall prominence within the system (d + r). Only relationships exceeding the threshold value are displayed to enhance visual interpretability.

The ForceAtlas2 layout in LinLog mode is used to visually emphasise differences in influence and connectivity by separating dominant causal drivers from dependent mechanisms and clustering strongly interconnected

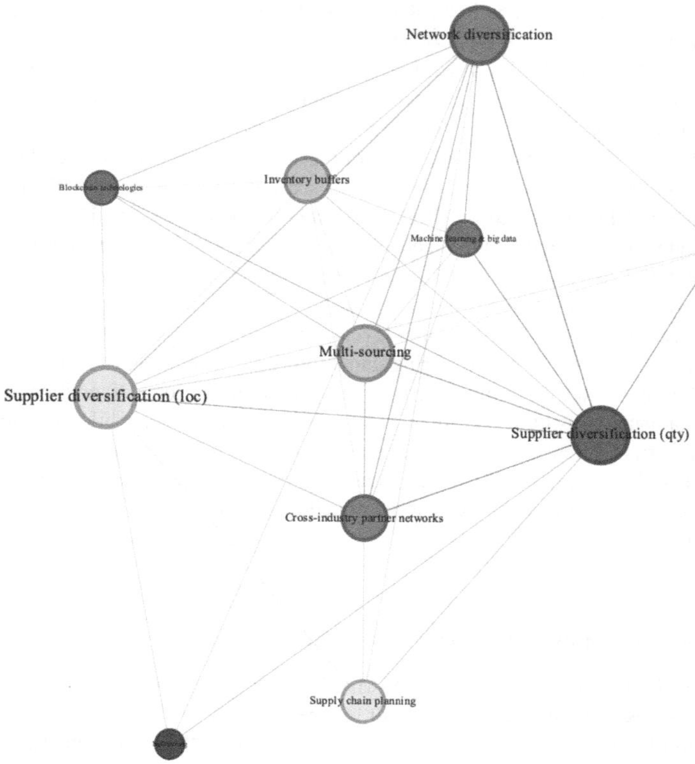

Figure 5.1 Cause–effect network of supply chain resilience strategies under geopolitical disruption (DEMATEL–Gephi visualisation).

strategies. Within this representation, digital capabilities (MLBD, BLCH) and production-location reconfiguration mechanisms (NEAR, RESH) occupy structurally central positions, consistent with their role as primary causal drivers identified in the DEMATEL analysis.

Diversification-oriented mechanisms—including SDQ, diversification of the production network, and multi-sourcing—appear as highly prominent but predominantly dependent elements. Their larger node size reflects strong systemic embeddedness, while their relative positioning indicates that they are shaped by upstream technological and locational drivers rather than initiating system-wide adjustment. Collaborative mechanisms occupy intermediate positions, facilitating the transmission of influence across layers of the system.

Overall, the visualisation corroborates the DEMATEL results by illustrating a layered and tightly coupled resilience system in which digital readiness and locational reconfiguration function as primary leverage points that condition the effectiveness of diversification, collaboration, and operational buffering mechanisms.

PHASE 4. Developing strategies based on causal insights

This phase translates the DEMATEL-derived causal structure into a capability-based sequencing of resilience-building actions. The objective is not to propose additional mitigation mechanisms, but to clarify how those already identified in Chapters 2–4 interact and how they should be prioritised given their position within a geopolitically constrained supply chain system. In doing so, the analysis integrates the conceptual framework introduced in Chapter 2, the thematic patterns identified in the systematic literature review in Chapter 3, and the firm-level adjustment mechanisms documented in Chapter 4. In the Central and Eastern European context, this prioritisation is shaped by firms' intermediate positioning in global value chains, high dependence on extra-regional inputs, and partial reliance on externally governed technological and regulatory infrastructures.

The causal hierarchy identified by DEMATEL indicates that digital capabilities and production-location decisions constitute the primary drivers of resilience formation, reflecting the CEE region's exposure to geopolitical chokepoints combined with limited upstream control over critical technologies and inputs. Investments in data analytics, visibility, traceability, and advanced digital infrastructure establish the informational and organisational foundations required for effective adjustment. Similarly, nearshoring and reshoring decisions reshape exposure to geopolitical risk and condition the feasibility of subsequent structural responses. These mechanisms align with the digital readiness and strategic reconfiguration domains articulated in Chapter 2 and correspond to upstream clusters identified in the literature, where they consistently function as enabling conditions rather than as reactive responses.

Structural diversification mechanisms—such as supplier diversification, multi-sourcing, and production network dispersion—become effective once these foundational conditions are in place. In the DEMATEL results, these strategies emerge primarily as effect mechanisms whose impact depends on prior technological and locational choices. This sequencing mirrors patterns observed in the literature, where buffering and redundancy are typically framed as operational responses to disruption rather than as initiators of systemic adjustment. When implemented without upstream enablers, diversification remains fragmented and yields limited system-wide benefits; when appropriately sequenced, it enhances flexibility and distributes risk across the network. In CEE-based firms, the effectiveness of diversification is further constrained by capital intensity, supplier availability, and uneven access to industrial policy support, reinforcing its dependence on prior digital and locational enablers.

Collaborative arrangements constitute an additional layer linking firm-level capabilities to network-level resilience. Shared data infrastructures, coordinated contingency planning, and relational governance amplify the effects of digital and structural adjustments, particularly in disruptions that propagate across organisational and national boundaries. In causal terms, collaboration reinforces resilience once internal capabilities are sufficiently developed, rather than operating as an autonomous driver of adaptation. This role is consistent with the collaborative ecosystem perspective identified in the literature review.

Overall, the findings indicate that resilience emerges through a structured progression of adjustments rather than through simultaneous or isolated interventions. Digital readiness and production-location reconfiguration act as catalytic conditions; diversification mechanisms deepen adaptive capacity; and collaboration extends resilience beyond the focal firm. This sequencing provides an integrated explanation of how resilience mechanisms interact under persistent geopolitical uncertainty.

The triangulation of methods strengthens this interpretation. The primary causal drivers identified through DEMATEL—digital technologies, transparency tools such as blockchain, and locational reconfiguration—were also evident in the case studies of firms that achieved operational stabilisation and broader reconfiguration (Cases A, C, D, and F). Firms lacking these foundations relied predominantly on downstream measures such as diversification or incremental optimisation, consistent with their classification as effect mechanisms in the causal model. This convergence across literature synthesis, case evidence, and causal modelling supports the robustness of the proposed sequencing in the context of CEE-based firms operating under persistent geopolitical exposure.

To consolidate these insights within the resilience capability architecture developed earlier in the monograph, Table 5.8 summarises the causal role of each capability domain and its empirical grounding in the DEMATEL analysis.

The capability-oriented synthesis presented in Table 5.8 confirms that readiness, responsiveness, resurgence, and collaboration contribute to resilience through distinct but interdependent functions. Readiness initiates adjustment by enabling sensing and anticipation, responsiveness stabilises short-term operations, resurgence provides structural leverage for longer-term adaptation, and collaboration reinforces coordination and learning at the network level. These domains form a sequential and mutually enabling process that integrates insights from the literature, qualitative evidence, and causal modelling, rather than a set of independent or interchangeable interventions.

Interpretation of causal pathways and leverage points

The DEMATEL analysis provides a direct empirical answer to **RQ3** by specifying both the structure and the relative strength of causal relationships among resilience mechanisms under geopolitical disruption. The results indicate that

Table 5.8 Capability domains, causal roles, and DEMATEL-supported evidence

Capability domain	*Causal role in resilience system*	*DEMATEL evidence*	*Strategic implication*
Readiness	Upstream driver	Digital technologies (AI, ML, analytics, blockchain) have the highest net causal influence, enabling visibility, early warning, and scenario-based anticipation. Readiness variables display strong outgoing influence and weak incoming influence.	Investments in digital infrastructure and sensing tools must precede most structural or diversification strategies. Firms with weak readiness remain locked in reactive modes.
Responsiveness	Transitional capability	Responsiveness-related actions (short-term tactical adjustments, initial geographic diversification) show moderate causal influence and are sensitive to readiness inputs. They receive strong influence from digital readiness but exert limited downstream force without structural enablers.	Responsiveness is necessary but insufficient; without prior readiness and subsequent resurgence, effects remain short-lived and operational only.
Resurgence	Structural reconfiguration driver	Reshoring, nearshoring, and production-footprint changes show the second-highest net causal influence after digital readiness. They act as structural leverage points that reshape the entire system.	Strategic reconfiguration multiplies downstream effects and reduces vulnerability. Resurgence capabilities should be treated as long-term strategic levers rather than reactive crisis responses.
Collaboration	Network-level reinforcement mechanism	Collaboration mechanisms have relatively high incoming influence but low outgoing influence. They depend on readiness, responsiveness, and resurgence to function but increase system stability once activated.	Collaboration strengthens capability accumulation and produces network effects, but must be sequenced after internal capabilities are sufficiently established.

Source: Own elaboration.

SCRES does not arise from a flat set of parallel responses, but from a hierarchically organised system of interdependent mechanisms characterised by asymmetric influence patterns.

At the top of this structure, advanced digital technologies and production-location adjustments exhibit the strongest net causal influence, identifying them as first-order drivers within the resilience system, particularly salient in the CEE context, where firms combine high exposure to extra-regional supply risks with limited upstream control over critical technologies and logistics corridors. These mechanisms exert substantial outbound influence while receiving relatively limited feedback, indicating that they shape the informational, organisational, and governance conditions under which other mechanisms operate. By improving visibility, reducing information asymmetries, and altering spatial exposure to geopolitical risk, they function as leverage points that condition the feasibility and effectiveness of subsequent adjustments.

Mechanisms occupying intermediate positions, such as early-stage geographic diversification and selective partner reconfiguration, display more balanced influence profiles, reflecting the constrained adjustment space of many CEE-based firms operating between global lead firms and downstream markets. They transmit causal effects from upstream drivers to downstream practices, translating digital readiness and locational change into operational sourcing and coordination responses. Their role is therefore not to initiate system-wide adjustment independently, but to mediate and propagate influence across the resilience architecture.

In contrast, downstream strategies including multi-sourcing, supplier-base expansion, and PND are characterised by negative net causal values, identifying them primarily as effect mechanisms. While these practices remain highly embedded within the system, their performance depends on the prior activation of upstream digital and locational capabilities. This finding clarifies why diversification-oriented strategies, although prominent in both practice and prior research, rarely function as independent drivers of resilience when implemented in isolation.

By making these asymmetric influence patterns explicit, the chapter advances resilience research beyond cataloguing mitigation practices towards explaining how and why certain mechanisms exert greater systemic impact than others. The DEMATEL results show that digital readiness and production-location reconfiguration condition the effectiveness of commonly emphasised downstream strategies such as diversification and collaboration. In this way, the analysis extends transaction-cost reasoning by demonstrating how firms first relax binding information and coordination constraints before reallocating transactional relationships under conditions of uncertainty.

In direct response to **RQ3**, the analysis therefore identifies not only which mechanisms matter, but where they sit within the causal hierarchy and how strongly they shape system behaviour. The resulting causal logic is consistent with dynamic capabilities reasoning, in which sensing and seizing through digital and structural reconfiguration enable subsequent reorganisation of supply networks and inter-firm governance arrangements. In the CEE context, this hierarchy helps explain why firms with stronger upstream capabilities progress towards more integrated and cumulative resilience trajectories, while others remain constrained to reactive or incremental responses.

Together with the systematic literature review in Chapter 3 and the case-based evidence in Chapter 4, this chapter completes the empirical examination of the causal foundations of SCRES. Chapter 6 builds on these findings to integrate insights across methods and discuss their implications for theory development, future research, and policy in geopolitically exposed supply chains.

Note

1 Factors with d − r values close to zero (e.g. SDL) occupy borderline positions in the cause–effect structure and should therefore be interpreted with caution, as small variations in expert judgement or threshold specification may shift their classification between causal and effect roles.

References

Agi, M. A. N., & Jha, A. K. (2022). Blockchain technology in the supply chain: An integrated theoretical perspective of organizational adoption. *International Journal of Production Economics*, *247*. https://doi.org/10.1016/j.ijpe.2022.108458

Alam, S. T., Ahmed, S., Ali, S. M., Sarker, S., Kabir, G., & Ul-Islam, A. (2021). Challenges to COVID-19 vaccine supply chain: Implications for sustainable development goals. *International Journal of Production Economics*, *239*. https://doi.org/10.1016/j.ijpe.2021.108193

Belhadi, A., Kamble, S. S., Venkatesh, M., Chiappetta Jabbour, C. J., & Benkhati, I. (2022). Building supply chain resilience and efficiency through additive manufacturing: An ambidextrous perspective on the dynamic capability view. *International Journal of Production Economics*, *249*. https://doi.org/10.1016/j.ijpe.2022.108516

Belhadi, A., Mani, V., Kamble, S. S., Khan, S. A. R., & Verma, S. (2024). Artificial intelligence-driven innovation for enhancing supply chain resilience and performance under the effect of supply chain dynamism: An empirical investigation. *Annals of Operations Research*, *333*(2), 627–652. https://doi.org/10.1007/s10479-021-03956-x

Britsche, A., & Fekete, M. (2024). Supply chain resilience in the European Automotive Industry. *Management Systems in Production Engineering*, *32*(3), 380–400. https://doi.org/10.2478/mspe-2024-0036

Chen, H., Hsu, C. W., Shih, Y. Y., & Caskey, D. (2022). The reshoring decision under uncertainty in the post-COVID-19 era. *Journal of Business & Industrial Marketing*, *37*(10), 2064–2074. https://doi.org/10.1108/JBIM-01-2021-0066

Choi, T. Y., Netland, T. H., Sanders, N., Sodhi, M. S., & Wagner, S. M. (2023). Just-in-time for supply chains in turbulent times. *Production and Operations Management*, *32*(7), 2331–2340. https://doi.org/10.1111/poms.13979

Fontela, E., & Gabus, A. (1976). *The DEMATEL observer*. Battelle Geneva Research Center.

Govindan, K., & Sivakumar, R. (2016). Green supplier selection and order allocation using a hybrid MCDM approach: A case study. *Computers & Industrial Engineering, 101*, 10–24. https://doi.org/10.1016/j.cie.2016.08.015

Ivanov, D. (2021). Supply chain viability and the COVID-19 pandemic: A conceptual and formal generalisation of four major adaptation strategies. *International Journal of Production Research, 59*(12), 3535–3552. https://doi.org/10.1080/00207543.2021.1890852

Ivanov, D., Dolgui, A., & Sokolov, B. (2019). The impact of digital technology and Industry 4.0 on the ripple effect and supply chain risk analytics. *International Journal of Production Research, 57*(3), 829–846. https://doi.org/10.1080/00207543.2018.1488086

Jiang, B., Rigobon, D., & Rigobon, R. (2022). From just-in-time, to just-in-case, to just-in-worst-case: Simple models of a global supply chain under uncertain aggregate shocks. *IMF Economic Review, 70*(1), 141–184. https://doi.org/10.1057/s41308-021-00148-2

Kazancoglu, Y., Lafci, C., Berberoglu, Y., Upadhyay, A., Rocha-Lona, L., & Kumar, V. (2024). The effects of globalization on supply chain resilience: Outsourcing techniques as interventionism, protectionism, and regionalization strategies. *Operations Management Research, 17*(2), 505–522. https://doi.org/10.1007/s12063-023-00429-1

Kouhizadeh, M., Saberi, S., & Sarkis, J. (2021). Blockchain technology and the sustainable supply chain: Theoretically exploring adoption barriers. *International Journal of Production Economics, 231*. https://doi.org/10.1016/j.ijpe.2020.107831

Li, C. W., & Tzeng, G. H. (2009). Identification of a threshold value for the DEMATEL method using the maximum mean de-entropy algorithm to find critical services provided by a semiconductor intellectual property mall. *Expert Systems with Applications, 36*(6), 9891–9898. https://doi.org/10.1016/j.eswa.2009.01.073

Liu, J., Gu, B., & Chen, J. (2023). Enablers for maritime supply chain resilience during pandemic: An integrated MCDM approach. *Transportation Research Part A: Policy and Practice, 175*, 103777. https://doi.org/10.1016/j.tra.2023.103777

Lohmer, J., Bugert, N., & Lasch, R. (2020). Analysis of resilience strategies and ripple effect in blockchain-coordinated supply chains: An agent-based simulation study. *International Journal of Production Economics, 228*. https://doi.org/10.1016/j.ijpe.2020.107882

Luthra, S., Kumar, A., Zavadskas, E. K., Mangla, S. K., & Garza-Reyes, J. A. (2020). Industry 4.0 as an enabler of sustainability diffusion in supply chain: An analysis of influential strength of drivers in an emerging economy. *International Journal of Production Research, 58*(5), 1505–1521. https://doi.org/10.1080/00207543.2019.1660828

Mamun, M. (2024). Building supply chain resilience in small and medium-sized clothing retailers in Australia: An empirical study. *Measuring Business Excellence, 28*(3/4), 277–292. https://doi.org/10.1108/MBE-04-2023-0064

Min, H. (2019). Blockchain technology for enhancing supply chain resilience. *Business Horizons, 62*(1), 35–45. https://doi.org/10.1016/j.bushor.2018.08.012

Modgil, S., Singh, R. K., & Hannibal, C. (2022). Artificial intelligence for supply chain resilience: Learning from COVID-19. *The International Journal of Logistics Management, 33*(4), 1246–1268. https://doi.org/10.1108/IJLM-02-2021-0094

Namdar, J., Li, X., Sawhney, R., & Pradhan, N. (2018). Supply chain resilience for single and multiple sourcing in the presence of disruption risks. *International Journal of Production Research, 56*(6), 2339–2360. https://doi.org/10.1080/00207543.2017.1370149

Paul, S. K., Chowdhury, P., Moktadir, Md. A., & Lau, K. H. (2021). Supply chain recovery challenges in the wake of COVID-19 pandemic. *Journal of Business Research*, 136, 316–329. https://doi.org/10.1016/j.jbusres.2021.07.056

Raj, A., Mukherjee, A. A., de Sousa Jabbour, A. B. L., & Srivastava, S. K. (2022). Supply chain management during and post-COVID-19 pandemic: Mitigation strategies and practical lessons learned. *Journal of Business Research*, 142, 1125–1139. https://doi.org/10.1016/j.jbusres.2022.01.037

Sawik, T. (2022). Stochastic optimization of supply chain resilience under ripple effect: A COVID-19 pandemic related study. *Omega*, *109*, 102596. https://doi.org/10.1016/j.omega.2022.102596

Scheibe, K. P., & Blackhurst, J. (2018). Supply chain disruption propagation: A systemic risk and normal accident theory perspective. *International Journal of Production Research*, *56*(1–2), 43–59. https://doi.org/10.1080/00207543.2017.1355123

Si, S. L., You, X. Y., Liu, H. C., & Zhang, P. (2018). DEMATEL technique: A systematic review of the state-of-the-art literature on methodologies and applications. *Mathematical Problems in Engineering*, 2018(1). https://doi.org/10.1155/2018/3696457

Sonar, H., Ghag, N., & Sharma, I. (2025). Reshaping industry 5.0: Unveiling supply chain resilience for a carbon-neutral future. *Sustainable Futures*, 9. https://doi.org/10.1016/j.sftr.2025.100513

Suryadi, A., & Rau, H. (2023). Considering region risks and mitigation strategies in the supplier selection process for improving supply chain resilience. *Computers & Industrial Engineering*, 181, 109288. https://doi.org/10.1016/j.cie.2023.109288

Swink, M., Kovach, J. J., & Roh, J. (2025). Inventory and supply chain planning systems as drivers of supply chain resilience: Analyses of firm performance through the COVID-19 pandemic. *Production and Operations Management*, *34*, 8. https://doi.org/10.1177/10591478251320528

Tang, C. S. (2006). Robust strategies for mitigating supply chain disruptions. *International Journal of Logistics Research and Applications*, *9*(1), 33–45. https://doi.org/10.1080/13675560500405584

Tzeng, G. H., Chiang, C. H., & Li, C. W. (2007). Evaluating intertwined effects in e-learning programs: A novel hybrid MCDM model based on factor analysis and DEMATEL. *Expert Systems with Applications*, *32*(4), 1028–1044. https://doi.org/10.1016/j.eswa.2006.02.004

Zaman, S. I., Khan, S. A., Qabool, S., & Gupta, H. (2023). How digitalization in banking improve service supply chain resilience of e-commerce sector? A technological adoption model approach. *Operations Management Research*, *16*(2), 904–930. https://doi.org/10.1007/s12063-022-00341-0

Zhang, H., & Doan, H. (2023). *From just-in-time to just-in-case? Changing global supply chains after the COVID-19 pandemic*. Research Institute of Economy, Trade and Industry (RIETI). https://www.rieti.go.jp/en/columns/v01_0204.html

Zhong, J., Cheng, H., & Jia, F. (2024). Supply chain resilience capability factors in agri-food supply chains. *Operations Management Research*, *17*(3), 850–868. https://doi.org/10.1007/s12063-024-00470-8

Zhou, J., Hu, L., Yu, Y., Zhang, J. Z., & Zheng, L. J. (2024). Impacts of IT capability and supply chain collaboration on supply chain resilience: Empirical evidence from China in COVID-19 pandemic. *Journal of Enterprise Information Management*, *37*(2), 777–803. https://doi.org/10.1108/JEIM-03-2022-0091

6 Towards an integrated understanding of supply chain resilience

Introduction

SCRES has emerged as a defining organisational capability in an era marked by geopolitical turbulence, regulatory divergence, energy insecurity, and increasingly interconnected global risks. Firms operate in environments where operational challenges are inseparable from political forces such as sanctions, trade realignment, technological rivalry, and regional conflict. These forces reshape the economic and institutional conditions under which supply chains are organised, governed, and adjusted. Evidence presented throughout this monograph shows that resilience extends beyond operational robustness and depends on firms' capacity to interpret geopolitical signals, anticipate cascading disruption, and reconfigure activities in ways that preserve continuity and competitiveness.

Geopolitical disruptions rarely occur in isolation. Recent research highlights how global risks reinforce one another, with climate stress, pandemics, and armed conflict interacting to generate disruptions of greater scale and persistence (Lawrence *et al.*, 2024). This pattern is reflected in the empirical material analysed in this study, where firms operating in Central and Eastern Europe confronted overlapping political, logistical, and economic pressures. Such conditions intensify uncertainty, raise coordination costs, and constrain feasible adjustment paths, underscoring the need for resilience capabilities that span technological, structural, and organisational domains rather than isolated or ad hoc responses.

Against this backdrop, systems thinking provides the unifying analytical perspective of the monograph. SCRES is not treated as a discrete intervention or equilibrium outcome, but as an emergent property arising from interactions among firm capabilities, governance arrangements, institutional constraints, and geopolitical conditions. This concluding chapter synthesises the insights generated across the study's triangulated research design and revisits the three guiding research questions in order to consolidate the monograph's explanatory contributions.

DOI: 10.4324/9781003733089-6

The bibliometric-systematic literature review maps the evolving conceptual landscape and identifies dominant thematic clusters in resilience research under geopolitical disruption, addressing **RQ1**. The qualitative case studies examine how firms operating in a high-exposure regional context interpret geopolitical uncertainty and translate it into concrete adjustment mechanisms, addressing **RQ2**. The DEMATEL-based causal analysis models interdependencies among these mechanisms, revealing their relative influence and systemic roles, addressing **RQ3**.

These analytical components do not form a linear sequence. Instead, each examines the same underlying resilience phenomena at a different analytical level—conceptual, organisational, and systemic—enabling convergent interpretation across methods. This structure supports an integrated understanding of resilience formation that captures both firm-level adjustment processes and system-level causal structures.

By integrating these perspectives, the chapter consolidates the monograph's analytical contributions, situates them within broader economic and supply chain theory, and develops an integrated framework of SCRES organised around readiness, responsiveness, resurgence, and collaboration. The chapter concludes by articulating the study's core contribution, discussing its limitations, and outlining directions for future research on resilience in geopolitically volatile environments.

An integrated capability model of supply chain resilience under geopolitical volatility

The integrated model conceptualises SCRES in geopolitically exposed environments as a cumulative capability system composed of readiness, responsiveness, resurgence, and collaboration. Each domain represents a distinct adaptive function whose effectiveness depends on its alignment with prevailing geopolitical pressures and institutional conditions, as illustrated in Figure 6.1. These capabilities do not operate independently or follow a fixed sequence. Instead, they interact through conditional and recursive relationships that shape firms' adjustment trajectories over time.

Readiness constitutes the foundational capability of the system. Digital technologies—including artificial intelligence, machine learning, advanced analytics, and blockchain—support supply chain visibility, early warning, and geopolitical scanning. As demonstrated in Chapter 5, readiness exerts the strongest causal influence within the resilience architecture. Firms with more developed readiness capabilities are better positioned to detect external change, interpret potential impacts, and assess feasible adjustment options. The realisation of readiness is conditioned by institutional factors such

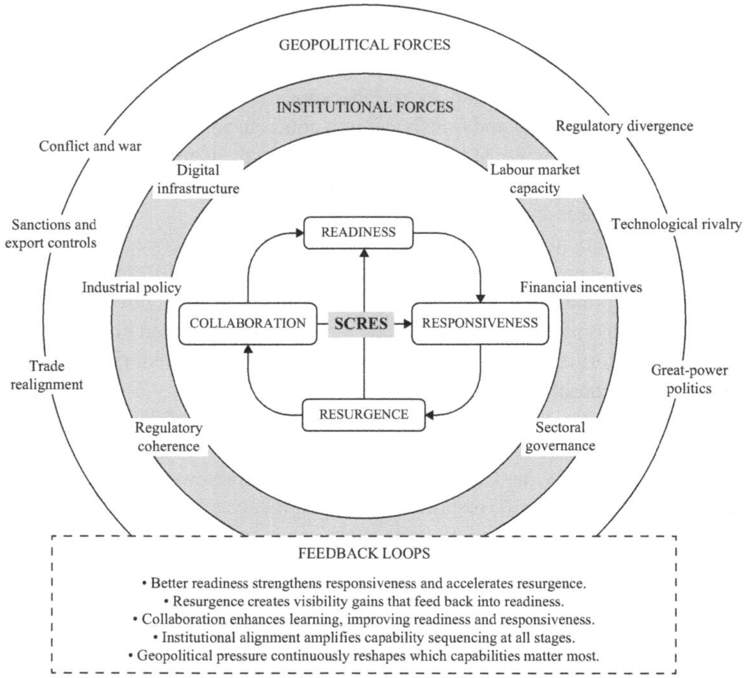

Figure 6.1 Integrated model of SCRES in the face of geopolitical disruptions.

as digital infrastructure quality, regulatory coherence, and cybersecurity maturity.

Responsiveness reflects firms' capacity to stabilise operations once disruptions materialise. Typical responses include tactical substitution, short-term diversification, and intensified coordination with logistics and sourcing partners. These actions function as adaptive mechanisms that build on prior readiness while shaping the scope and direction of subsequent adjustment. The DEMATEL analysis indicates that responsiveness is strongly influenced by digital readiness and performs a mediating role between immediate operational continuity and longer-term structural change.

Resurgence captures longer-term strategic adaptation through changes in supply chain configuration. This domain encompasses nearshoring, reshoring, and broader redesign of production footprints. Causal modelling results show that resurgence-related mechanisms exert significant upstream influence by reshaping supply chain architectures and future coordination patterns. Firms that undertake locational and structural adjustments demonstrate a greater capacity to move beyond reactive responses, a pattern consistent with the qualitative evidence presented in Chapter 4.

Collaboration operates primarily at the network level and includes cross-industry partnerships, information-sharing arrangements, joint contingency planning, and engagement with public authorities and regulatory bodies. Although collaborative mechanisms often depend on prior technological and structural enablers, they play a reinforcing role by diffusing information, reducing uncertainty, and enabling coordinated responses across interconnected ecosystems. Collaboration therefore consolidates and amplifies resilience outcomes rather than initiating adjustment in isolation.

Feedback loops connect all four capability domains, reflecting interdependent adjustment processes in which earlier responses reshape information availability, cost structures, and feasible reconfiguration options. Readiness strengthens responsiveness; responsiveness influences the scope and direction of resurgence; and structural reconfiguration may alter visibility and network configuration, feeding back into readiness. Collaborative arrangements reinforce these dynamics by supporting collective learning and shared problem-solving across organisational boundaries.

SCRES outcomes emerge when these capabilities are coherently aligned with geopolitical pressures and institutional arrangements. The model highlights the cumulative and conditional nature of resilience formation and clarifies why isolated interventions frequently produce limited or unstable results. By integrating conceptual reasoning, literature-based synthesis, qualitative evidence, and DEMATEL-based causal analysis, the model provides a coherent explanation of how SCRES develops and evolves under conditions of sustained geopolitical volatility.

Contribution to the discipline

This monograph advances the state of the art in SCRES research by moving beyond fragmented and predominantly practice-oriented accounts of resilience to provide a theoretically integrated explanation of how firms adjust supply chain structures under conditions of persistent geopolitical disruption. While existing research has generated a growing body of empirical insights into resilience practices, it has remained limited in its capacity to explain how such practices interact over time, how they are conditioned by geopolitical and institutional constraints, and why similar strategies generate divergent outcomes across contexts. The present study addresses these limitations by developing an integrated, capability-based and systems-oriented account of resilience formation.

The primary theoretical contribution lies in the development of an integrated capability architecture for SCRES that conceptualises readiness, responsiveness, resurgence, and collaboration as interdependent domains activated through conditional and path-dependent processes. Prior SCRES frameworks typically enumerate resilience dimensions or practices without specifying their functional roles, causal ordering, or interdependencies. In contrast, the architecture introduced in Chapter 2 provides a coherent explanatory structure grounded in the economic logic of coordination and governance. By doing so, it extends insights from the theory of the firm by demonstrating how resilience-related adjustments reflect changing coordination costs, governance hazards, and institutional constraints under geopolitical volatility, rather than representing universally optimal or purely technology-driven responses.

At the conceptual level, the monograph departs from the dominant treatment of geopolitical disruption as an episodic external shock. It reconceptualises geopolitics as a structural condition that persistently reshapes institutional environments, contractual risk, and adjustment costs. This reframing advances resilience research by aligning it more closely with transaction cost economics and institutional analysis. Although prior studies frequently acknowledge geopolitical risk as contextual background, they rarely theorise its implications for the sequencing, feasibility, and durability of resilience-building processes. By embedding geopolitical disruption within the core explanatory logic, the monograph offers a more robust account of why resilience formation is gradual, uneven, and context-dependent.

The study also contributes to the organisation of knowledge in the field through the bibliometric and systematic literature review presented in Chapter 3. Rather than providing a purely descriptive mapping of themes or methods, the review demonstrates that research on SCRES under geopolitical disruption is structured around four interrelated clusters—digital readiness, operational resilience, strategic reconfiguration, and collaborative ecosystems—and clarifies how these clusters correspond to distinct functional roles and temporal horizons of adjustment. This moves the literature beyond thematic enumeration towards an explanatory synthesis that shows how dispersed research streams collectively address different mechanisms and phases of resilience formation.

Empirically, the monograph contributes original evidence from a high-exposure but under-researched regional context. Much of the existing SCRES literature focuses on firms located in core economies characterised by relatively strong institutional buffers and policy autonomy. The qualitative case studies presented in Chapter 4 extend this evidence base by examining firms operating in Central and Eastern Europe, where geopolitical exposure is immediate and adjustment options are more constrained. These findings enrich SCRES research by illustrating how firms positioned outside core governance centres recalibrate sourcing, production, and coordination arrangements within externally shaped institutional frameworks.

Methodologically, the study advances SCRES research by demonstrating the value of combining mechanism-based qualitative analysis with causal modelling. Whereas prior studies tend to rely either on case-based narratives or on variance-based quantitative approaches, the integration of realist-informed case evidence with DEMATEL analysis in Chapter 5 reveals the hierarchical influence structure among resilience mechanisms. This approach clarifies why certain strategies function as upstream causal drivers while others operate as dependent or reinforcing mechanisms, addressing a persistent limitation of the literature: the lack of insight into causal ordering and interdependence among resilience practices.

At an epistemological level, the monograph contributes by advancing a non-linear, triangulation-based approach to theory development. Rather than deriving its integrated model from a sequential application of methods, the study develops theoretical insight through iterative reconciliation of conceptual reasoning, literature-based patterns, qualitative mechanisms, and causal modelling results. This demonstrates a viable pathway for building mid-range theory in resilience research that remains analytically rigorous without relying on methodological reductionism.

Finally, at the level of synthesis, the monograph delivers an integrated model of SCRES formation under geopolitical volatility that identifies leverage points, interdependencies, and feedback effects within complex supply networks. Unlike many existing frameworks, this model does not prescribe best practices or normative solutions. Its contribution lies in providing an analytical structure that explains why resilience outcomes differ across firms and contexts, and how sequencing, prioritisation, and constraint shape adaptive capacity under persistent geopolitical uncertainty. Table 6.1 summarises these contributions by explicitly linking each to the state of the art, the analytical approach adopted, and the specific element of originality introduced in this study.

Future scenarios and resilience trajectories

Recent crises highlight the importance of forward-looking approaches to SCRES. The COVID-19 pandemic exposed the fragility of efficiency-oriented production models, the Russia–Ukraine conflict revealed the structural nature of energy and critical materials dependencies, and intensifying rivalry between the United States and China underscored the strategic significance of technological access, standards, and regulatory asymmetries. These developments demonstrate that geopolitical forces shape not only episodic disruption but also the longer-term constraints within which supply chains are designed, governed, and reconfigured.

Scenario-based reasoning offers a useful lens for examining how alternative geopolitical trajectories may condition firms' adaptive capacity. Rather than forecasting a single outcome, scenario analysis enables assessment of how different constellations of political, regulatory, and technological forces influence the viability and prioritisation of resilience capabilities. Looking towards 2030, three broad geopolitical trajectories appear particularly relevant.

Table 6.1 Mapping of contributions to chapters, analytical basis, and novelty

Contribution	*Chapter(s)*	*Analytical basis*	*Novelty and originality*
Theoretical contribution: integrated capability architecture of SCRES	2	Integration of economic and organisational perspectives on coordination and adjustment	Develops a coherent capability architecture (readiness, responsiveness, resurgence, collaboration), whereas prior SCRES frameworks typically treated resilience dimensions as parallel, loosely specified, or weakly interconnected
Conceptual contribution: geopolitical disruption as a structural condition	2 and 4	Institutional and political–economic interpretation of geopolitical constraints	Reconceptualises geopolitics as an endogenous, structuring condition shaping capability development, governance choices, and adjustment costs rather than as an episodic external shock
Knowledge-mapping contribution: structuring the SCRES–geopolitics literature	3	Combined quantitative mapping and qualitative synthesis of the literature	Provides a structured mapping of an intellectually fragmented field and identifies functional research streams linked to adjustment roles and temporal horizons rather than isolated thematic clusters
Empirical contribution: firm-level adjustment under geopolitical pressure in CEE	4	In-depth analysis of firm behaviour in a high-exposure regional context	Generates original empirical insight from a peripheral and semi-core region, extending SCRES research beyond dominant Western European, North American, and East Asian settings
Methodological contribution: causal analysis of resilience mechanisms	5	Systematic examination of cause–effect relationships among adjustment mechanisms	Introduces causal modelling to SCRES–geopolitics research, revealing hierarchical influence structures, asymmetries, and conditional dependencies among resilience mechanisms
Epistemological implication: triangulated explanation of resilience formation	3–5	Cross-comparison of patterns, mechanisms, and system interactions	Demonstrates how resilience theory can be developed through triangulated synthesis rather than linear sequencing or single-method dominance
Synthetic contribution: integrated model of resilience formation under geopolitical volatility	6	System-level integration of conceptual, empirical, and causal insights	Produces an integrated model clarifying cumulative, conditional, and path-dependent processes of resilience formation under persistent geopolitical pressure
Analytical–practical contribution: leverage points and feedback effects	5 and 6	Interpretation of system interactions and adjustment dynamics	Identifies leverage points, sequencing effects, and feedback mechanisms without reducing findings to prescriptive best-practice recommendations

Source: Own elaboration.

One trajectory is characterised by deepening fragmentation, marked by rival regulatory regimes, competing technology ecosystems, and declining cross-border interoperability. Under such conditions, firms face elevated uncertainty and rising coordination costs across jurisdictions. Pressure falls primarily on readiness and resurgence, as enhanced geopolitical scanning, rapid interpretation of external signals, and flexible production footprints become central to navigating fractured operating environments.

A second trajectory reflects selective realignment. Geopolitical tensions persist but stabilise around negotiated boundaries, producing clearer—though still contested—zones of political risk. Within this context, responsiveness and collaboration assume greater importance. Firms must balance exposure across blocs while maintaining operational continuity, relying on short-term adaptive responses, relational coordination, and targeted structural adjustments to manage bounded uncertainty.

A third trajectory centres on coordinated adaptation, driven by climate imperatives, decarbonisation policies, and large-scale investment in energy and infrastructure transformation. Although geopolitical competition remains present, coordination increases around shared environmental and technological objectives. This scenario places stronger emphasis on long-term resurgence and network-level collaboration, as supply chains reconfigure around new technologies, regulatory coalitions, and sustainability-oriented standards.

Across these scenarios, the integrated capability model developed in this monograph provides a framework for interpreting divergent resilience trajectories. Each geopolitical logic stresses different domains of the capability system and alters the relative importance of readiness, responsiveness, resurgence, and collaboration. The analysis also suggests that firms investing in digital readiness, production footprint flexibility, and collaborative capacity are more likely to remain resilient across multiple trajectories, even as geopolitical dynamics evolve in uncertain and uneven ways.

Implications for managerial decision-making

The findings point to a reconceptualisation of managerial decision-making in geopolitically exposed supply chains. Rather than identifying discrete best practices, the analysis underscores the importance of sequencing, alignment, and orchestration of capabilities under conditions of persistent uncertainty. Resilience emerges not from isolated interventions but from the cumulative interaction of technological, structural, and organisational adjustments implemented over time.

Digital readiness functions as a foundational condition for effective resilience formation. Capabilities supporting visibility, forecasting, and data-driven analysis enable earlier recognition of disruption signals and more informed assessment of their implications. In their absence, firms face informational delays and are pushed towards reactive adjustment. Investments in digital infrastructure and analytical capacity therefore condition the feasibility and effectiveness of subsequent resilience measures, rather than constituting one option among many.

Decisions concerning production footprint configuration represent a further critical lever. Nearshoring, reshoring, and selective regionalisation reshape exposure to geopolitical risk by altering coordination costs, supplier reliability, and response times. The analysis indicates that such decisions exert influence across the broader resilience system and should be evaluated not solely in terms of short-term efficiency, but with reference to longer-term adaptability and systemic stability under geopolitical constraint.

Diversification emerges as a contingent rather than universally beneficial strategy. Expanding supplier bases or increasing geographic dispersion can reduce dependency, but when pursued without sufficient coordination mechanisms, and decision-support capabilities, diversification may introduce additional complexity and new vulnerabilities. Effective diversification therefore presupposes an adequate technological and organisational foundation for governing increasingly heterogeneous networks.

Collaborative arrangements across organisational boundaries reinforce these processes by facilitating learning, coordination, and adaptive response during disruption. Evidence from the case studies indicates that trust-based relationships, structured information sharing, and joint contingency planning contribute to more timely and coherent responses to geopolitical shocks. Collaboration does not substitute for internal capabilities but amplifies their effects once they are in place.

Institutional awareness constitutes an additional condition for sustained adaptability. Firms operating in Central and Eastern Europe and comparable environments must continuously navigate heterogeneous regulatory regimes and shifting geopolitical pressures. Integrating geopolitical scanning and institutional monitoring into supply chain governance supports anticipation of policy change, adjustment of coordination arrangements, and preservation of strategic flexibility under evolving external constraints.

Collectively, these implications suggest a shift away from event-driven, reactive responses towards deliberate orchestration of capability development. Resilience-oriented decision-making involves aligning digital readiness, structural configuration, diversification, collaboration, and institutional awareness within a coherent adjustment logic that reflects both geopolitical exposure and organisational constraints, rather than treating these elements as independent managerial choices.

Implications for industrial and regulatory policy

The findings indicate that geopolitical disruption should be understood as a persistent condition shaping supply chain organisation rather than as an episodic external shock. Political forces alter uncertainty, coordination requirements, and adjustment costs in ways that progressively reshape how firms configure sourcing, production, and governance arrangements. From a policy perspective, this implies that resilience cannot be addressed through short-term crisis instruments alone but requires sustained institutional frameworks capable of accommodating prolonged geopolitical volatility.

Within this context, the resilience-building mechanisms observed in the study can be interpreted as adaptive responses to heightened uncertainty and coordination complexity. Investments in digital readiness, adjustments to production location, and changes in sourcing structures reflect firms' efforts to manage information asymmetries, stabilise coordination, and retain control over critical activities. These responses do not eliminate risk but redistribute it across organisational boundaries and network structures, producing differentiated resilience outcomes that are contingent on firms' institutional environments.

Institutional context plays a decisive conditioning role in these processes. Formal regulatory frameworks, industrial policy instruments, and compliance regimes shape which resilience strategies are feasible, while informal institutional constraints influence firms' expectations, risk perceptions, and coordination practices. In the Central and Eastern European context, institutional asymmetries and externally anchored geopolitical alignments constrain adjustment paths and contribute to uneven development of resilience capabilities across firms and sectors. This helps explain why similar levels of geopolitical exposure generate divergent organisational responses.

The sequencing of capabilities identified in the analysis further refines understanding of resilience formation. Readiness, responsiveness, resurgence, and collaboration function as interdependent layers rather than interchangeable tools. Early investments in information processing and visibility enable subsequent structural adjustments, which in turn reshape coordination requirements and future strategic options. This cumulative logic highlights the path-dependent nature of adaptation under sustained uncertainty and suggests limits to policy interventions that focus on isolated capability development.

Digital technologies occupy a particularly influential position within this process. Beyond efficiency gains, data-driven systems affect how firms detect disruption, coordinate decisions, and allocate control within supply networks. By reshaping information flows and decision speed, digitalisation alters the practical conditions under which coordination takes place, with implications for both firm behaviour and the effectiveness of industrial and regulatory initiatives aimed at strengthening resilience.

Overall, the findings suggest that resilience outcomes emerge from the interaction between firm-level adjustment mechanisms and broader institutional conditions. Industrial and regulatory policies therefore influence resilience primarily by shaping coordination environments, incentive structures, and constraint sets rather than by directing specific organisational choices. This points to the need for analytically grounded policy approaches that recognise institutional diversity, path dependence, and the cumulative nature of resilience formation under persistent geopolitical volatility.

Study limitations

Several limitations should be considered when interpreting the findings of this study. First, the empirical focus on firms operating in Central and Eastern Europe provides insight into a geopolitically exposed yet under-researched context, but it may limit the transferability of results to economies characterised by different institutional configurations, market sizes, or positions within global production networks. Firms embedded in highly diversified, resource-abundant, or institutionally stable environments may face different coordination constraints and adjustment incentives. Future comparative research across regions and levels of development could assess whether the identified sequencing of readiness, responsiveness, resurgence, and collaboration holds under alternative geopolitical and institutional conditions.

Second, managerial data were collected during a period of acute and overlapping disruptions, including the COVID-19 pandemic, Russia's invasion of Ukraine, and major shifts in trade, energy, and industrial policy. Interpretations formed under such conditions may place greater weight on immediate operational continuity and risk containment than on longer-term strategic recalibration. In addition, the causal relationships identified through DEMATEL reflect perceived influence structures at a specific point in time rather than dynamic adjustment processes unfolding longitudinally. Panel-based or repeated-measure designs could offer deeper insight into how resilience capabilities evolve, stabilise, or weaken as geopolitical pressures persist, intensify, or subside.

Third, while DEMATEL is well suited to identifying causal hierarchies and influence pathways in complex systems, it does not explicitly model temporal dynamics, non-linear interactions, or threshold effects. Consequently, feedback loops and tipping points may be only partially captured. Complementary approaches, such as system dynamics modelling, or agent-based simulation could enhance understanding of how supply chain adjustments propagate over time under prolonged uncertainty.

Fourth, digital readiness was operationalised primarily through analytics- and AI-enabled tools that support visibility, monitoring, and decision support. Although this captures a central dimension of contemporary resilience, it remains a relatively aggregated construct. More fine-grained analysis distinguishing data governance arrangements, cybersecurity maturity, interoperability across partners, and human–machine coordination could yield additional insight into how digital capabilities condition resilience outcomes.

Finally, although the analysis recognises the conditioning role of institutional and policy environments, it does not undertake a systematic comparison of regulatory regimes or industrial policy configurations. A more explicit political economy perspective—focusing on variation in trade regulation, security alignment, and digital governance across countries—could strengthen understanding of how public institutions shape firm-level adjustment paths and longer-term resilience trajectories. While sustainability-related policies emerged in the literature review, they are not treated here as primary explanatory drivers, and future research could more clearly disentangle their indirect effects from those associated with geopolitical and institutional constraints.

Future research agenda

Several avenues for future research emerge directly from the findings and limitations of this study. One promising direction concerns how firms balance resilience and efficiency in increasingly fragmented geopolitical environments, where supply networks must be redesigned while maintaining cost competitiveness. While this study highlights the importance of capability sequencing, the economic mechanisms through which firms negotiate resilience–efficiency trade-offs under institutional, regulatory, and political constraints remain insufficiently explored. Future research could examine how cost structures, pricing power, and access to public support condition these trade-offs.

AI-enabled resilience represents a second area requiring deeper investigation. Although digital readiness emerges as a primary causal driver, the implications of artificial intelligence for risk perception, contractual governance, and inter-organisational coordination are not yet well understood. In particular, future studies could examine how algorithmic tools influence managerial judgement, information asymmetries, accountability, and exposure to misinformation or systemic bias across supply networks.

Furthermore, longitudinal research offers significant potential to advance understanding of resilience dynamics. Tracking firms across successive disruptions could reveal how resilience capabilities accumulate, erode, or transform over time, and under what conditions firms transition between readiness, responsiveness, and resurgence. Such designs would help capture adjustment processes that remain invisible in cross-sectional analyses.

Comparative regional analysis constitutes another important avenue. While this study focuses on Central and Eastern Europe, regions such as East Asia, Latin America, or North America face distinct geopolitical pressures and institutional configurations. Comparative studies could test the generalisability of the integrated model and identify region-specific resilience pathways shaped by differing policy regimes and geopolitical exposure.

Further research at the network level is also needed. Collaboration emerges as a reinforcing capability, yet the analysis concentrates primarily on firm-level decisions. Approaches drawing on social network analysis, cluster dynamics, and ecosystem governance could deepen understanding of how resilience evolves across interconnected production systems and how collective adjustment mechanisms emerge.

Moreover, interactions between sustainability and resilience warrant closer attention. While certain sustainability strategies may strengthen resilience, others may introduce new constraints or trade-offs. Clarifying these interactions could support more coherent organisational strategies and inform policy frameworks aimed at aligning environmental objectives with resilience outcomes.

Finally, methodological innovation presents further opportunities. Mixed-method designs combining causal modelling with longitudinal data, natural experiments, machine-learning analysis of policy discourse, or scenario-based stress testing could enrich understanding of how geopolitical narratives translate into organisational adjustment and strategic reconfiguration.

Concluding synthesis

This monograph advances theoretical and empirical understanding of SCRES as an adaptive response to persistent geopolitical disruption rather than to episodic shock. As introduced in Chapter 1, geopolitical forces reshape the institutional, regulatory, and cost conditions under which firms organise cross-border production and exchange. Supply chains are therefore not merely exposed to geopolitical disruption, but are structurally shaped by it over time. The findings demonstrate that resilience in geopolitically exposed supply chains emerges from the alignment and interaction of digital, structural, organisational, and relational capabilities, not from isolated responses to discrete events. Adaptation unfolds under sustained geopolitical pressure and is conditioned by institutional environments that shape firms' feasible adjustment paths, influencing how resilience is formed, stabilised, or eroded over time.

The integrated model developed in this chapter conceptualises resilience as a cumulative and path-dependent capability system rather than as a normative management objective. Consistent with the capability-based framework outlined in Chapter 2, readiness enables firms to sense geopolitical and regulatory change and anticipate economic implications; responsiveness stabilises operations through short-term tactical adjustment; resurgence reflects deeper structural reconfiguration aimed at restoring strategic coherence; and collaboration consolidates adaptive capacity across interconnected supply networks. These domains explain how firms reallocate resources, redesign governance arrangements, and reconfigure production and sourcing structures as the conditions of international exchange evolve.

A systems-thinking perspective, introduced at the outset of the monograph, is essential for interpreting these dynamics. Capability complementarities, feedback effects, and contextual dependencies shape how firms interpret geopolitical disruption and how resilience evolves across successive adjustment phases. Evidence assembled across the empirical chapters indicates that resilience formation is constrained by path dependence: early investments in digital readiness, structural flexibility, and relational embeddedness expand future reconfiguration options, whereas delayed or fragmented responses narrow adaptive space and increase adjustment costs. Resilience therefore cannot be reduced to a catalogue of best practices, but must be understood as an evolving configuration of capabilities embedded in broader political–economic structures.

The study addresses its three guiding research questions through an integrated mixed-method design based on triangulation rather than linear methodological progression, as articulated in Chapter 1. In response to **RQ1**, the systematic literature review clarifies how scholarly understanding of SCRES under geopolitical disruption has developed unevenly across thematic domains, revealing persistent gaps related to long-term structural adjustment, institutional conditioning, and capability interdependence. In response to **RQ2**, the qualitative case analysis explains how multinational enterprises operating in a high-exposure Central and Eastern European context interpret geopolitical pressures and activate mitigation mechanisms, generating heterogeneous resilience outcomes shaped by institutional constraints and pre-existing capability endowments. In response to **RQ3**, the DEMATEL-based causal modelling identifies hierarchical influence structures, interdependencies, and leverage points among resilience mechanisms, clarifying which adjustments exert the strongest systemic influence on adaptive capacity.

These complementary analytical strands are reconciled in the integrated model presented in this chapter, which explains resilience as an adaptive, cumulative, and path-dependent capability system encompassing readiness, responsiveness, resurgence, and collaboration. By aligning conceptual synthesis, realist explanation, and causal modelling, the monograph fulfils its research objectives and provides a coherent system-level explanation of how SCRES is formed, constrained, and transformed under sustained geopolitical disruption.

The integrated perspective developed here offers a coherent analytical framework for advancing research on SCRES in geopolitically volatile environments. It supports further theoretical refinement of capability sequencing and interdependence, facilitates context-sensitive empirical investigation across regions and institutional settings, and provides a structured basis for examining how geopolitical forces shape the adaptive logic of globally interconnected production systems.

Reference

Lawrence, M., Homer-Dixon, T., Janzwood, S., Rockström, J., Renn, O., & Donges, J. F. (2024). Global polycrisis: The causal mechanisms of crisis entanglement. *Global Sustainability*, *7*, 6. https://doi.org/10.1017/sus.2024.1

Appendix A

Expert survey for DEMATEL-based analysis of SCRES under geopolitical disruption

General respondent information
Position (current role/title)
Industry/sector
Total years of professional experience

PART 1. Identification of mitigation strategies supporting supply chain adjustment under geopolitical disruption (e.g. the armed conflict in Ukraine, U.S.-China trade war, tensions surrounding Taiwan)

Please indicate which of the following mitigation strategies your firm has adopted in response to geopolitical disruptions affecting its supply chain. If applicable, you may add additional strategies not listed. For each strategy, assess its economic and strategic relevance for your firm by assigning a score from 0 to 4, where 0 denotes "no relevance" and 4 denotes "very high relevance".

Mitigation strategy	**Description**	**0**	**1**	**2**	**3**	**4**
1. Creating surplus production capacity and inventory	Transition from a just-in-time (JIT) to a just-in-case approach by building surplus capacity and stock rather than minimising inventory.					
2. Production optimisation with supply chain planning	Synchronisation of all elements of the supply chain.					
3. Nearshoring of production	Relocating production activities to locations close to the company's headquarters.					
4. Reshoring of production	Relocating production activities back to the company's headquarters.					

5. Diversification of the production network	Diversifying production bases by forming new partnerships or requesting existing partners to supply from different locations.					
6. Supplier diversification by quantity	Expanding the supplier portfolio in terms of the number of suppliers.					
7. Supplier diversification by location	Expanding the supplier portfolio in terms of geographic distribution.					
8. Multi-sourcing	Maintaining an existing supplier base by cooperating with multiple suppliers.					
9. Creation of cross-industry partner networks	Cooperating with strategic raw material suppliers and external service partners.					
10. Implementation of machine learning, AI, and big data	Understanding and utilising data to increase efficiency and effectiveness.					
11. Technology improvement (e.g. blockchain)	Automating processes through improved digitalisation.					
12. Alternative components (e.g. 3D printing)	On-demand manufacturing of certain products/components using 3D printing techniques to fill crisis gaps without long-term disruption to normal business processes.					

PART 2. Interdependencies between mitigation strategies

Please rate the impact of each factor on the scale 0–4, where 0 = no influence, 4 = strong influence.

Creating surplus production capacity and inventory affects:	**0**	**1**	**2**	**3**	**4**
Production optimisation with supply chain planning					
Nearshoring of production					
Reshoring of production					
Diversification of the production network					
Supplier diversification by quantity					
Supplier diversification by location					
Multi-sourcing					
Creation of cross-industry partner networks					
Implementation of machine learning, AI, and big data					
Technology improvement (e.g. blockchain)					
Alternative components (e.g. 3D printing)					
Production optimisation with supply chain planning affects:	**0**	**1**	**2**	**3**	**4**
Creating surplus production capacity and inventory					
Nearshoring of production					

Reshoring of production					
Diversification of the production network					
Supplier diversification by quantity					
Supplier diversification by location					
Multi-sourcing					
Creation of cross-industry partner networks					
Implementation of machine learning, AI, and big data					
Technology improvement (e.g. blockchain)					
Alternative components (e.g. 3D printing)					
Nearshoring of production affects:	**0**	**1**	**2**	**3**	**4**
Creating surplus production capacity and inventory					
Production optimisation with supply chain planning					
Reshoring of production					
Diversification of the production network					
Supplier diversification by quantity					
Supplier diversification by location					
Multi-sourcing					
Creation of cross-industry partner networks					
Implementation of machine learning, AI, and big data					
Technology improvement (e.g. blockchain)					
Alternative components (e.g. 3D printing)					
Reshoring of production affects:	**0**	**1**	**2**	**3**	**4**
Creating surplus production capacity and inventory					
Production optimisation with supply chain planning					
Nearshoring of production					
Diversification of the production network					
Supplier diversification by quantity					
Supplier diversification by location					
Multi-sourcing					
Creation of cross-industry partner networks					
Implementation of machine learning, AI, and big data					
Technology improvement (e.g. blockchain)					
Alternative components (e.g. 3D printing)					
Diversification of the production network affects:	**0**	**1**	**2**	**3**	**4**
Creating surplus production capacity and inventory					
Production optimisation with supply chain planning					
Nearshoring of production					
Reshoring of production					
Supplier diversification by quantity					
Supplier diversification by location					
Multi-sourcing					
Creation of cross-industry partner networks					
Implementation of machine learning, AI, and big data					

Technology improvement (e.g. blockchain)					
Alternative components (e.g. 3D printing)					
Supplier diversification by quantity affects:	**0**	**1**	**2**	**3**	**4**
Creating surplus production capacity and inventory					
Production optimisation with supply chain planning					
Nearshoring of production					
Reshoring of production					
Diversification of the production network					
Supplier diversification by location					
Multi-sourcing					
Creation of cross-industry partner networks					
Implementation of machine learning, AI, and big data					
Technology improvement (e.g. blockchain)					
Alternative components (e.g. 3D printing)					
Supplier diversification by location affects:	**0**	**1**	**2**	**3**	**4**
Creating surplus production capacity and inventory					
Production optimisation with supply chain planning					
Nearshoring of production					
Reshoring of production					
Diversification of the production network					
Supplier diversification by quantity					
Multi-sourcing					
Creation of cross-industry partner networks					
Implementation of machine learning, AI, and big data					
Technology improvement (e.g. blockchain)					
Alternative components (e.g. 3D printing)					
Multi-sourcing affects:	**0**	**1**	**2**	**3**	**4**
Creating surplus production capacity and inventory					
Production optimisation with supply chain planning					
Nearshoring of production					
Reshoring of production					
Diversification of the production network					
Supplier diversification by quantity					
Supplier diversification by location					
Creation of cross-industry partner networks					
Implementation of machine learning, AI, and big data					
Technology improvement (e.g. blockchain)					
Alternative components (e.g. 3D printing)					
Creation of cross-industry partner networks affects:	**0**	**1**	**2**	**3**	**4**
Creating surplus production capacity and inventory					
Production optimisation with supply chain planning					
Nearshoring of production					
Reshoring of production					

Diversification of the production network					
Supplier diversification by quantity					
Supplier diversification by location					
Multi-sourcing					
Implementation of machine learning, AI, and big data					
Technology improvement (e.g. blockchain)					
Alternative components (e.g. 3D printing)					
Implementation of machine learning, AI, and big data affects:	**0**	**1**	**2**	**3**	**4**
Creating surplus production capacity and inventory					
Production optimisation with supply chain planning					
Nearshoring of production					
Reshoring of production					
Diversification of the production network					
Supplier diversification by quantity					
Supplier diversification by location					
Multi-sourcing					
Creation of cross-industry partner networks					
Technology improvement (e.g. blockchain)					
Alternative components (e.g. 3D printing)					
Technology improvement (e.g. blockchain) affects:	**0**	**1**	**2**	**3**	**4**
Creating surplus production capacity and inventory					
Production optimisation with supply chain planning					
Nearshoring of production					
Reshoring of production					
Diversification of the production network					
Supplier diversification by quantity					
Supplier diversification by location					
Multi-sourcing					
Creation of cross-industry partner networks					
Implementation of machine learning, AI, and big data					
Alternative components (e.g. 3D printing)					
Alternative components (e.g. 3D printing) affect:	**0**	**1**	**2**	**3**	**4**
Creating surplus production capacity and inventory					
Production optimisation with supply chain planning					
Nearshoring of production					
Reshoring of production					
Diversification of the production network					
Supplier diversification by quantity					
Supplier diversification by location					
Multi-sourcing					
Creation of cross-industry partner networks					
Implementation of machine learning, AI, and big data					
Technology improvement (e.g. blockchain)					

Index